CLASSIC FRENCH RECIPES

CLASSIC

FRENCH

RECIPES

GINETTE MATHIOT

PREFACE

When I packed up to move to France in 2003, my new home was a tiny rooftop apartment in Paris, which was filled with charm (after a good scrubbing and a few coats of paint), but its *petite* proportions meant that I'd have to drastically cut down my cookbook collection. I decided to ship my very favorite cookbooks, the ones that meant the most to me, in two boxes and keep a few especially useful cookbooks in my suitcase so I was sure to have them. Fortunately, I'd packed my copy of the *Joy of Cooking* with me, as twenty years later, I'm still waiting for my other cookbooks to arrive.

It might seem silly to bring an American cookbook to France, the home of one of the world's greatest cuisines, but the book is a classic reference for everything *américain*, from making pies and roasting a whole turkey, to eviscerating a squirrel, which I figured would come in handy when I needed a taste of "home." (Confession: I've made a few pies in Paris but have yet to cook a squirrel.)

My daily life in Paris soon revolved around joining the locals and shopping at the local markets, buying what looked best that day. It also gave me a chance to learn about ingredients that were unfamiliar to me. In those cases, I'd ask the vendor how to use mirabelles (tiny yellow plums) or sweet lemons known as bergamots. I also learned what else Belgian endive was good for, other than salad. And that if you wanted a whole turkey for Thanksgiving, you'd need to put in a special order for one.

My favorite moments (when my French got better) were when I was shopping and someone else in line would chime in with a favorite recipe. I felt like I was getting "insider" information that made me feel more French, even though I made gaffes like asking for some "brain" (rather than brine) with my olives, or saying I needed a basket of *grosses selles* (big poop), rather than *groseilles*, which are red currants.

I'd bring my brain-free basket (which was also free of other things…) home, loaded with herbs, lettuce, cheese, plums, strawberries, and perhaps something I'd never cooked before, such as duck thighs or salt cod or salsify, and read up on how to use them.

Two decades later, I'm now French-American and cook like the French, being particularly *exigeant* (discerning) about buying the best ingredients and referencing traditional French recipes, which have stood the test of time and are still enjoyed today in homes and bistros across the country.

The recipes in *Je sais cuisiner* have been used by French people since 1932. The name translates to "I Know How to Cook," and Ginette Mathiot's best-selling book has indeed lived up to its name, teaching generations of French people how to cook. The original volume contained nearly 2,000 recipes, which for this edition have been culled down to the recipes French people make the most. (I'm not sure if the original version of her book had a recipe for *écureuil*, or squirrel, but don't worry – there isn't one in here.)

What you will find are French sauces and pastry doughs, as well as local favorites such as croque-monsieur, duck terrine, coq au vin, clafoutis, île flottante, and Belgian endive gratin, which was the recipe that taught me what I normally tossed into a salad wasn't just for salads; it is the base for a cheesy, creamy casserole that is now one of my favorite dishes to dig into on a cold winter night.

If you want to cook like the French, find the best ingredients you can, which you can do at farmer's markets and greenmarkets bursting with vibrant fruits and vegetables, leafy lettuces for green salads (essential at any French meal), free-range eggs, and meats and poultry raised by small producers. And no offense to my adopted country, but there are amazing cheeses produced elsewhere, where the quality is just as high as it is in France.

Cuisine fait maison is the French version of cozy, "comfort" cooking, and these are the time-honored dishes that French people enjoy. Ask even the most esteemed multi-starred chef who the best cook they know is, and without hesitation, they'll say, "Ma grand-mère." You may not be a French grandmother (or grandfather—French men cook too!), but with this book, no matter who or where you are, you'll not only see how easy it is to make the same traditional dishes at home, but you'll also taste how delicious these classic French dishes are.

David Lebovitz
Paris, France

HOW TO COOK
THE FRENCH WAY

This book is for anyone who wants to produce the perfect omelet *aux fines herbes* as a quick lunch, whip up an impromptu aïoli to accompany some cold fish, or prepare a hearty coq au vin for a table of friends. In a nutshell, it's for anyone who wants to cook the French way. Inside you will find a collection of 170 carefully selected recipes, *la crème de la crème*, as the French would say—the best of the best. In a globalized world, where every cuisine is accessible to the curious home cook, French cooking continues to hold a timeless appeal. Justifiably so, since its history and influence on chefs all over the world means it is widely referenced in terms of basic techniques and recipes. To make a court-bouillon for poaching sea bream and then prepare a classic beurre blanc sauce to enhance its delicate taste is to understand how flavor is created and layered in the simplest dishes. Not to mention the fact that the simple luxury of French food also evokes a desirable *art de vivre* (art of living), encouraging a pleasure-oriented approach to eating, where every meal is as much a social occasion as a joyful act of nourishment.

To instruct readers in how to cook the French way, it made sense to draw knowledge from a trusted reference. Ginette Mathiot's *Je sais cuisiner* (*I Know How to Cook*) was first published in 1932. The young home-economics teacher had been enrolled by a publisher to conduct the selection, testing, and writing of almost two thousand recipes. The book would become a cooking bible for three generations of French households, and through revising work, was constantly adapted to contemporary life without losing its original essence or giving in to passing trends. Ginette Mathiot worked on many later editions and wrote other books, including volumes about pastry and preserving. Over the years, her magnum opus became a bestseller, with several million copies sold by the turn of the century, continuing its life even though she passed away in 1998. It was translated into English in 2009.

The recipes in this book, all Ginette's, are meant for everyday use but are also suitable to cater to special occasions and include regional dishes as well as seasonal treats. This edition also includes advice adapted from her writings about planning menus, shopping for food, and organizing a kitchen. It all strikes as thoroughly modern, perhaps because it meets our renewed require-ments for a globally sensible way of eating. We want affordable, nourishing, additive-free, and delicious food. We know the value of recycling leftovers and preserving abundant produce. No frills, no waste: the beauty of French cooking may reside in its ability to make the most of a varied but moderate range of ingredients and flavorings. A softly sophisticated minimalism that requires the careful choice of seasonal produce and some guidance in the kitchen.

HOW TO PLAN A MENU

This book is structured along traditional lines, starting with basic recipes, followed by starters, main courses, and desserts to finish. Though many households skip the starter in everyday meals, the three-course structure still reflects the classic French way to eat. It remains the norm at restaurants, and when hosting guests at home. In fact, eating reasonable servings of an array of different dishes is not only a pleasurable experience but also can help strike a nutritional balance. In quite a novel way for her times, Ginette Mathiot insisted on the dietary function of food and the physical needs it should fulfil by providing the right quantities of carbohydrates, protein, fats, vitamins, minerals, fiber, and water. This is unar-guably a concern shared by modern cooks and does justify planning varied menus but not obsessively calcu-lating nutritional values. As she instructed, harmony should be created within a meal—primarily between flavors, which should be distinct but not clashing, and never overpowering, instead enhancing the main ingredient of each dish against a backdrop of secondary flavors. Although this idea is a little theoretical, keep it in mind when planning a menu. If you want to host a dinner party "à la française," compose the meal sensibly. French cooking is not all about extravagant dishes and heavy sauces. Serve a light starter of raw vegetables or oysters before a hearty dish, or follow a more opulent beginning, such as foie gras, with something less rich but coherent—perhaps braised or roast poultry, with greens.

On a more practical note, try not to work yourself too hard: modern French hosts develop strategies to spend the right amount of time in the kitchen. Some dishes, such as casseroles, can be made well in advance, and it's completely acceptable to ask friends to bring a dessert. If you enjoy baking fancy pastries, choose dishes that are easier and quicker to prepare for the rest of the meal: for example, a baked fish with herbs will leave room for your Paris-Brest (page 324). On the other hand, dessert could be a thoughtful combination of high-quality shop-bought ice cream and poached fruit. Remember that no French meal goes without fresh bread to mop up sauces and accompany the cheese course. Set a nice table, if you like, but don't overdo it: nowadays, fancy crockery and complicated sets of cutlery are not a requirement for entertaining. A simple, thoughtfully set table with a vase of pretty flowers, plainly folded napkins, and good wine glasses is all you need to make your guests enjoy the meal you have prepared for them.

In everyday life, the French keep it simple but usually do set a table for the members of a household to eat together. Menu-wise, you may structure most meals around a single dish, which you can pick from either the main courses or the starters—for example, a Quiche Lorraine (page 68), or some Eggs in Cocottes (page 82)—and serve it with a salad as a green counterpart. Remember also that balance can be achieved over one or several days, so make sure to plan varied dishes over a week. Ideally, the heartier meal in France is lunch, while supper should be a lighter affair.

HOW TO SHOP FOR FOOD

By all means, plan your meals over a few days if you can and make a list before you go shopping, but remain open to inspiration and be prepared to make changes depending on what is available. Ginette Mathiot always insisted on one of the most important factors in devising a menu: whether the ingredients are in season. Most fruit and vegetables are now available all year round and it is very tempting to use them out of season. Remember, however, that they will generally be more expensive and will not have as much flavor or nutritional value. French cooking relies on a limited selection of pantry items, and on great fresh produce. This is usually shopped for once or twice a week, ideally from the market or specialist shops that sell produce from local, small-scale farms. Cheese, meat, and fish also have seasons.

It is not necessary to spend too much. Some ingredients have a higher price justified by their rarity or the time and resources it took to produce them, and should remain occasional treats. It's better to buy an excellent-quality "lower" cut of meat rather than discounted steak from the supermarket. It will simply require longer and slower cooking time. More abundant, affordable fish (such as mackerel or sardines), if prepared the right way, are quite as delicious as more delicately flavoured species such as sole or bass. Remember that meat and fish should be consumed responsibly, as they are a limited resource.

EQUIPMENT AND ORGANIZATION

Organize your cooking space according to a logical workflow and to your actual use of utensils and ingredients. Do not clutter your work counter, so adjust your choice of equipment to the storage and space available. Choose quality over quantity. Limit your range of electrical appliances. When cooking, always have a bowl serving as a temporary bin to discard anything as you work (separating compost if relevant) to keep your counter clean.

Cooking vessels
Keep two to five sizes of heavy pans made of stainless steel, an excellent conductor and easy to clean. Copper is great but expensive, and hard work to maintain.

A cast-iron Dutch oven (casserole) is a good investment as it lasts forever and holds in the heat very efficiently. A cast-iron sauté pan is also a good choice, yet a little heavy to manipulate. Select skillets (frying pans) of various depths and sizes according to the type of dishes you make: omelets (page 84), Crêpes (page 294), pan-fried fish (page 180), etc. Earthenware (especially in dark colors to absorb the heat) and enamelware (handy and light) are both good for the oven. Baking sheets need to be solid and heavy so they do not warp.

Utensils
Only keep the tools that you actually use. Have several vegetable peelers, to share the chore. As a home cook, you will not need more than three to four knifes: a big chopping knife, a small paring knife, a serrated bread knife, and maybe a filleting knife for fish. Ideally, teach yourself to use a sharpener. Never put any wooden tools in the dishwasher or throw sharp knives in the sink, which could damage them. A modern extra-fine (rasp) grater is really useful for zesting citrus or reducing garlic to pulp.

COOKING METHODS

These methods are not specific to French cooking. However, each of them is involved in classic dishes, so understanding how they work is essential to the process of learning how to cook the French way.

Boiling and poaching
When food is added directly to boiling water, the flavors are less likely to seep into the water, so this method is suitable for preserving maximum flavor through rapid cooking, such as for vegetables *en jardinière* (page 240). On the contrary, when food is added to cold water that is gradually heated, the juices are slowly released into the liquid, so the flavor and nutritional value of the liquid is increased at the same time as it is lost from the food. Broths (stocks, page 24) are prepared in this manner.

Deep-frying
This method is not truly emblematic of French cooking yet is used for Fries (chips, page 228), a staple of bistro lunches, typically served with steak and Béarnaise Sauce (page 39). For deep-frying, the fat needs to be brought to a temperature of about 350°F/180°C, so only oils or animal fats with a high burning point, such as peanut (groundnut), can be used. Beef drippings (in the north) and duck fat (in the southwest) are also used for potatoes. The oil should never be allowed to smoke. The food must be dry with no moisture clinging to it and be added in small batches—carefully. Fried foods are often coated in breadcrumbs, batter, or flour, which contain starch. The heat of the fat rapidly caramelizes this

outside layer while the inside cooks in its own juices, such as with Apple Fritters (page 274). Fries are cooked twice, once to cook the inside and the second time to crisp the outside. Once cooked, the food should be drained immediately on paper towels to absorb the excess fat.

Roasting

Roasting means cooking food in a hot oven with a little fat. It is used for large pieces of meat, such as leg or shoulder of lamb, or poultry—for example, chestnut-stuffed turkey for Christmas (page 166). The cooking temperature is usually quite high, around 425–475°F/220–240°C/Gas Mark 7–8 to brown the surface, then sometimes reduced to 350°F/180°C/Gas Mark 4 or even lower to complete the cooking if necessary. Foods should be basted in their own juices during cooking so they do not dry out.

Grilling and broiling

Raw ingredients are often marinated, then usually lightly brushed with oil before being exposed to direct heat: under a broiler (grill) in a preheated oven, or over a charcoal, a woodfire, or a gas barbecue. Once one side is cooked, most food is turned over to cook on the other side. Sausages, such as *boudin* (page 174), are pierced to avoid bursting. The food is usually placed about 4 inches (10 cm) from the heat source. Food grilled over a wood fire is permeated by smoke and takes on a delicious flavor. Any food being grilled should be closely watched because the rapidity of cooking is not predict-able. Crème brûlée (page 280) or Hot Chavignol Crottins (page 72) are cooked under a broiler. A variation of grilling is to cook lightly oiled food on a hot griddle placed on a stove, such as with Entrecôte Steak (page 134).

Pot-roasting

Pot-roasting involves cooking meat in a covered Dutch oven (casserole) or heavy pan on the stove with a little fat, such as butter, and on a bed of sliced carrots, onions, or other aromatic vegetables. This cooking technique is used mainly for large or tough cuts of veal and large birds such as chickens, capons, or turkeys, which risk drying out if roasted in an oven. During cooking, the aromatic vegetables release steam and this reduces the risk of the cut drying out. Start by browning the roast on all sides, then salt it lightly and continue cooking, tightly covered, turning the meat about every 15 minutes.

Stewing

Many French classics are made following this method. A stew is very practical since it does not need a lot of attention and is even better the next day. The meat and vegetables cook slowly together on a very low heat or in a low oven in a sauce thickened with flour in a tightly covered casserole. The food becomes deliciously infused with the flavorings, wine, and broth (stock) with which it is cooked. For a white stew, or Veal Blanquette (page 142), the pieces of meat or poultry are not browned, and the sauce is made with a white broth (stock). For a brown stew, the pieces of meat or poultry are browned first, then a liquid such as red wine or brown broth (stock) is added, such as for a Navarin (page 148), Daube of Beef (page 128), or Coq au Vin (page 156).

Sautéing (shallow-frying)

Sautéing should be done quite quickly. The food is placed in hot fat in a deep skillet, frying pan, or sauté pan. Brown the food on one side; when it is half cooked, turn it over to brown the other side. This method is suitable for Tournedos Rossini (page 132), Sole Meunière (page 180), or sweetbreads (page 144). The deep sides of the pan help keep in the heat and the moisture. While cooking, catch the juices in a spoon by slightly tilting the pan, and keep basting the item. When shallow-frying smaller, chopped ingredients such as vegetables or mushrooms, move them around with a wooden spoon or shake the pan to help them brown without catching at the bottom. Once the food and fat are removed, the frying pan may be deglazed.

PANTRY AND FLAVORINGS

French cooking functions with a limited range of basic fats, flavorings, acidic ingredients (souring agents), and pantry items, some of which significantly vary depending on the region. The following paragraphs list most of the essentials.

The pantry

– A French kitchen shelf will usually hold two or three different types of oil: a neutral vegetable oil for seasoning and frying such as grapeseed, canola (rapeseed), or sunflower; olive oil (originally in the Mediterranean area) for cooking and seasoning; and maybe an oil for deep frying. Walnut or hazelnut oils are not specifically used in this book, but they are present regionally (for instance around the town of Grenoble and in the southwest) and can be used in a classic Vinaigrette (page 32) for an interesting twist.
– Vinegars come in many varieties, plain or flavored, but the essentials would be a white wine (for sauces) and a sherry vinegar. Choose good-quality, artisanal vinegars when possible. They are used in Court-Bouillon (page 26–27) and many sauces. Vinaigrette is a good way to experiment with other vinegars, such as cider or raspberry-flavored red wine vinegar.
– Strong Dijon mustard is an essential. Whole-grain mustard can be considered a basic as well.
– Rock salt is indispensable, as well as fine salt or *fleur de sel*. Choose additive-free sea salt. In France, salts

from Guérande or the region of Camargue are used a lot, but any good-quality salt will do.
- You will need butter for a lot of recipes, although the regional divide between butter and olive oil as cooking fats is still a reality. People in the Mediterranean area are less inclined to make *cuisine au beurre* and, indeed, you would never cook a Provençal ratatouille with anything other than olive oil.
- Cream is almost a must unless you stick to the southern style.
- Eggs, milk, flour, and corn or rice flour are needed for pastry but also for sauces.
- Capers and pickles (gherkins) are present in French cooking as acidic ingredients (souring agents), for example to cut through the fat, such as in gribiche (page 34), an egg-based, cold emulsified sauce.
- Long-grain and short-grain (pudding) rice is used as an accompaniment or in stuffing or desserts.
- Different varieties of dried white haricot beans are regional staples and the base of traditional dishes such as Cassoulet (page 170).

Of course, baking requires some specific items (chocolate, dried fruit, baking powder, yeast, etc.), but French-style pastry is renowned for its creativity based on a limited range of ingredients.

Flavorings: aromatic vegetables, herbs, and spices
The following range of flavorings complement the basic pantry list. As Ginette Mathiot explained, these are an essential part of the art of French cooking. They stimulate the appetite, add depth of flavor, and often serve as a garnish.

Aromatic vegetables
These four ingredients are the flavor base of many dishes. They are used very frequently.
- Celery stalks and leaves are frequently used to flavor broth (stock), Pot-au-Feu (page 124), and purées.
- Onions are essential to French cuisine. Cooking moderates their pungent flavor so their natural sweetness can develop. For cooking, use standard yellow onions. When a recipe requests onions to be sweated, cook them with a pinch of salt and some fat on low heat, until they turn transparent and tender without coloring. When they need to be sautéed, cook on high heat, moving them around with a wooden spoon so they brown without burning. Red onions have a crisp, sharp taste, which is good raw, while white or spring onions are milder and sweeter.
- Garlic cloves are covered in a fine skin; to remove this, crush each clove under the wide part of the blade of a knife. The skin can then be easily removed, as can the germ (the green part in the center).
- Shallots, which form the base of a great many sauces, have a subtler flavor than onions and garlic.

Although not a vegetable, lemon is also quite widely used, mostly in the south of France, for its souring role as well as to flavor dishes with its very aromatic zest.

Herbs
They play a starring role in many dishes, but they should be used sensibly.
- Fresh leafy herbs are best added torn or chopped toward the end of the cooking process or just before serving, so they don't lose their delicate flavor.
- Woody herbs such as thyme, bay, and rosemary retain a good flavor when dried and are better suited to long, slow cooking.
- Thyme is very emblematic of French cooking: it appears often and goes with almost everything, but try not to use it too systematically to avoid uniformity of taste.
- Parsley is commonly used as a garnish, even if the curly leaf variety now seems a little old-fashioned and tends to make way for the more peppery flat leaf.
- Another important herb in French cooking is tarragon, the star of béarnaise sauce. It has a strong anise-like flavor and should be used sparingly.
- Though they are less representative of French cooking, basil, dill, fennel, marjoram, mint, lemon balm, sage, and savory also appear regionally.
- *Fines herbes*, known for example as an omelet filling, is a classic mix including chervil, parsley, and chives, each of which can also be used individually. Chervil has a subtle aniseed flavor, while chives are part of the onion family but with a much more delicate flavor.
- Bouquet garni is a bunch of herbs tied together and used to flavor soups, broths (stocks), and stews, then removed before serving. It almost always includes a bay leaf, some parsley stalks, and thyme, but can also feature sturdier herbs.

Spices
Their strong aroma can overpower the taste of main ingredients, which is why they are used sparingly in French cooking, and only to impart subtle background aromatic notes. Although other spices may appear (for example in processed pork products), the following are the most frequently encountered in French recipes.
- Cinnamon mostly flavors fruit or milk and egg desserts.
- Cloves are often stuck into an onion or shallot, which is then simmered in a pot-au-feu or court-bouillon.
- Juniper berries are used in sauerkraut, marinades, and with game.
- Whole nutmeg, grated, appears as a distinct flavor in mashed potatoes, white sauces, omelets, and soufflés, and goes well with spinach.
- Saffron, obtained from the stigma of certain crocus flowers (which can be grown in France), adds depth to Bouillabaisse (page 176), a fish soup from the south.
- Pepper is perhaps the most important spice in French cooking. Green pepper is the unripe berry, often sold

in brine and infused in sauces. White is the shelled berry, warm yet not spicy. Red and black pepper are dried berries that have been picked at various degrees of maturity. Pepper aromas can range from fresh and citrussy to really strong and leathery, according to their origin and variety. Use only whole berries and grind them in a pepper mill, as ground spices lose their potency.

CHEESE

The French are very fond of their cheeses. At dinner parties, a cheese course almost always appears after the main dish and before desserts, with more bread and often appropriate wines. Cheese remains a daily staple in many French households. It is a delicious and nutritious addition to a light, vegetable-based meal—such as soup on a winter night. It's also a celebration of regionality, with so many (more than four hundred!) different varieties, tastes, and textures.

On a dinner party cheese platter, three to seven different cheeses are commonly served, following seasonality. Fresh goat or sheep cheeses or raw milk "alpages" cheeses (from rich grass prairies in the mountains) are better enjoyed in the spring and summer, while the bloomy and washed rinds are good for the winter. A typical platter will often include a hard or semihard cheese (like Comté from the Alps, Cantal, or Saint-Nectaire from Auvergne), a soft cheese (with a bloomy white rind such as Normandy Camembert, or a semisoft washed rind like Alsatian Munster or Savoie Reblochon), and, finally, a blue (maybe Aveyronnais Roquefort) or a goat cheese (a Languedocian Pélardon, for example). Guests will help themselves to every variety they fancy; no one really knows the perfect way to cut cheese but a good principle to follow is to cut leaving the same proportion of rind to inside for other guests. Cheeses are usually presented clockwise from the milder tasting ones to the stronger, which is obviously the order in which it makes sense to taste them.

WINE

Wine is inseparable from cooking and eating. The French will easily say yes to a glass of wine with a nice—or informal—meal, and several wines are frequently served at dinner parties to go with the different dishes. This does not necessarily mean drinking a lot; it is more about tasting and experimenting, pairing with food in a relaxed and sociable way. Do not be intimidated by wine vocabulary: the trend today is toward unpretentious wines, with a focus on pleasure and taste sensations.

Some young wines benefit from being poured into flared carafes, to increase contact with the oxygen in the air, which amplifies the wine's aromatic palette. This is entirely different from the decanting of certain aged red wines, which is meant to separate solid residues from the liquid and should be done in a much narrower carafe to avoid contact with air. To appreciate wine in the best way, it is important to have a set of actual wine glasses, even inexpensive ones.

Food and wine pairing is a very subjective matter and there are few absolute rules. Nowadays, the approach to wine is more relaxed and open. Ginette Mathiot generally recommended matching mild-flavored foods with light and/or young wines and strongly flavored dishes and sauces with more full-bodied wines, which of course still makes sense as basic advice. Interest in smaller-scale vineyards has grown, and you are no longer restricted to the prestigious wine regions of Bordeaux and Burgundy or to a few well-known grape varieties. Give chenin blanc or viognier a chance instead of chardonnay or sauvignon blanc. Try bold, sun-exposed wines from the south for a change from expensive châteaux. Enjoy easy, drinkable gamays from Beaujolais. Pair a festive meal with an unbranded, extra-brut Champagne. Remember that regional associations often make sense: a dish of sauerkraut goes well with a riesling, both from Alsace, as does a *crottin de Chavignol* with a Sancerre, also from the Loire region. Camembert is good with a cider of the same terroir, on the tart rather than the sweet side. Sometimes, audacious, anti-geographical pairings like Breton lobster with vin jaune (yellow wine) from Jura, a mountainous region in the east of France, work exceptionally well.

When shopping for wine, the French like to discuss choices with the *caviste* (the person in charge of the wine store), keeping their budget in mind and remaining open to many options, which is also an enjoyable way to learn.

Now is time to pour yourself a glass, which may be the best possible way to start cooking the French way.

Keda Black

GLOSSARY

ASPIC
A clear jelly made from clarified meat or fish broth (stock).

BAIN-MARIE
A vessel used for a gentle method of heating in which the dish to be cooked is placed in, or over, a pan of hot water, which is then placed in the oven or simmered very gently on the stove.

BARD
To cover a joint (cut) of meat or line a pan with strips of bacon or bacon rind known as bards, to prevent it from drying out.

BEURRE MANIÉ
A mixture of equal parts softened butter and flour. It is used to thicken sauces.

BIND
To add egg yolks or other thickening agents to a sauce, stuffing, or other preparation to thicken it and help it cohere.

BLANCH
To cook food briefly in boiling water, often vegetables. It is usually followed by "refreshing," or plunging straight into cold water to stop the cooking. The food should not stay in the cold water longer than it has in the boiling liquid while cooking. Blanching is sometimes done to help remove the skin (for example, from tomatoes or peaches) more easily.

BLEND
To combine ingredients together until homogeneously mixed. This can be done by hand or with the help of a food processor, mixer, or blender.

BONE
To remove the bones from a piece of meat or fish.

BOUQUET GARNI
A small bunch of herbs, tied together with string. It is added to sauces and broths (stocks) to add flavor.

BRAISE
To cook gently in a sealed pan such as a Dutch oven (casserole) with a small quantity of broth (stock) or thickened sauce. This method is mostly used for red meats, poultry, or game.

BROTH (or STOCK)
A flavored cooking liquid obtained by simmering beef, veal, or poultry meat and bones with vegetables and aromatics for 2–3 hours. The fat is skimmed off before use. For speed, a meat bouillon cube can be dissolved in hot water, and good liquid stocks are also available.

BROWN
To fry ingredients in very hot fat to color the surface.

CARAMELIZE
To cook an ingredient in a pan over quite a high heat until the sugar it contains becomes brown, like caramel. The term is often used for onions and meats. To caramelize sugar is to heat it until it melts into a syrup, becomes golden, and then turns to caramel.

CARVE (POULTRY)
To cut a cooked bird in order to serve. To carve poultry, stick a fork in the leg. Apply pressure to lift it and slide a knife along the carcass to detach the meat. Cut off at the joint. Stick a fork under the wings. Find the joint with a knife and cut through it. Press down on the fork to remove the wing. Use the knife to hold the chicken steady. For breasts, cut along both sides of the breastbone. You can do this in the kitchen or at the table if you feel confident.

CHANTILLY CREAM
The name given to (generally sweetened) whipped cream.

CHARLOTTE MOLD
A deep circular mold, usually made from nonreactive metal, used for many French cakes and puddings. It tapers towards the bottom and is sometimes gently fluted. A deep, round dish can usually be substituted.

CHINOIS
A fine-mesh conical sieve.

CHOP
To cut vegetables, meat, or other ingredients, usually with a large knife.

CLARIFY
To pass a liquid through a fine-mesh sieve or heat it with egg whites to remove any solid particles and leave a perfectly clear liquid.

CLARIFIED BUTTER
Butter from which the white milk solids have been removed, usually by heating and skimming. To be clarified, butter is melted in a saucepan over a gentle heat. Scum will appear on the surface, which may be skimmed or allowed to settle. In the latter case, the sediment will remain at the bottom of the pan. The clear liquid is poured off, leaving the sediment behind.

CLEAN (FISH)
To clean a whole fish, insert your index finger into the gill-slit and pull out the innards and the gills. With larger fish, make a slit in the belly and pull out all the insides. Rinse under cold water.

COAT
To cover a dish with a sauce or a cake pan with caramel. A sauce coats a spoon when it is thick enough to cover it.

COVER
To put a lid on a pan for cooking. A piece of foil can also be used. This stops evaporation and enables the ingredients to cook in liquid or their own juices. It also makes the cooking process faster and is recommended when boiling water to save time and energy.

CURDLE
This happens when the eggs in a mixture coagulate rather than blend smoothly with the other ingredients. This may happen in sauces such as mayonnaise or custard and in cake batters. To avoid it, you should add ingredients in a slow trickle while constantly beating.

CREAM
To beat egg yolks or soft butter and sugar together with a whisk or wooden spoon until they become thick and pale in color.

CRUSH
Crushing of ingredients can be done with a mortar and pestle, in a small coffee or spice mill, or under the blade of a knife, the ends of a rolling pin, a large spoon, or the flat bottom of a jar. Garlic cloves are crushed under the side of a large knife's blade, for easier peeling or to release their flavor when added whole to a stew or a roast.

DEEP-FRY
To cook ingredients by immersion into very hot oil or beef, or duck, or pork drippings. To test whether your deep-frying oil is hot enough, add a cube of stale bread. If it browns in 30 seconds, the temperature is 350–375°F/180–190°C, which is about right for most frying.

DEGLAZE
To pour a liquid (usually water, broth/stock, or wine) into a hot pan in which meat has been sautéed and removed, and to scrape and dissolve the brown caramelized morsels stuck to the bottom. The resulting flavored liquid can then be boiled to slightly reduce it and used as the base for a sauce.

DICE
To cut ingredients into even-size small cubes.

DUST
To lightly coat fish, meat, or vegetables with flour before frying. To sprinkle flour on a work counter before turning out a pastry or dough to prevent it from sticking.

DUXELLES
A mixture of chopped mushrooms, shallots, and parsley used as a forcemeat or stuffing.

EMULSIFY
To mix liquids of different densities together to form a thicker liquid, often with the help of an emulsifier such as mustard. This is what happens with mayonnaise, for instance.

EVAPORATE
To dry off excess liquid by boiling it, to concentrate the flavor and make it thicker.

FILLET (FISH)
To cut a fish in order to cook it. To fillet flat fish, cut off the fins all around the fish with scissors. Make a cut down the middle from the tail to the head to detach the flesh from the bones. Slide the blade of a filleting knife (or other knife with a thin, flexible blade) between the fillet and the bones. Remove all four fillets. For round fish, make a cut along the backbone of the fish from the head to the tail. Cut off the head and remove the fillets by sliding a filleting knife between the bones and the flesh. You will probably not be able to do this as

neatly as a fishmonger, but you will become better with practice. You can use the trimmings for broth (stock), see page 24.

FINES HERBES
This mixture of finely chopped fresh herbs, including chervil, parsley, tarragon and chives, is a classic addition to many French dishes.

FROST (or ICE)
To decorate a cake with frosting (icing), a glossy preparation made of sugar and other ingredients such as egg white, lemon juice, chocolate, or fruit purées.

GARNISH
To decorate a dish with herbs, cut lemons, or cut vegetables to make it attractive while adding ingredients that are also useful to achieve the right taste balance.

GIBLETS
The culinary term for the edible offal—feet, wings, neck, head, liver, and gizzard—of poultry. They are often used in making broths (stocks).

GLAZE
To brush the surface of food with a liquid, usually pastry with a mixture of water and egg yolk. Or, to coat a dish with a thick sauce or syrup before serving.

GRATIN
A dish that has been sprinkled with dried breadcrumbs or grated cheese and browned in a hot oven.

GREASE
To brush the inside of a baking pan with oil or butter in order to prevent the ingredients from sticking to it when cooking. Butter should be soft or melted, then chilled until it becomes solid but still soft enough to be brushed inside the pan.

GRILL (or BROIL)
To cook ingredients, lightly brushed with oil, by exposing them to the direct heat of a burner, charcoals, or flame.

GRIND (or MINCE)
To reduce meat to a fine mince by passing it through a mechanic or electrical grinder (mincer).

INFUSION
A liquid obtained by pouring boiling water over parts of a plant to extract the flavor.

JOINT (POULTRY)
Cutting poultry into smaller pieces (usually 6–8) for more convenient cooking.

JULIENNE
To cut vegetables such as carrots, turnips, celery, or the white part of leeks into very thin strips.

KNEAD
To work a dough against a work counter (or inside a bowl if the dough is quite wet) with the palm of the hand, until smooth and elastic. Bread and brioche dough should be kneaded vigorously to activate the gluten contained in the flour, while pastry should be kneaded very lightly, just to bring it together.

LARD
To insert strips of bacon fat into meat at even intervals in the direction of the grain, using a larding needle.

LINE
To cover the inside of a pan with pastry or slices of vegetables, meat, or bacon before filling. Or to cover the inside of a tin or the surface of a baking sheet with parchment (baking) paper so the ingredients don't stick.

LOOSEN
To add some liquid to a stiff preparation to make the texture looser or softer. It is sometimes necessary to loosen a preparation a little before adding a larger quantity of liquid, so it can absorb it more easily.

MACÉDOINE
A mixture of vegetables or fruit cut into dice.

MARINATE
To place raw meat or other foods in an aromatic liquid to tenderize it prior to cooking, or to add extra flavor.

MIREPOIX
Diced vegetables and herbs fried until brown. This is used to intensify the flavor of gravies and sauces.

MOISTEN
To add a liquid, such as water, milk, or broth (stock).

MUSLIN
A very fine cloth used to strain sauces and jams (jellies).

POACH
To cook gently in a liquid such as broth (stock), water, milk, or sugar syrup.

POUND
To make a piece of meat finer by applying the pressure of a mallet to it (usually by banging the mallet against the meat). Or to crush ingredients in a mortar with a pestle to mash them and bind them together.

PURÉE
To reduce ingredients to a smooth paste in a food processor or blender. Also, the name given to the paste itself.

QUENELLE
Small dumplings, often in the characteristic oval shape of the same name, poached in water or broth (stock).

REDUCE
To boil or simmer a liquid to evaporate the water it contains, thereby concentrating the flavor and thickening it.

RIBBON STAGE
When a mixture falls like ribbons from a spoon or whisk (usually when beating a batter).

ROAST
To cook food, such as meat or vegetables, in a hot oven with a little fat.

ROLL OUT
To roll out pastry or dough with a rolling pin on a work counter, which may be sprinkled with flour to prevent the pastry from sticking to it. Regular pressure should be applied to the rolling pin, which should always be moved in the same direction, while the dough or pastry is moved by quarter turns.

ROUX
A paste made from melted butter and flour, which forms the basis of many thickened sauces. Also sometimes used to describe the sauce itself.

SALT
To sprinkle salt, in particular on moist vegetables that are left to rest in a colander until some of their juices are drawn out, making them easier to cook or prepare for certain dishes. This is used for cucumbers, sometimes grated zucchini (courgettes), and squash, shredded spinach, etc.

SAUTÉ
To cook food in a high-sided frying pan or sauté pan with very little fat over a high heat.

SCALE (FISH)
To scale, hold a fish by the tail and scrape from the tail to the head with a flat knife or a scaler. Do it on the paper the fish was wrapped in to catch the scales.

SEASON
To improve the taste of food by adding the necessary quantity of salt and other flavorings such as acidic ingredients/souring agents (lemon, vinegar), spices, or other condiments.

SHRED
To cut leafy vegetables such as cabbage or spinach into thin strips. This can be done by layering the leaves, rolling them in together into a tube, then chopping them.

SIFT
To pass dry ingredients such as flour, sugar, or cocoa powder through a sieve to remove lumps before mixing with liquids.

SIMMER
To cook slowly over a gentle heat. Simmering takes place at the point at which a liquid is about to boil, with just a few bubbles breaking the surface.

SINGE
To pass plucked poultry or game birds over an open flame to remove any small feathers.

SKIM
To remove the froth or scum that forms on the surface of simmering liquids such as pot-au-feu or broths (stocks) with a skimmer or slotted spoon. This helps obtain a clear, clean broth (stock). Fat can also be skimmed with a spoon off the surface of broth (stock).

S–Z

SKIN (FISH)
For fish (apart from sole), it is better to skin after filleting. To skin sole, make a slit and cut the skin just above the tail. Take hold of the skin using a cloth and pull hard from top to bottom.

SLASH
To make a diagonal cut, usually done to a piece of fish to prevent it from bursting during cooking.

SOAK
To soften certain foods in water or milk: in order to rehydrate them in the case of dried or dehydrated ingredients such as raisins, gelatin, or dried mushrooms; or to clean and remove an unpleasant flavor such as bitterness, or excessive saltiness in the case of salted ingredients such as cod.

SOFTEN
To make an ingredient (such as butter or pastry) softer, usually by increasing its temperature, either by bringing it to room temperature or sometimes by working it with a spatula.

STEW
To cook meat, fish, or vegetables immersed in a liquid on a low heat and in a covered pan.

STIR IN
To add an ingredient or ingredients to a mixture while stirring in order to completely incorporate it. This is usually done in several stages, so the ingredient(s) can blend into the mixture smoothly. To "stir in" butter, cream, or egg yolks to a sauce or soup helps bind it, making it thicker and often glossier.

STUFF
To fill the inside of a piece of meat or poultry or a vegetable with stuffing (below).

STUFFING
A mixture of finely chopped ingredients and flavorings, often bound with breadcrumbs, egg, or bread soaked in milk. It is used as a filling for meat, poultry, or vegetables.

SUGAR-SYRUP STAGES
The different stages in consistency of a sugar syrup is tested usin a candy (sugar) thermomether.
- **Long thread stage**: this occurs at 228–230°F (109–110°C).
- **Feather stage**: This occurs at 232°F (111°C).
- **Firm-ball stage:** This occurs at 248°F (120°C).
- **Hard-crack stage:** This occurs at 293–302°F (145–150°C).

THICKEN
To add ingredients such as egg yolks to make a sauce or soup thicker.

TRIM (FISH)
To cut off the fins with kitchen scissors.

TRUSS
To fasten a piece of meat, often a bird, with kitchen twine (string) passed through the wings and legs with a trussing needle to keep it in place during cooking.

TURN (PASTRY)
Giving turns to a puff pastry refers to the technique of rolling out the pastry to a rectangle, folding it, then giving it a quarter turn before rolling out and folding again.

WELL
A hole hollowed out of a mound of flour, into which liquids are added.

WHISK
To vigorously beat a liquid or soft ingredient with a whisk, usually to incorporate air, thus increasing its volume and making it frothier and lighter. Other ingredients can be incorporated in the process. This method is also used to emulsify a sauce.

ZEST
The thin, aromatic outer layer of a citrus fruit, on top of the white pith. Zest also refers to removing this layer, usuallly by grating it with an extra-fine (rasp) grater or peeling it and cutting into thin strips. Citrus zest can also be dried and added to meat stews.

✹	GLUTEN-FREE
⌇	VEGAN
v	VEGETARIAN
Ⓓ	DAIRY-FREE
Ⓝ	NUT-FREE
✳	5 INGREDIENTS OR FEWER
㉚	30 MINUTES OR LESS
⌷	ONE POT

BASIC RECIPES
RECETTES DE BASE

The following chapter contains essential recipes you will need to refer to when using this book: different types of sauces and marinades, broths (stocks), doughs for sweet or savory baking, and basic creams and custards for desserts.

Broths and sauces are often considered to be the backbones of French cooking. Broths and court-bouillon are flavored liquids used in soups, stews, or sauces, or for cooking ingredients, to add an extra layer of flavor. They are best homemade, and a great way to use up scraps that would otherwise be discarded and yet are full of flavor, for example fish trimmings or meat bones. Some broths need to be simmered for a long time, but they don't require much effort to make and can be stored in smaller portions in the freezer. However, if you don't have broth at hand, you can use good-quality shop-bought liquid broth, bouillon (stock powder), or bouillon cubes.

Marinades are used to improve the texture and taste of meat, especially beef or game or firm-fleshed fish such as herring, before cooking. They are also highly adaptable and you can adjust or add flavorings to your liking.

Sauces coat or surround the dish they accompany, or may be served separately in a sauce boat. They are often quite rich, but eaten in moderation within balanced meals, they form part of a healthy diet. The recipes included in this chapter are the most frequently encountered classics such as Béarnaise Sauce (page 39), Beurre Blanc (page 29), or Vinaigrette (page 32). But of course, an endless range of other sauces can be made using the same methods, for example by varying the flavorings and thickening agents.

Sauces can be categorized according to how they are prepared: roux-based (like béchamel), emulsified (such as mayonnaise), or made with an aromatic liquid (such as jus which is the juices from roasted or braised meat, or a reduction of aromatic ingredients in wine), and thickened with starchy ingredients or fat. Sometimes a sauce is made using a combination of these methods.

Thickening agents help improve the body and smoothness of a sauce. When adding a starch-based thickener such as flour, potato flour, corn flour, or rice flour, mix it with a little cold liquid and pour into the boiling sauce, stirring constantly, then allow to boil for a few moments. If using egg yolk, pour the hot sauce into the yolks, stirring brisky with a whisk, then put the sauce on a very low heat and stir constantly until it thickens. Stop before it coagulates completely and do not let it boil. Fats, such as butter or cream, form an emulsion that gives a sauce flavor and consistency. They should be beaten into a liquid that is hot but not boiling, otherwise the emulsion will be destroyed.

Roux-based sauces are made from a mixture of flour and fat (usually butter)—which together make the roux—to which hot liquid (water, milk, broth, wine, or cooking liquid) is added. Roux can be white, blond, or brown, depending on how long the fat and flour mixture is cooked before the liquid is added.

Emulsified sauces are unstable, delicate preparations in which a fat-rich ingredient (usually cream, butter, or oil) is vigorously stirred into a liquid, forming fine droplets that become suspended in the liquid, which appears thick and smooth. Usually, an emulsified sauce is made by gradually adding the fat or the liquid by steadily beating. The sauce can be hot or cold, but it must be kept at an even temperature. Making an emulsified sauce always requires care. Mayonnaise (page 35), Béarnaise Sauce, and Hollandaise Sauce (page 37) are all made according to these principles.

This chapter also contains the three basic types of pastry dough—puff, pie dough (shortcrust pastry), and choux—that you need for making any French savory or sweet classic, from Pâté in Pastry (page 90) to Pommes Dauphine (page 222), from Apple Turnovers (page 332) to Chocolate Éclairs (page 322). Pie dough and puff can be made in batches and stocked in the freezer, either rolled out or not. Take them out of the freezer the day before you need them and defrost in the fridge. There are many variations of pie dough, but the recipe in this book, which is an easy, sugar-less version, is suitable for any sweet or savory tart. Homemade puff pastry is worth a try, but if you don't have the time for the lengthy process, replace it by good-quality, all-butter shop-bought puff. Mastering choux pastry paves the way to making not only patisserie-style desserts such as Paris-Brest (page 324), Saint-Honoré (page 326), and many more, but also some savory preparations like Gougère (page 74).

You will also find here the recipes for the essential creams used in French pastry. Once you learn how to make them, and master a simple jam and caramel, you will be able to prepare any dessert, as fancy as you care.

FISH BROTH

FUMET DE POISSON

Preparation time: 10 minutes
Cooking time: 30–35 minutes
Makes 2 cups plus 1 tablespoon/17 fl oz (500 ml)

When filleting fish, do not discard the bones and trimmings but save them for making a basic broth (stock). It is very easy and quick to make and will bring depth of flavor when used in fish soups such as Bouillabaisse (page 176). Try swapping the fish bones and trimmings for crustacean shells. To turn this into a creamy sauce, simmer until reduced a little, then whisk in some soft butter or cream and serve with seafood. It will keep for 2–3 days in the refrigerator, or can be frozen in small portions.

3½ tablespoons/1¾ oz (50 g) butter
⅓ cup/1¾ oz (50 g) sliced onion
1 lb 2 oz–1 lb 5 oz (500–600 g) fish bones
 and trimmings, such as from sole,
 silver hake (whiting), or brill
scant 1 cup/7 fl oz (200 ml) dry white wine
2 teaspoons lemon juice
4 parsley stalks, roughly chopped
salt

Melt the butter in a large pot over medium–low heat and add the onion and fish bones and trimmings. Gently cook for about 8 minutes, or until the onion has softened.

Add the wine and just enough water to cover. Add the lemon juice and parsley stalks and lightly season with salt. Cover and gently cook for 20–25 minutes.

Strain and let cool, then store in the refrigerator or freezer. The broth (stock) can be used for sauces or fish soups.

RICH BEEF BROTH (POT-AU-FEU)

BOUILLON GRAS (POT-AU-FEU)

Preparation time: 25 minutes
Cooking time: 3½ hours
Serves 6

Starting with the meat and aromatic vegetables in cold water and gradually heating them allows the juices to slowly release, creating a flavorsome and nutritious broth (stock) that you can simply pour over toast and eat as a soup. The cooked meat is good for Shepherd's Pie (page 130) and the broth (stock) can also be used in place of water in recipes such as Pot-au-Feu (page 124).

1¾ lb (800 g) stewing beef on the bone
2½ tablespoons/1 oz (30 g) salt
scant 1 cup/7 oz (200 g) diced carrots
½ cup/4½ oz (125 g) diced turnips
¾ cup/3½ oz (100 g) coarsely chopped leeks
¼ cup/2 oz (60 g) diced parsnips
1 celery stalk, diced
6 slices of toast, to serve

Put the beef in a large Dutch oven (casserole) with the salt. Cover with water. Bring to a boil, then reduce the heat and simmer for 15 minutes. Skim to remove the scum, and then add all the vegetables. Bring back to a boil, then reduce the heat to low and simmer for 3 hours.

Just before serving, skim off the fat. Put a slice of toast in the bottom of each soup tureen or bowl. Strain the broth (stock) into the tureens over the toast.

BASIC MARINADE

MARINADE CRUE

Preparation time: 10 minutes
Makes 6¼ cups/2½ pints (1.5 liters)

With its strong flavor and acidity from the wine and vinegar, this marinade is more suited to tenderizing robust meat and fish, such as stewing cuts of beef, rabbit, or game, before braising or roasting. It also works well with fish such as red mullet, tuna, or skate, before sautéing or grilling. If using on fish, don't marinate for too long, otherwise the acidity of the marinade can "cook" the flesh. The sweet marinade version below has milder flavors and is better suited to more delicate-flavoured meats such as veal.

½ cup/4 oz (100 g) sliced carrot
scant 1 cup/3½ oz (100 g) sliced onion
1 tablespoon/¼ oz (10 g) sliced shallot
1–2 cloves garlic, sliced
1–2 cloves, ground
1 bay leaf, broken up
2–3 sprigs thyme, chopped
3 cups/25 fl oz (750 ml) white wine
¾ cup/6 fl oz (175 ml) white wine vinegar
2 tablespoons olive or sunflower oil
salt and pepper

Cover the meat or fish to be marinated with the carrot, onion, shallot, and garlic, then sprinkle with the ground cloves, salt and pepper to taste, bay leaf, and thyme. Pour over the wine, vinegar, and oil. Marinate in the refrigerator for up to 3 days for meat (depending on the type and freshness), or 2–3 hours for fish, turning it regularly.

SWEET MARINADE / MARINADE DOUCE
For a sweet marinade, mix together ½ cup/3½ oz (100 g) chopped smoked bacon, 1½ tablespoon/1 oz (30 g) chopped onion, 1 tablespoon/¼ oz (10 g) chopped shallot, 1 small clove garlic, chopped, a few sprigs of flat-leaf parsley, chopped, a few sprigs of chervil, chopped, 1 tablespoon olive or sunflower oil, 4 tablespoons/2 fl oz (50 ml) white wine vinegar, salt and pepper.

COURT-BOUILLON

COURT-BOUILLON

Preparation: 10 minutes
Cooking time: 1 hour

A court-bouillon is a highly seasoned liquid used for cooking fish and seafood. Unlike fish broth (stock), it is not usually consumed, as it's often too salty or vinegary. *Court* means "short," which refers to the short time required to poach the ingredients. You can use it to poach lobster for Lobster Thermidor (page 204), Snails (page 56), or herrings before they are marinated (page 190). The fish or other food being poached should be completely covered by the court-bouillon, so adjust the quantity according to the shape and size of the ingredients and the pan.

Combine all the ingredients (see opposite) in a pan. Bring to a boil and simmer gently for 1 hour, stirring from time to time. Strain and use as desired.

COURT-BOUILLON WITH SALT
COURT-BOUILLON AU SEL
—

for mackerel, sea bream, or striped (gray) mullet

1 tablespoon/½ oz (15 g) salt
4 cups/32 fl oz (1 liter) water

COURT-BOUILLON WITH VINEGAR
COURT-BOUILLON AU VINAIGRE
—

for hake, pike, or carp

scant 1 cup/7 oz (200 ml) white wine vinegar
¼ cup/1¾ oz (50 g) sliced carrot
⅓ cup/1¾ oz (50 g) sliced onion
1 clove
1 sprig flat-leaf parsley, roughly chopped
12 cups/5¼ pints (3 liters) water
salt and pepper

COURT-BOUILLON WITH WHITE WINE
COURT-BOUILLON AU VIN BLANC
—

*for salmon or trout—or pike, carp, or trout,
if using red wine*

4 cups/1¾ pints (1 liter) dry white (or red) wine
¼ cup/1¾ oz (50 g) sliced carrot
⅓ cup/1¾ oz (50 g) sliced onion
1 large sprig thyme
1 large bay leaf
several sprigs flat-leaf parsley, roughly chopped
8 cups/3½ pints (2 liters) water
salt and pepper

COURT-BOUILLON WITH MILK
COURT-BOUILLON AU LAIT
—

for turbot, brill, or sole

12 cups/5¼ pints (3 liters) water
2 cups plus 1 tablespoon/17 fl oz (500 ml) milk
1 slice lemon
salt and pepper

MAÎTRE D'HÔTEL BUTTER

BEURRE MAÎTRE D'HÔTEL

Preparation time: 15 minutes,
  plus chilling time
Makes 6 tablespoons/3¼ oz (90 g)

Compound (herb) butters are an easy way to season a simple griddled Entrecôte Steak (page 134) or pan-fried fillet of sole, for example, without having to prepare a sauce. When making compound butter, it's important to take the butter out of the refrigerator in advance, as it needs to be soft enough to be mixed with the other ingredients. You can make many variations of compound butters; try using garlic, anchovies, lemon zest, and/or a variety of herbs. Well-wrapped, this will keep in the refrigerator for a few days, or several months in the freezer, so you can always have some at hand for an impromptu meal.

5½ tablespoons/2¾ oz (80 g) butter, softened
1 small handful flat-leaf parsley, chopped
1 teaspoon lemon juice
salt and pepper

In a bowl, beat the butter with the parsley and lemon juice, and season with salt and pepper.

Put the mixture in the center of a small sheet of wax (greaseproof) paper or aluminum foil and use this to roll the mixture into a log. Chill until required, at least 3 hours.

When ready to serve, unwrap the butter, cut it cross-wise into coin shapes, and place one on top of each serving. The butter will melt immediately to provide a rich sauce and goes particularly well with grilled meats such as steaks.

BEURRE BLANC

BEURRE BLANC

Preparation time: 15 minutes
Cooking time: 20 minutes
Makes 2 cups plus 1 tablespoon/17 fl oz (500 ml)

This subtly flavored sauce offers the perfect balance of creaminess and acidity. It is excellent served with delicately flavored fish like baked bass or sea bream. If you prefer a smooth sauce, strain out the shallot after reducing the liquid. The butter is whisked in quickly and vigorously so it doesn't have a chance to fully melt before it is incorporated, and so that the sauce has a creamy, slightly runny texture. Serve as soon as possible, as it firms up quite quickly. Solidified leftovers may be used to season rice.

scant ½ cup/3½ oz (100 g) chopped shallots
5 tablespoons/¾ oz (20 g) tarragon leaves,
    plus extra, chopped, to serve
⅓ cup/3½ fl oz (100 ml) white wine
4 tablespoons/2 fl oz (50 ml) white
    wine vinegar
4 tablespoons/2 fl oz (50 ml) heavy
    (double) cream
generous 1 cup/9 oz (250 g) butter,
    slightly softened
salt and pepper

Place a small, dry pan over low heat, and add the shallots with the tarragon leaves. Dry-fry for a few minutes.

Stir in the wine and all but a little of the vinegar. Bring to a simmer and cook gently over low heat for about 10 minutes to reduce.

Add the cream and bring to a boil.

Add the butter in small pieces, beating vigorously with a whisk between additions.

Remove from the heat and pour into a blender. Blend, then add the remaining vinegar to make the sauce smoother. Season with salt and pepper. A little chopped tarragon may be added at the last moment. Serve immediately.

BÉCHAMEL SAUCE

SAUCE BÉCHAMEL

Preparation time: 5 minutes
Cooking time: 20 minutes
Makes 2 cups plus 1 tablespoon/17 fl oz (500 ml)

2 tablespoons/1 oz (30 g) butter
⅓ cup/1½ oz (40 g) all-purpose (plain) flour
2 cups plus 1 tablespoon/17 fl oz
   (500 ml) milk
salt and pepper

This essential sauce is a roux, which is butter and flour mixed together and cooked with milk. It was perfected by La Varenne, a famous seventeenth-century cook, and named after the nobleman Louis Béchameil. It is considered a "mother" sauce: a base for other sauces, like Mornay, which is béchamel with egg yolk and Gruyère added to it. The consistency of béchamel is often adjusted depending on the recipe in which it is being used; for gratins, where it is poured over vegetables like cauliflower, endive, or zucchinis/courgettes (page 246), and sprinkled with grated cheese, it is more liquid; for the classic Cheese Soufflé (page 66), which is based on a béchamel sauce, you make it thicker. Depending on how it is to be used, it is also often flavored with freshly grated nutmeg.

Melt the butter in a pan over medium–low heat. Stir in the flour and cook for 2–3 minutes to form a paste.

Gradually add the milk, a little at a time, stirring all the time to prevent lumps forming. You may not need all the milk (see note). Simmer for 10 minutes over low heat, stirring constantly. Season with salt and pepper.

Notes
Since the absorbency of different flours can vary, it is difficult to specify the exact quantity of liquid needed, so add just enough milk to achieve the required consistency.

POIVRADE SAUCE

SAUCE POIVRADE

Preparation time: 15 minutes
Cooking time: 40 minutes
Makes 2 cups plus 1 tablespoon/17 fl oz (500 ml)

Poivrade is well rooted in French culinary history; its modern form is an evolution of a sauce that has been mentioned in culinary treaties since the Middle Ages. Poivrade is a derivation of a brown sauce—itself based on a brown roux—which is made with butter and flour mixed together and cooked until brown. Poivrade should be generously seasoned with freshly ground black pepper. Its spicy character makes it fit to enliven the taste of a simple Entrecôte Steak (page 134), or to accompany more robustly flavored cuts of meat, such as kidneys, game, or rabbit (page 152).

For the vinegar mixture
⅓ cup/3½ fl oz (100 ml) white wine vinegar
1 bay leaf
1 sprig thyme
1 carrot, sliced
1 shallot, chopped
1 onion, chopped
⅓ cup/3½ fl oz (100 ml) dry white wine
scant 1 cup/7 fl oz (200 ml) any broth (stock)
salt and pepper

For the brown sauce
3½ tablespoons/1¾ oz (50 g) butter
2 oz (60 g) onion, quartered
⅓ cup/2 oz (60 g) diced lean (streaky) bacon
½ cup/2 oz (60 g) all-purpose (plain) flour
1¼ cups/10 fl oz (300 ml) any broth (stock),
   or water
1 bouquet garni

Make the vinegar mixture: Put the vinegar, bay leaf, thyme, carrot, shallot, and onion in a pan with a pinch of pepper. Bring to a boil, then simmer over low heat for about 20 minutes, or until reduced by half.

Meanwhile, make the brown sauce. Melt the butter in a large, heavy pan. Add the onion and bacon and cook over medium heat until browned. Remove the onion and bacon, set them aside, and slightly increase the heat. When the butter begins to smoke, add the flour to the pan, all at once. Stir with a wooden spoon until the butter and flour mixture browns.

Stirring all the time, gradually add the broth (stock), then season with salt and pepper. Return the onion and bacon to the pan with the bouquet garni and gently cook for 20 minutes.

Remove the onion, bacon and bouquet garni from the brown sauce. Strain the reduced vinegar mixture and discard the solids. Pour into the brown sauce, along with the wine and broth. Bring to a simmer and cook for 15 minutes.

Pass through a fine strainer and add more pepper to taste. Serve with meat or game.

VINAIGRETTE

SAUCE VINAIGRETTE

Preparation time: 5 minutes
Makes ¼ cup/2 fl oz (60 ml)

1 tablespoon white wine vinegar, or more
  to taste
3 tablespoons good-quality olive, peanut
  (groundnut), or canola (rapeseed) oil,
  or a combination
salt

Nothing is simpler to make, yet a good vinaigrette will make any green lettuce sing. In fact, many types of cold dishes and salads call for it, whether they are made with cooked or raw vegetables, pulses such as lentils; or leftover poultry or cold fish and shellfish. The recipe below is just a template you can adapt: the types of oils and vinegars can be swapped to suit the ingredients you are seasoning (see Notes, below). It is important to taste the vinaigrette to determine if the ratio of fat, acidity, and salt seems right for your dish.

Dissolve a pinch of salt in the vinegar in a small bowl, then add the oil. Mix everything together well, either by whisking them in the bowl or by putting them in a clean jar with a tight-fitting lid and vigorously shaking.

Taste the vinaigrette and, if it seems too oily, add a little more salt or vinegar, and whisk or shake it again.

Notes
Try adding a teaspoon of Dijon or other mustard for a mustard vinaigrette (the mustard will also help the ingredients emulsify), a small handful of chopped herbs such as chives, chervil, parsley, tarragon, or basil (or a mixture) for a herb vinaigrette, or 1–2 crushed or chopped cloves of garlic for a garlic vinaigrette.

Depending on the food the vinaigrette is to dress, the vinegar can be replaced with an acidic fruit juice, such as lemon or orange.

ROQUEFORT SAUCE

SAUCE AU ROQUEFORT

Preparation time: 10 minutes
Makes ½ cup/4 fl oz (120 ml)

This cold sauce is very quick to make and good for serving to guests as an appetizer with raw vegetables. Roquefort is a blue sheep cheese from the south of France, known for its crumbly texture and pronounced taste, which is mellowed in this recipe by the addition of cream. You can also serve this warm by melting the cheese and cream together on low heat before adding the herbs and a dash a lemon: it is very good with entrecôte (page 134).

2 oz (60 g) Roquefort cheese
juice of ½ lemon
3 tablespoons heavy (double) cream
several basil leaves, torn, or 2 sage leaves,
    finely chopped
greens (salad leaves) or crudités,
    to serve (optional)

In a bowl, mash the Roquefort with a fork until smooth. Stir in the lemon juice and cream, and then whisk to emulsify. Stir in the basil or sage, and serve with greens (salad leaves) or as a dip with crudités.

GRIBICHE SAUCE

SAUCE GRIBICHE

Preparation time: 10 minutes
Makes 1¼ cups/10 fl oz (300 ml)

Gribiche is prepared like a mayonnaise, only with cooked yolks, and with herbs, chopped egg whites, and pickles (gherkins) added at the end to balance out the fat and give it texture. The origin of its name is uncertain: one theory is that it was named after nineteenth-century theater's caricature of gaudy female characters—which were also called "gribiche"—to reflect the sauce's strong 'personality.' Today, it retains an old-school charm as the classic accompaniment to calf's head but is also good with cold fish or vegetable dishes.

---

3 eggs
1 teaspoon Dijon mustard
1 cup/8 fl oz (250 ml) olive, peanut
   (groundnut), or sunflower oil,
   or a combination
2 tablespoons white wine vinegar
¼ cup/1¼ oz (30 g) pickles (gherkins),
   finely chopped
1 tablespoon chopped herbs, such as parsley,
   chervil, or tarragon, or a mixture
salt and pepper

Bring a pan of water to the boil, then gently add the eggs. Boil for about 10 minutes (to hard boil).

Using a slotted spoon, transfer the eggs into a bowl of cold water to quickly cool them, then remove their shells, halve, and separate the yolks from the whites. Finely chop the whites and set aside.

Separately, mash the yolks to a smooth paste with the mustard in a bowl. Gradually add the oil, a little at a time, as if making mayonnaise (see opposite), then add the vinegar.

Finish by adding the pickles (gherkins), chopped egg whites and herbs. Season with salt and pepper and serve.

MAYONNAISE

Preparation time: 10 minutes
Makes 1 cup/8 fl oz (250 ml)

1 egg yolk
¾ cup/6 fl oz (180 ml) olive, peanut
    (groundnut), or sunflower oil,
    or a combination
1½ tablespoons (20 ml) white wine vinegar
salt and pepper

One of the most emblematic French sauces, a "real" mayonnaise is made of only egg yolk, neutral vegetable oil, vinegar, salt, and pepper. There can be, however, multiple variations in the choices of oil, acidic ingredients (souring agents), and added flavorings. It should be gently mustardy for egg salad (egg mayonnaise) or Eggs Mimosa (page 76) or flavored with shallots when served with celery root/celeriac (page 116). In both cases, herbs may be added. Making it with all olive oil gives a more pungent taste, so you may prefer to use one-third olive with two-thirds of a more neutral vegetable oil, such as peanut (groundnut) or sunflower. Or go all the way by adding garlic and lemon, turning it into its cousin from the south, Aïoli (page 36).

In a large bowl, beat the egg yolk until creamy, using a wooden spoon or a whisk. Add the oil gradually and in small quantities, whisking between additions and adding more only when the mixture is completely emulsified.

When the mayonnaise is thick, add the vinegar. Season with salt and pepper and serve.

Notes
To make this recipe mustardy, add 1–3 teaspoons mustard, to taste.

Make sure all ingredients are at room temperature to avoid curdling.

If your mayonnaise curdles (which can happen if the oil is added too quickly), you can try to rescue it; place a teaspoon of mustard, or a droplet of vinegar, or ½ teaspoon of cold water, or a fresh egg yolk in a clean bowl, then gradually beat in the curdled mixture.

AÏOLI

AÏOLI

Preparation time: 10 minutes
Cooking time: 20 minutes
Makes 1¼ cups/10 fl oz (300 ml)

1 baking (floury) potato, unpeeled
   (about 3½ oz/100 g)
4–6 cloves garlic
2 egg yolks
1 cup/8 fl oz (250 ml) olive oil
2 teaspoons lemon juice
salt and pepper

Boldly flavored with garlic, aïoli is typical of the regions along the Mediterranean coast. It accompanies all kinds of raw or cooked vegetables, salt cod, and shellfish, sometimes presented together as a "*grand aïoli*," and traditionally served on Fridays. It is also served with snails (page 56) or with bourride, a Provençale or Languedocian fish stew. Made like mayonnaise, but with olive oil, it may or may not contain boiled potato or soaked stale bread, both of which give it a more full-bodied texture.

Bring a large pan of water to a boil and boil the potato in its skin until just tender, about 20 minutes. Drain and carefully peel while still hot.

Crush the garlic using a mortar and pestle or in a bowl, add the potato, and pound it to a purée with the garlic. Stir in the egg yolks with some salt and pepper. Gradually add the olive oil, stirring constantly as if you are making mayonnaise (see page 35). Finish by adding the lemon juice.

Note
The potato can be replaced with a piece of stale bread soaked in milk. (Squeeze out the milk when the bread has softened.)

HOLLANDAISE SAUCE

SAUCE HOLLANDAISE

Preparation time: 10 minutes
Cooking time: 10 minutes
Makes 1 cup/8 fl oz (250 ml)

Warm, luscious, and buttery, hollandaise is served with grilled meat or fish, eggs, and boiled or steamed vegetables. One of the classic French sauces, its principle, if not its name, was codified in François Pierre de La Varenne's 1651 *Le Cuisinier françois*. To achieve the hot emulsion of lemon juice, butter, and egg yolks, temperature control is critical. This is why it is cooked in a bain-marie. The temperature should never rise above 150°F/65°C: you can use a thermometer if you don't feel confident, but it's perfectly possible to succeed without. You will need careful observation and practice. Hollandaise made with blood orange juice and zest instead of lemon is called *maltaise* and goes very well with green asparagus.

---

3 egg yolks
¾ cup/6 oz (175 g) butter, cut into small pieces
2 teaspoons lemon juice, warmed
salt and pepper

Bring a pan of water just to a simmer over gentle heat. Put the egg yolks with a little salt in a heatproof bowl with 1 tablespoon of water and set over the pan. Stir vigorously to mix thoroughly. Take the pan off the heat and stir the butter pieces into the yolks gradually.

When all the butter is stirred in, put the pan back on a very gentle heat and stir until the sauce thickens; this is a delicate procedure, so it may be necessary to remove the pan from the heat from time to time if it looks as though the sauce may separate or curdle (see Note, below). You may need to do this several times, if needed.

Pour in the lemon juice, and season with salt and pepper. Serve immediately.

Note
To rescue a curdled hollandaise, put 1 teaspoon hot water into a clean bowl and gradually mix in the curdled sauce.

MOUSSELINE SAUCE   SAUCE MOUSSELINE

Preparation time: 15 minutes
Cooking time: 10 minutes
Makes 1 cup/8 fl oz (250 ml)

Mousseline is a variation of hollandaise (page 37) but with a mousse-like texture due to the whipped cream. The method is mostly the same, although the addition of cornstarch (corn flour) makes it a little more stable. It pairs well with the same types of ingredients, however the subtle lactic acidity from the cream and its fluffier quality makes it even more well suited for finer-textured fish like bass or delicately flavored vegetables, such as cooked leeks or asparagus.

4 tablespoons/¼ oz (10 g) cornstarch
   (corn flour)
2 egg yolks
⅔ cup/5½ oz (150 g) butter
¼ cup/2 fl oz (60 ml) heavy (double) cream,
   whipped to stiff peaks
salt

Put the cornstarch (corn flour), egg yolks, a pinch of salt, and 1 tablespoon of water in a heatproof bowl set over a pan of barely simmering water on a very gentle heat. Stir vigorously to mix thoroughly. Take the pan off the heat and stir the butter into the yolks in small pieces.

When all the butter is stirred in, put the pan back on the heat and stir until the sauce thickens; this is a delicate procedure, so it may be necessary to remove the pan from the heat from time to time if it looks as though the sauce may separate, or turn into scrambled eggs.

When the sauce has thickened, add the whipped cream and season with salt. Keep the sauce hot in the bain-marie or roasting pan, and whisk it lightly just before serving.

BÉARNAISE SAUCE

SAUCE BÉARNAISE

Preparation time: 15 minutes
Cooking time: 1 hour
Makes 1¼ cups/10 fl oz (300 ml)

Béarnaise sauce is a derivation of hollandaise (page 37) that is flavored prominently with tarragon. The invention of béarnaise was claimed in part by nineteenth-century author Alexandre Dumas, who was not only famous for *The Three Musketeers* novels, but also for his *Dictionary of Cuisine.* Steak béarnaise with fries is a French bistro staple. If you make this sauce quite often, you might find it helpful to make a batch of béarnaise essence (the initial reduction of vinegar, shallots, and tarragon) to keep at hand in the freezer. You can also add chopped onion and white wine (about a third of the volume of vinegar).

⅓ cup/3½ fl oz (100 ml) white wine vinegar
2 shallots, finely chopped
½ clove garlic, finely chopped
1 sprig of tarragon, finely chopped
3 egg yolks
⅔ cup/5½ oz (150 g) butter

In a pan, add the vinegar, shallots, garlic, and a little of the tarragon. Bring to a simmer over very low heat and cook for 20–30 minutes to reduce.

Strain the reduced liquid. Put the egg yolks and the reduction in a heatproof bowl set over a pan of barely simmering water on a very gentle heat. Stirring constantly, add the butter in small pieces. Add the rest of the chopped tarragon.

PUFF PASTRY

PÂTE FEUILLETÉE

Preparation time: 2 hours, plus resting time
Makes 1 puff pastry

1¾ cups/7 oz (200 g) all-purpose (plain) flour,
    sifted, plus extra for dusting
⅓ cup/3½ fl oz (100 ml) ice-cold water
scant ½ cup/3½ oz (100 g) butter, diced
    and softened
salt

The beautiful principle of puff is to create multiple layers of butter caged in a flour-and-water dough by rolling it out, folding it, and turning it, repeatedly. The process can be intimidating but is actually not complicated, just quite lengthy. The only difficulty is maintaining the overall temperature of the dough and butter, so the resting times in the refrigerator are essential. Mastering puff means you can make Mille-Feuilles (page 328), Apple Turnovers (page 332), and more, as well as savory items such as Vol-au-Vent (page 62), all from scratch.

In a bowl, mix the flour with a pinch of salt, and most of the water until you have a smooth, elastic dough, adding the rest of the water only if necessary; the dough should be firm and not feel too wet or sticky. Flour a work counter and roll the dough out to a rectangle ¼ inch (5 mm) thick. Put the butter in the middle of the dough and fold over the 4 corners so that they meet in the middle and the butter is covered, pinching the edges of the dough together to ensure the butter is completely enclosed. Let rest for 10 minutes in the refrigerator.

Remove the dough from the refrigerator, flouring the counter again if needed, then turn the dough 90 degrees clockwise and roll out, taking care not to let the butter escape, into a long rectangle ¼ inch (5 mm) thick. Fold both short ends to overlap in the center to make a smaller rectangle with 3 layers. Rest again for 15 minutes in the refrigerator. This stage is called a "turn."

Turn another 90 degrees, then roll out the dough again and repeat the folds. Rest for 15 minutes in the refrigerator.

Do this 6 more times. After the sixth turn, the pastry is ready, but the more it is worked, the lighter it will be.

Note
The butter should be as soft as the dough, or it will tear the carefully constructed layers.

BASIC PIE DOUGH

PÂTE BRISÉE

Preparation time: 20 minutes,
  plus resting time
Makes 1 pastry shell

2¼ cups/9 oz (250 g) all-purpose (plain) flour,
  plus extra for dusting
1 tablespoon flavorless oil, such as sunflower
  or canola (rapeseed)
½ teaspoon salt
9 tablespoons/4½ oz (125 g) butter, chilled
  and diced
4–6 tablespoons ice-cold water

This versatile recipe for a crunchy pastry is an essential for many savory and sweet pastries: Quiche Lorraine (page 68), Pâté in Pastry (page 90), Tarte Tatin (page 336), etc. Homemade pie dough (shortcrust pastry) does make a difference and is well worth the extra effort. It is in fact very quick to put together, although the resting time is important as it allows the gluten in the flour to relax, which avoids shrinkage when baking. Moreover, the dough freezes very well, so it's a good idea to make a larger batch and freeze it for future baking. Blind baking, explained below, is important to avoid soggy bottoms of tarts and pies.

Put the flour into a bowl. Make a well in the middle and add the oil, salt, and butter. Rub the butter into the flour. Moisten with enough of the water to just bring the dough together. Briefly knead the dough by hand; the more quickly this is done, the better the pastry will be. Cover the pastry with plastic wrap (clingfilm) and let rest in the refrigerator for between 30 minutes and 24 hours.

To line and bake a pastry shell
Bring it back to room temperature before rolling out. On a lightly floured counter, roll it out to a round, about ¼ inch (5 mm) thick and use to line a tart pan, preferably one with a removable bottom.
  To blind-bake the pastry shell (case), preheat the oven to 400°F/200°C/Gas Mark 6. Line the pastry shell with wax (greaseproof) paper and fill with pie weights (baking beans) or uncooked rice. Bake for 10 minutes, then gently remove the wax paper and pie weights or rice and return the pastry shell to the oven for another 10–15 minutes until it is light golden brown and cooked throughout.

Notes
Keep the ingredients and utensils as cool as possible. This will help the pastry retain a short, crumbly texture.
  The pastry may also be used to line small round or boat-shaped pans (barquettes).

CHOUX PASTRY

PÂTE À CHOUX

Preparation time: 20 minutes
Cooking time: 15 minutes
Makes about 6 buns

This twice-cooked pastry is said to have been brought to the French royal court by one of Catherine de Medici's Italian cooks. Piped in different shapes and sizes, then baked, it becomes a vessel for creams and fillings in pastries like Chocolate Éclairs (page 322), Saint-Honoré (page 326), and Paris-Brest (page 324). To make straightforward choux buns, cook as explained below, cool down, and fill with plain or flavored Crème Pâtissière (page 46) or Sweetened Whipped Cream (page 44). Choux pastry is also used in savory preparations like Gougère (page 74), or mixed with mashed potatoes for Pommes Dauphine (page 222).

1½ tablespoons/¾ oz (20 g) superfine
  (caster) sugar
scant ½ cup/3½ oz (100 g) butter, plus extra
  for greasing
1 teaspoon salt
1 cup/4 oz (120 g) all-purpose (plain) flour
4 eggs, beaten

In a large pan, gently heat ½ cup/4 fl oz (120 ml) water and the sugar, butter, and salt until the butter has melted, then bring to a boil. Quickly add the flour all at once, and beat with a wooden spoon. Reduce the heat and continue to beat the dough for about 1 minute, until it comes away easily from the sides of the pan.

Remove from the heat and let cool to room temperature. Gradually beat in the eggs until the dough is smooth and glossy.

Preheat the oven to 425°F/220°C/Gas Mark 7 and butter a baking sheet.

Pipe or spoon egg-size pieces of choux pastry dough onto the buttered baking sheet. Turn the oven down to 400°F/200°C/Gas Mark 6, then bake for 20 minutes until well risen and golden. Fill as required and serve hot or cold.

SWEETENED WHIPPED CREAM

CRÈME CHANTILLY

Preparation time: 10 minutes
Makes 1⅓ cups/11 fl oz (330 ml)

Sweetened whipped cream, or Chantilly cream (crème Chantilly), is appreciated for its fluffy texture, obtained by whisking air bubbles into cream. The use of the word "Chantilly" for whipped cream is often associated with the eponymous château, but the name could also be an allusion to a type of very white china produced in the area during the same period. Either way, the cream must be cold to ensure the correct consistency: to do this easily, place the mixing bowl in a larger bowl full of ice cubes. This cream is usually served with ice cream and pies or used as a filling for choux buns (page 42).

1⅓ cups/11 fl oz (330 ml) heavy (double or whipping) cream
superfine (caster) sugar, to taste
the seeds of 1 vanilla bean, to taste

Whisk the cream, which should be very cold, until stiff, frothy, and light. Take care not to overwhip it or allow it to become too warm, as the cream may turn to butter. Add sugar and vanilla to taste.

CRÈME ANGLAISE

CRÈME ANGLAISE

Preparation time: 5 minutes
Cooking time: 20 minutes
Makes 2 cups plus 1 tablespoon/17 fl oz (500 ml)

2 cups plus 1 tablespoon/17 fl oz (500 ml) milk
scant ⅓ cup/2 oz (60 g) sugar
6 egg yolks

A French equivalent of custard, crème anglaise generally has a pouring consistency and is served as a sauce for warm cakes, pies, and cooked fruit. It is also a base for making ice cream (page 298). Floating Island (page 284), made with the remaining egg whites from the recipe, swims in a pool of crème anglaise.

In a large pan, mix together the milk and sugar, then bring to a simmer over low heat.

Place the egg yolks into a large bowl and, beating constantly with a whisk, add the hot milk a little at a time.

Once fully incorporated, pour back into the pan. Place over low heat and, stirring all the time, gradually cook until thickened enough to coat the back of a spoon—about 10 minutes. Do not allow it to boil. Alternatively, set the bowl of custard over a pan of simmering water, ensuring the bowl does not touch the water, then cook for 10 minutes, stirring all the time, until thick. If the custard separates and curdles, pour small quantities into a bottle; cover with a clean cloth and shake vigorously for several minutes, after which the custard will thicken. Alternatively, process in a blender.

Strain the custard through a fine sieve and serve.

Note
Crème anglaise can also be made with whole eggs. Use 4 whole eggs per 2 cups plus 1 tablespoon/17 fl oz (500 ml) milk and take even greater care to thicken over the lowest heat possible.

This crème can be flavored with vanilla, coffee extract, lemon, or orange zest: add to the milk and sugar and proceed as above. For chocolate crème anglaise, replace the sugar with 200 g (7 oz) semisweet (dark) chocolate and use only 5 yolks.

CRÈME PÂTISSIÈRE

CRÈME PÂTISSIÈRE

Preparation time: 15 minutes
Cooking time: 10–15 minutes
Makes 2 cups plus 1 tablespoon/17 fl oz (500 ml)

½ vanilla bean, split
2 cups plus 1 tablespoon/17 fl oz (500 ml) milk
heaped ¼ cup/1¾ oz (50 g) all-purpose
   (plain) flour
⅓ cup/2½ oz (75 g) superfine (caster) sugar
1 whole egg
3 egg yolks

Chocolate Éclairs (page 322), Paris-Brest (page 324), Saint-Honoré (page 326), Mille-Feuilles (page 328), Raspberry Tartlets (page 340), Quick Rum Baba (page 330), etc. Crème pâtissière is a must for anyone who decides to bake the French way. Once the cream is cooked, transfer to a clean container. To avoid a skin forming on the top, gently rub a piece of butter over the surface of the cream; as the butter touches the hot cream, it will melt, leaving a thin layer of butter, which prevents the cream from forming a skin. Once chilled, beat the cream to smooth it out before using. Crème pâtissière can be flavored in many ways. Grated chocolate may be incorporated while the cream is still hot. To add liquor such as kirsch, the cream needs to have cooled down completely before you beat in the alcohol.

Scrape the seeds out of the vanilla bean with the tip of a sharp knife, then add along with the bean to the milk in a large pan and bring to a boil.

Beat the flour, sugar, whole egg, and egg yolks together in a large bowl. Stirring constantly, pour the boiling milk over the egg mixture, a little at a time.

Once fully incorporated, pour back into the pan. Place over low heat and, stirring constantly, gently cook until it just comes to a boil and thickens— 10–15 minutes. Immediately remove from the heat.

ALMOND CUSTARD

CRÈME FRANGIPANE

Preparation time: 15 minutes
Cooking time: 20 minutes
Makes 1¼ cups/10 fl oz (300 ml)

v

⅓ cup/2½ oz (75 g) superfine (caster) sugar
2 whole eggs
2 egg yolks
¾ cup/3¼ oz (90 g) all-purpose (plain) flour
6½ tablespoons/3¼ oz (90 g) butter, softened
1 teaspoon salt
1¼ cups/10 fl oz (300 ml) milk
½ cup/2 oz (60 g) ground almonds

Frangipane is a crème pâtissière enriched with ground almonds. In France, it is the traditional filling for *galette des rois* (see Note, below), a pastry traditionally shared for Twelfth night. The *fève*, a lucky charm—originally a dried fava (broad) bean—is hidden inside the cake and whoever finds it becomes the king or queen for the day. Frangipane can also be used to fill Chocolate Éclairs (page 322) or a pie dough (shortcrust pastry) base to make almond tart.

In a bowl, mix together the sugar, whole eggs, egg yolks, and flour with 4 tablespoons/2 oz (60 g) of the butter and the salt. Bring the milk to a boil in a large pan, and pour into the egg mixture, a little at a time.

Once fully incorporated, pour back into the pan. Place over medium heat and, stirring constantly, cook until the mixture thickens—about 5 minutes.

Mix in the remaining butter and the almonds. Gently stir until cool, then use as desired.

Notes
To make *galette des rois*, spread the frangipane on a round layer of puff pastry (page 40), put the charm on top, and close with a second layer of pastry, sealing the edges well and cutting them neatly. Trace a lattice shape with a knife before brushing with an egg yolk beaten with 1 teaspoon water. Bake for 30 minutes at 350°F/180°C/Gas Mark 4, brushing the top 5 minutes before the end with a mixture of ½ cup/2 oz (60 g) confectioners' (icing) sugar and 2 teaspoons water.

BUTTERCREAM

CRÈME AU BEURRE

Preparation time: 30 minutes
Cooking time: 10 minutes
Makes 2 cups/16 fl oz (475 ml)

Crème au beurre is a very rich cake filling that comes in different flavors and is found in fancy layered pâtisserie cakes like *fraisier*, *opéra*, *moka*, etc. Nowadays, it is considered a little old fashioned for modern tastes or dietary concerns, so today's pastry chefs tend to replace it with lighter creams; but it is actually very delicious and deserves a comeback. Start by enjoying it in a Chocolate Log (page 316), a roulade with a chocolate or coffee buttercream filling. There are several ways to make buttercream, and the following method is just one of them. For this version, it is imperative the eggs are at room temperature before you begin.

---

3 eggs, at room temperature
scant ⅔ cup/4 oz (120 g) superfine (caster) sugar
1¼ cups/10 oz (270 g) butter, softened
grated orange or lemon zest, coffee extract, vanilla extract, crushed praline, or cooled melted chocolate, to flavor (optional)

Place the eggs and sugar in a large bowl. Set the bowl over a pan of simmering water, and whisk together with an electric whisk until thick and creamy.

Remove from the heat and continue whisking until the mixture has almost completely cooled. Whisk in the butter, a little at a time, and continue whisking until the cream is thick, glossy, and completely cool. If desired, add your chosen flavoring.

Store in the refrigerator until required.

CARAMEL

CARAMEL

Preparation time: 2 minutes
Cooking time: 25 minutes
Makes 5 cups/2 pints (1.2 liters)

Caramel is merely sugar cooked to a precise temperature and that changes its texture, color, and taste to become a delicious, golden, thick syrup. The process in itself is extremely simple, but it's actually quite difficult to know when to stop. Even the best cooks sometimes burn their caramel: it does happen very quickly. Practice makes perfect, and a candy (sugar) thermometer can help if you don't feel confident. Always be very careful, especially if children are around, as caramel is dangerously hot. Pour caramel into a mold or pan to make Crème Caramel (page 282), or drizzle on top of a Floating Island (page 284).

5 cups/2¼ lb (1 kg) superfine (caster) or granulated sugar

Pour 1 cup/8 fl oz (250 ml) water into a large, clean pan. Add the sugar and place over low heat, stirring constantly, until the sugar dissolves.

Increase the heat and bring to a boil, without stirring, until all the water has evaporated and the sugar is starting to caramelize, moving from light gold to deeper brown: 155–165°C (311–329°F) for a light caramel; or 166–175°C (330–347°F) for a dark caramel.

When the correct temperature has been reached, carefully remove the pan from the heat and stop the cooking by adding one or two drops of ice water to the pan.

APRICOT JAM

CONFITURE D'ABRICOTS

Preparation time: 20 minutes
Cooking time: 45 minutes

apricots (see recipe)
sugar (see recipe)

When fruit is abundant and inexpensive, it's time to prepare jam, a wonderful way to make the most of the season's bounty, and to put summer in a jar for the colder months. It's also a good pantry staple with many uses. For breakfast, the French—children and adults alike—often enjoy tartines of fresh bread with butter and jam. It is also used to sweeten and flavor fromage frais for dessert. Melted in a pan and strained through a sieve, apricot jam can also be brushed as a glaze on fruit pies. This recipe also works for cherry jam, strawberry jam, mirabelle plum jam, and greengage plum jam. Strawberry jam is lovely spread on a basic jelly roll cake (Swiss roll), such as the one used for the Chocolate Log (page 316), before it's rolled up.

Cut the apricots in half lengthwise and remove the pits. Weigh the raw fruit.

Prepare a sugar syrup using the same weight of sugar as fruit and add the appropriate amount of water (see Notes, below): place the sugar in a pot, add water and place over low heat to dissolve the sugar.

Raise the heat and bring to a boil, without stirring, until the sugar reaches 232°F (111°C) on a candy (sugar) thermometer—the feather stage. Alternatively, to check the consistency without a thermometer, remove a small quantity of syrup with a teaspoon, then dip your fingers in cold water and immediately into the syrup on the spoon: the water should form small round beads on the surface; and, when taken between your fingers, the syrup should form a 1–2-inch (4–5-cm) long thread.

When the syrup reaches the feather stage, add the fruit. Continue heating, then as soon as it comes to a boil, remove the fruit. Boil the syrup until it reaches the feather stage again. Return the apricots to the pan. Bring to a boil again and add a few pits. Remove from the heat and put into sterilized jars, leaving a ½-inch (1 cm) head space, let cool, cover, and seal. Store in the fridge for up to 1 month.

Notes
The sugar:water volume ratio for a sugar syrup is 3:2—or if weighing, the sugar (grams):water (fl oz) ratio is 5:4—so if you have ¾ cup/5½ oz (150 g) sugar, you will need ½ cup/4 fl oz (120 ml) water.

Do not use brown sugar, as it changes the flavour and colour of the jam and may cause it to ferment. Choose superfine (caster) sugar instead.

STARTERS

ENTRÉES

French meals traditionally begin with a first course, called an "entrée," which you can choose either from the recipes in this chapter or from those within the fish or vegetable recipes across the book. There are so many different types of starters in French cuisine, some are relatively complex dishes and some of these are very rich: think Vol-au-Vent (page 62) or Cheese Soufflé (page 66). These types of starters are usually served as small portions and balanced out by the next course, which could be something more simple to make, like a roast. Other starters are much lighter, such as fish in aspic or poached egg with asparagus. Keep that in mind when planning a menu (page 9). Many of the dishes in this chapter could also be served as a single dish for an informal meal: Quiche Lorraine (page 68), Herb Omelet (page 84), or Croque-Monsieur (page 64) are all ideal for lunch with a green salad. The latter are frequently served as quick meals in cafés.

Sometimes, often at parties, several different starters are served as hors d'oeuvres before the first course, or as an alternative to it: they usually consist of small portions of some of the entrées in this chapter, with some fresh vegetable crudités (seasoned raw vegetables such as cucumber, tomato, carrot salad, etc.) and sometimes canapés (little toasts topped with spreads and various ingredients). Shellfish and crustaceans may also be served at this point of the meal, for instance oysters presented with *mignonette*—shallot mixed with vinegar—bread, and butter.

Starters fall into four main categories: fish starters (and frogs' legs and snails); cheese, milk, and egg starters; pâtés and terrines; and soups and vegetable starters.

Fish or shellfish dishes are often served as a first course, and some recipes from the fish section in this book also work well as starters: for example, Sea Scallop Gratin (page 200) or Stuffed Oysters (page 202) for special occasions, or Marinated Herring Fillets (page 190) for a simpler meal. Snails (page 56) and Sautéed Frogs' Legs (page 54) are delicacies most often served in small portions as specialty first courses.

Eggs are inexpensive, quick to cook, and so versatile that they can easily be the star ingredient of a first course. Eggs in Cocottes (page 82), Eggs in Meurette Sauce (page 78), or Poached Eggs with Asparagus (page 88) are elegant starters for a fancy dinner. Eggs are also a good source of protein. Combined with milk, often cheese, and sometimes vegetables, they can make deliciously substantial and comforting dishes such as Leek Pie (page 70) or Quiche Lorraine (page 68), but also refined food like soufflés and gougères (page 74). If serving a cheese starter (such as Hot Chavignol Crottins, page 72) for an informal meal you will probably want to skip the cheese course later.

In France, pâtés and terrines are often bought from a charcuterie, but they are not complicated to make at home. They are usually prepared a few days in advance and sometimes require ordering ingredients from the butcher. Pork Rillettes (page 98) or Liver Pâté (page 92) are good with pickles (gherkins) and good bread as a first course, but can also be brought to picnics or served as part of a buffet. Foie gras is for festive occasions and is usually served with thin toast and sometimes an onion chutney or fig chutney.

Soups come in many varieties: smooth veloutés, hearty country soups—some so substantial they can be served as a main course, such as Garbure (page 112)—or elegant seafood bisques perfect to begin a dinner party meal. Vegetable soups make a comforting and healthy everyday first course, but can also be served on their own for supper with some bread and cheese. This chapter includes a short selection of vegetable dishes suitable as starters, but you can also check the Sides and Vegetables chapter (starting on page 210) for other ideas, such as Leeks Served Like Asparagus (page 238), Lentil Salad (page 212), and Artichokes à la Barigoule (page 256).

SAUTÉED FROGS' LEGS

CUISSES DE GRENOUILLES SAUTÉES

Preparation time: 8 minutes
Cooking time: 10 minutes
Serves 6

72 frogs' legs
heaped ¼ cup/1¾ oz (50 g) all-purpose
  (plain) flour
scant ½ cup/3½ oz (100 g) butter
3–4 tablespoons finely chopped shallot
  or garlic
salt and pepper

Frogs' legs are a delicacy mainly associated with Dombes, a marshland area not far from Lyon. Their meat is reminiscent of chicken but with a softer texture similar to fish. They are eaten skinless, which is generally how they are sold, and cooked to add crunch and taste—often fried or breaded and with garlic, as below. They are emblematic of French culinary culture in the sense that one of its main concerns is to make the most of any ingredient at hand. In reality, they are not eaten very often, and only by some as an occasional delicacy, even though nowadays frogs are farmed for their legs.

Thread the frogs' legs onto 12 skewers, then sprinkle with the flour.

Melt the butter in a large sauté pan, skillet, or frying pan. Add the legs and sauté for 8–10 minutes, or until browned all over.

Season with salt and pepper, sprinkle with the shallot or garlic, then transfer to a plate and serve.

SNAILS

ESCARGOTS

Preparation time: 20 minutes, plus 1 week
  fasting of the snails
Cooking time: 2¼ hours
Makes 12 snails

Collecting snails after the rain, then fasting and purging them, is still quite popular in the countryside. It is probably the most authentic and tasty way to enjoy them, but nowadays you do not have to go through that whole process to try them, as they come ready-blanched in jars, or frozen. The most common preparation is *à la bourguignonne*—with garlic butter. In restaurants, they are usually served on special plates with hollows for each snail, and with tongs to hold the shell while you pull out the meat. The recipe below will serve 1 person, or 2 as a small starter, so adjust the ingredients according to how many you are serving. It is based on cooking larger Bourgogne snails. If you are cooking petit gris, shorten the boiling time to around 45 minutes to 1½ hours. To prepare the snails, carefully wash them in water mixed with white vinegar and a little salt; check each snail and discard any that are in the bottom of the shell, not visible.

For the snails
12 snails
all-purpose (plain) flour, for purging
white wine vinegar, for purging
1 quantity Court-Bouillon with White
  Wine (page 27)
bread, for serving (optional)
salt

For the stuffing
4 tablespoons/2 oz (60 g) butter
1 teaspoon finely chopped shallot, to taste
½ clove garlic, finely chopped
2 tablespoons/¼ oz (10 g) finely
  chopped flat-leaf parsley
salt and pepper

This is the traditional French method for purging snails: Fast the snails for a week, then purge them by feeding them salt mixed with flour and a dash of white wine vinegar. Carefully wash the snails (see above).

Bring a large pan of salted water to a boil and drop in the snails. Blanch in the boiling water for 5 minutes. Remove with a slotted spoon and let cool enough to handle. Take each snail out of its shell and remove the black part of the tail. Wash the snails again in plenty of water.

Pour the court-bouillon into a large pan and bring to a boil. Add the snails and boil for 2 hours. Let cool in the liquid. Carefully wash each shell, then drain on a napkin.

Preheat the oven to 400°F/200°C/Gas Mark 6.

Make the stuffing: Mix all the ingredients together in a bowl. Put a little stuffing in each shell, replace the snail and add more stuffing. Place the snails in a snail dish and bake in the oven for 8 minutes, then serve.

Note
Canned, bottled, or frozen snails, and their shells, can be found in some specialty stores. If using these store-bought alternatives, you can skip the purging step.

FISH IN ASPIC

ASPIC DE POISSON

Preparation time: 30 minutes, plus 12 hours
   of setting time
Cooking time: 4¼ hours
Serves 6

Covering ingredients in aspic, or gelatin, is visually spectacular, and was especially fashionable in household
cooking from the 1950s to the 1970s. The first record of
this type of recipe dates back to the thirteenth-century
Viandier, a book written by a cook named Taillevent.
Originally, it was a simple preservation technique, but it
also adds interest in terms of taste and texture. The jelly
melts in the mouth, adding moisture and flavor to the
fish and vegetables. It can be a good way to reuse leftover
fish. Be careful that your macedoine vegetables are
correctly cooked, retaining a subtle bite and bright color.

For the aspic jelly
2¼ lb (1 kg) veal knuckle
1 lb 2 oz (500 g) beef silverside
5½ oz (150 g) bacon rind, fat removed
2 onions, chopped
1 carrot, chopped
1 bouquet garni
1½–2 tablespoons/½ oz (12–15 g) powdered
   gelatin or 3–4 platinum gelatin leaves
   (if needed)
2 egg whites
⅓ cup/3½ fl oz (100 ml) Madeira, port,
   or sherry, to flavor (optional)
salt and pepper

For serving
6 slices tomato
6 oz (175 g) macédoine of vegetables
   (page 118)
9 oz (250 g) cooked fish, skinned and cut
   into pieces

Make the aspic jelly: Put the veal, beef, bacon, onions,
carrot, and bouquet garni in a large pan with 10½ cups/5
pints (2.5 liters) water and bring to the boil. Skim the
scum from the surface and let simmer on a steady heat
for about 4 hours.

   Carefully strain through a sieve lined with muslin and
let cool completely. Remove the fat, which will solidify
on the top.

   When the broth (stock) is cold, check the consistency:
if it has not set, soak the 3–4 gelatin leaves in cold water.

   To clarify the aspic, lightly beat the egg whites. If you
did not need to add the gelatin, put the broth in a pan
over very low heat. Stir in the egg whites and gently
beat all the liquid, without stopping, so that the egg
whites turn frothy, until the liquid just comes to the boil.
If using, add the Madeira, port, or sherry. Add the
drained gelatin to the broth if using, and stir until
completely dissolved (or add the powdered gelatin,
if using). Pour the clarified liquid through a sieve lined
with damp muslin, then discard the solids.

   To serve: Place a slice of tomato at the bottom of each
of 6 small dishes or ramekins, cover with a little of the
macédoine of vegetables, and top with a piece of fish.
Pour the aspic jelly into each dish. Cover with plastic
wrap (clingfilm) and let set in the refrigerator for 12 hours.

   Run a knife carefully around the edge of each dish
to loosen, flip tomato-side up onto a serving plate, and
shake gently to unmold. Serve cold.

NANTUA-STYLE PIKE QUENELLES

QUENELLES DE BROCHET À LA NANTUA

Preparation time: 40 minutes,
   plus resting time
Cooking time: 1½ hours
Serves 6

Quenelles are light, oval dumplings, often made with puréed leftover meat (such as veal, poultry, or liver) or fish (especially pike or any oily fish). They may also be made with bread, mashed potato, or flour as the base. Meat and fish quenelles are often used to fill vol-au-vents, and starchy versions to top stews and blanquettes. In the north of France, small ball-shaped quenelles known as *fricadelles* are added to soups. This starter of pike quenelles in Nantua-style sauce is the most elegant version, a classic found in *bouchons*, typical Lyon bistros.

For the pike quenelles
7 oz (200 g) pike fillets, skinned and any pin
   bones removed, trimmings reserved
2¾ cup/7 oz (200 g) breadcrumbs, soaked
   in milk
scant 1 cup/7 oz (200 g) butter, softened
4 eggs
freshly grated nutmeg
salt and pepper

For the Nantua-style sauce
reserved pike trimmings
scant 1 cup/7 fl oz (200 ml) dry white wine
½ oz (15 g) chopped onion
1 bouquet garni
3 tablespoons/1½ oz (40 g) butter
heaped ¼ cup/1¾ oz (50 g) all-purpose
   (plain) flour
¼ cup/2 fl oz (60 ml) heavy (double) cream
5 shelled crayfish tails, cut into small pieces
salt and pepper

Make the pike quenelles: Place the pike in a food processor and process until finely mashed. Drain the breadcrumbs thoroughly. Put the breadcrumbs in a bowl or mortar and, one at a time, mix in the butter, pike, and eggs. Season with nutmeg, salt, and pepper. Mix everything together until the mixture is perfectly homogeneous. Let rest for a few hours in the refrigerator.

Make the Nantua-style sauce: Place the fish trimmings, wine, onion, bouquet garni, and ⅓ cup/3½ fl oz (100 ml) water in a pan and season with salt and pepper. Bring to a boil and simmer for 1 hour. Strain and reserve the liquid.

Meanwhile, remove the dough from the refrigerator and shape into oblong quenelles at least 4 inches (10 cm) long using two spoons. Bring a small pan of water to a boil, then reduce to a simmer. Add the quenelles, a few at a time, and poach in the simmering water for 3–5 minutes. Remove and set aside.

Melt the butter in a heavy pan over medium heat. When it is hot, on the point of smoking, add the flour and cook for a couple of minutes, stirring with a wooden spoon, until the roux is light golden and still sandy in texture.

Take the roux off the heat and gradually add the strained liquid, stirring constantly to avoid lumps. Return to the heat and slowly bring to a simmer, stirring all the time. Stir in the heavy (double) cream to bind and add the crayfish tails.

Put the pike quenelles in the sauce and simmer for 15 minutes to poach. Serve hot.

VOL-AU-VENT À LA FINANCIÈRE

VOL-AU-VENT À LA FINANCIÈRE

Preparation time: 1 hour 15 minutes,
  plus resting time
Cooking time: 1 hour
Serves 6

For the pastry cases
butter, for greasing
all-purpose (plain) flour, for dusting
11 oz (300 g) Puff Pastry (page 40)
1 egg yolk

For the veal quenelles
2 tablespoons/1 oz (30 g) butter, plus extra
  for greasing
⅔ cup/2¾ oz (80 g) all-purpose (plain) flour,
  plus extra for rolling
1 whole egg
2 egg yolks
7 oz (200 g) veal, cut into pieces
freshly grated nutmeg
salt and pepper

For the financière sauce
3½ tablespoons/1¾ oz (50 g) butter
½ cup/2 oz (60 g) all-purpose (plain) flour
2 cups plus 1 tablespoon/17 fl oz (500 ml)
  chicken broth (stock)
juice of 1 lemon or ⅓ cup/3½ fl oz
  (100 ml) Madeira
1½ cups/3½ oz (100 g) thinly sliced mushrooms
a few truffle slices, chopped (optional)
salt and pepper

Vol-au-vent is a large puff pastry vessel filled with an opulent sauce of poultry, calve's sweetbreads, or veal quenelles and mushrooms called *"financière,"* a name evocative of its richness. *Bouchées à la reine* are merely the individual version of vol-au-vent, and Marie Leszczynska, wife of Louis XV, may have been the queen after which they were named. Making the pastry cases at home does require some work and patience, but they are worth the effort, compared to the shop-bought versions. Serve as a starter for a fancy meal or as a main course for a less formal affair.

Make the pastry cases: Preheat the oven to 425°F/220°C/Gas Mark 7 and grease a baking sheet with butter.

On a floured work counter, roll out the puff pastry to 1 inch (2.5 cm) thick. Using a sharp knife, cut out 6 rounds to no more than 2–2½ inches (5–6 cm) in diameter. Mix the egg yolk with a little water in a bowl and use a pastry brush to glaze the pastry rounds.

Make small incisions all around the edges of the rounds with the point of a knife. Then mark a smaller round in the center, taking care not to press too deeply. This will make the lids. Score a crisscross pattern on the inner round, if desired. Put the pastries on the prepared sheet. Bake for 35 minutes until deep golden brown, then remove the pastries from the oven, carefully remove the lids, and reserve. Pull out any uncooked pastry from the middle and set aside.

Meanwhile, make the veal quenelles: Make the choux pastry (see page 42) with ⅔ cup/5 fl oz (150 ml) water, the butter, flour, whole egg, and egg yolks (omitting the sugar). Chop the veal in a food processor, season with salt and pepper, and stir it into the well-beaten choux pastry dough, until smooth. Add nutmeg to taste.

Mold tablespoons of the dough into small finger-shaped quenelles and roll in flour. Set aside.

Make the financière sauce: Melt the butter in a heavy pan over medium heat. When it is hot, add the flour and cook for a couple of minutes, stirring constantly, until the roux is light golden and still sandy in texture.

Take the roux off the heat and gradually add the broth (stock), stirring constantly to avoid lumps. Return to the heat and slowly bring to a simmer, stirring all the time. Add the lemon juice or Madeira, the mushrooms, and the truffle, if using. Add the veal quenelles and gently poach for 5–8 minutes. Season with salt and pepper.

To finish, fill the pastry cases with the financière sauce. Replace the pastry lid and serve hot.

CROQUE-MONSIEUR

CROQUE-MONSIEUR

Preparation time: 15 minutes
Cooking time: 10 minutes
Serves 6

9 oz (250 g) crustless white bread,
  preferably stale
scant ½ cup/3½ oz (100 g) butter
½ cup/2 oz (60 g) grated Gruyère cheese
3 oz (85 g) ham, sliced

Marcel Proust mentions the croque-monsieur in his novel
À l'ombre des jeunes filles en fleurs, published in 1919,
as a post-concert snack taken at a hotel restaurant.
A croque-monsieur is merely a grilled ham and cheese
sandwich, made especially good by browning in butter
on both sides in a frying pan. Warm and comforting,
it's a French café staple and is often cooked in French
households as a quick lunch, usually served with a
green salad. Sometimes a layer of béchamel sauce is
added. The croque-madame is a version topped with
a fried egg.

Cut the bread into thin, evenly shaped slices. Spread
all the slices with some of the butter on each side and
sprinkle with the cheese. Put a piece of ham on half
the bread slices. Cover each one with a buttered slice.
Tie together with kitchen twine (string).

Melt the remaining butter in a skillet or frying pan
over medium heat. Add the croque-monsieurs and
brown for 4 minutes on each side. Remove the twine
before eating

CHEESE SOUFFLÉ

SOUFFLÉ AU FROMAGE

Preparation time: 25 minutes
Cooking time: 1¼ hours
Serves 6

Bringing a well-risen soufflé to a table of admiring guests is such a cliché of culinary prowess that it has discouraged many home cooks to even give it a try. Regrettably so, because it is not difficult but, in fact, really wonderful, with a cloud-like and comforting texture. The beaten egg whites should be folded into the cheese mixture very carefully, cutting through it and lifting it with a spatula, to preserve their volume. The other trick is to plan the correct time to put it into the oven so that you can serve it straight away once it's ready.

scant ½ cup/3½ oz (100 g) butter, plus
    extra for greasing
scant 1 cup/3½ oz (100 g) all-purpose
    (plain) flour
2 cups plus 1 tablespoon /17 fl oz (500 ml) milk
generous 1 cup/4½ oz (125 g) grated
    Gruyère cheese
5 eggs, separated
salt and pepper

Preheat the oven to 350°F/180°C/Gas Mark 4 and grease a soufflé dish or 6 individual ramekins right up to the top.

Make a very thick béchamel sauce (see page 30) with the butter, flour, and milk. Add the cheese and stir until melted, then let cool. Add the egg yolks to the cheesy sauce.

In a separate clean bowl, whisk the egg whites to stiff peaks and fold into the cheese mixture. Season with salt and pepper, and pour into the prepared dish. If using a soufflé dish, bake in the oven for 30 minutes, then turn the heat up to 425°F/220°C/Gas Mark 7 and cook for another 15 minutes. If using individual ramekins, cook for 10 minutes, then turn up the heat and cook for another 5–10 minutes, or until the soufflé is golden and just set.

Remove from the oven and serve immediately.

QUICHE LORRAINE

QUICHE LORRAINE

Preparation time: 20 minutes
Cooking time: 40 minutes
Serves 6

7 oz (200 g) Basic Pie Dough (page 41)
all-purpose (plain) flour, for dusting
¾ cup/4½ oz (125 g) diced smoked bacon
4 eggs
2 cups plus 1 tablespoon/17 fl oz (500 ml)
  crème fraîche, or 1 cup/8 fl oz (250 ml)
  milk mixed with 1 cup/8 fl oz (250 ml)
  crème fraîche
salt and pepper

The story goes that during the Franco–Prussian War of 1870, people fled from Lorraine to Paris or Lyon, carrying their countryside quiche recipe to the big cities. Today, quiche Lorraine can be found everywhere. It is often bought ready-made, as a handy snack or a quick meal, in boulangeries and charcuteries, and industrial versions are also sold at supermarkets. Making it at home, though, with good-quality ingredients and a homemade pastry is not complicated and really makes a difference. It's great served warm as a light lunch, accompanied by a green salad seasoned with vinaigrette (page 32).

Preheat the oven to 400°F/200°C/Gas Mark 6.

Roll the dough out on a counter dusted with flour and use it to line a solid-bottom 9-inch (23-cm) tart pan. Sprinkle the bacon over the bottom.

Beat the eggs in a bowl, add the crème fraîche, or milk and crème fraiche, and season with salt and pepper. Pour the mixture into the pastry shell (case). Bake for 40 minutes, or until golden and set.

Remove from the oven and serve.

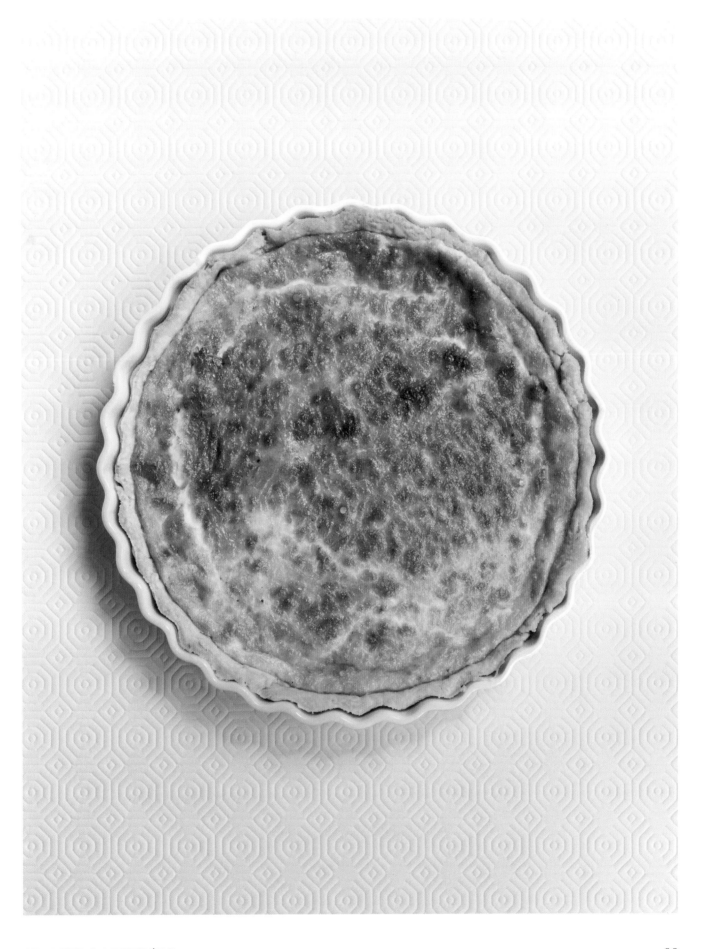

LEEK PIE

Preparation time: 10 minutes
Cooking time: 1 hour
Serves 6

v   ✳

scant ⅔ cup/5 oz (140 g) butter, softened
10 large leeks, white parts only, thinly sliced
3¾ cups/15 oz (420 g) all-purpose (plain)
   flour, plus extra for dusting
3 whole eggs
2 eggs, separated
½ cup/4 fl oz (125 ml) crème fraîche
salt and pepper

The French name of this dish comes from Picardie, a historical province located in the north of France, where leeks are a staple crop, and *flamiche*, which is the local name given to different kinds of pies or tarts, made with various types of pastries—leavened and slightly sweet, like brioche, puff, or pie dough (shortcrust pastry)—and fillings. The word *flamiche* probably refers to the small flame in a wood-fired oven, by which the pies were baked before the oven got hot enough for bread. This leek pie is officially classified as a starter but can also be served as a warm lunch.

In a large pan, gently melt 3 tablespoons/1½ oz (40 g) of the butter over very low heat. Add the leeks and season with salt and pepper. Cook for 30 minutes, stirring frequently.

Preheat the oven to 425°F/220°C/Gas Mark 7 and grease a pie dish with 1 tablespoon/½ oz (15 g) of the butter.

Meanwhile, in a bowl, combine the flour, the remaining 6 tablespoons/3 oz (85 g) butter, the whole eggs and egg whites (reserve the yolks), and a pinch of salt. Knead together with your hands until the mixture forms a dough.

Divide the dough into 2 balls, then thinly roll out each ball on a well-floured work counter. Line the prepared dish with one of the pieces of dough.

Remove the leeks from the heat, and stir in the reserved egg yolks and the crème fraîche. Taste and season again if necessary. Fill the pastry-lined dish with the leek and crème fraîche mixture. Cover with the remaining piece of dough and decorate by scoring patterns with a knife, if desired. Brush the edges of the pastry with a little water and gently press down to seal.

Bake for 30 minutes, or until brown. Serve hot.

HOT CHAVIGNOL CROTTINS

CROTTINS DE CHAVIGNOL CHAUDS

Preparation time: 10 minutes
Cooking time: 7–10 minutes
Serves 6

Crottin de Chavignol is a small, cylindric, firm-textured goat cheese from the Loire Valley area. Chavignol is the name of the village from which it takes its origins. When grilled, the surface of the cheese starts to melt, while the inside warms up but retains its shape. This *salade de chèvre chaud* became very popular in French cafés in the 1980s, as a starter or light lunch. It's easy to replicate at home, with any similar type of goat cheese. The authentic cheese is made using unpasteurized milk, but the pasteurized version Crottin de Champcol is also readily available. If you cannot find either, a *bijou* or any chèvre would also work with this recipe. Use fresh lettuce such as romaine or Little Gem, or lamb's lettuce (corn salad greens), which you can season with a little vinaigrette (page 32).

---

6 slices of crustless white bread
greens (salad leaves) of your choice
3 Crottin de Chavignol goat milk cheeses

Preheat the broiler (grill) to medium.

Brown the slices of bread on both sides under the hot broiler.

Place the greens (salad leaves) on each of 6 plates. Cut each cheese horizontally into 2 pieces. Place each piece of cheese on a slice of bread and return to the broiler. Cook for a few minutes until soft and golden. Place on top of the greens and serve immediately.

GOUGÈRE

GOUGÈRE

Preparation time: 20 minutes
Cooking time: 30 minutes
Serves 6

2 teaspoons/¼ oz (10 g) butter
11 oz (300 g) Choux Pastry (page 42; omitting the sugar)
generous 1 cup/4½ oz (125 g) grated Gruyère cheese (or cut it into thin strips), plus extra for sprinkling

According to Grimod de La Reynière, a celebrated food critic who published his *Almanach des gourmands* in 1804, gougères are a Burgundy specialty, although the regions of Flanders and Franche-Comté also claim them. These little savory choux traditionally accompany wine tastings in cellars, and they are lovely to make as an appetizer for a dinner party, served with a dry, aromatic or sparkling white wine. They melt in the mouth like little warm clouds. The ring shape in the recipe below, to be shared between guests, is more traditional but tends to be replaced by the pretty individual little choux, as pictured here.

Preheat the oven to 425°F/220°C/Gas Mark 7 and grease a baking sheet with the butter.

Mix in the cheese into the choux pastry. Pipe or spoon the dough in a ring shape (or place individual, well-spaced spoonfuls) on the prepared baking sheet. Sprinkle with extra cheese.

Bake for 25–30 minutes (or 15–20 minutes for individual gougères), until risen and golden brown. Serve immediately.

EGGS MIMOSA

ŒUFS MIMOSA

Preparation time: 30 minutes
Cooking time: 10 minutes
Serves 6

  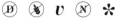

6 eggs
1 quantity Mayonnaise (page 35)
chopped parsley, to garnish
salt

The name Mimosa comes from the yellow flowery appearance the cooked yolks take on when passed through a sieve to decorate the eggs. They are a fancy version of a basic *œuf mayo*—a halved hard-boiled egg filled with a mixture of yolk and mayonnaise found at café counters—fit to be served on a silver platter for a Sunday lunch. Fancy, yet easy as child's play. The parsley for garnish can be swapped for chervil, chives, and even a little tarragon. The mayonnaise should be nicely but not overpoweringly mustardy.

To hard-boil the eggs: Bring a small pan of salted water to the boil. Gently lower the eggs into the boiling water. If you want the yolk to stay in the center of the white, stir constantly for a few minutes after lowering the eggs into the water. Boil for 10 minutes.

Remove the eggs with a slotted spoon, and plunge into cold water (this will make them easier to shell). Let cool completely, then peel and discard the shells. Cut them in half lengthwise, then carefully remove the yolks with a teaspoon and put them in a bowl. Mash the yolks and then stir two-thirds of them into the mayonnaise.

Arrange the white halves on a serving dish and fill with the egg and mayonnaise mixture. Pass the remaining yolks through a coarse sieve and sprinkle over the filled egg whites to cover the mayonnaise mixture. Garnish with chopped parsley.

EGGS IN MEURETTE SAUCE

ŒUFS EN MEURETTE

Preparation time: 10 minutes
Cooking time: 25 minutes
Serves 6

v

This specialty from Burgundy consists of poached, soft, or hard-boiled eggs served in a red wine sauce and garnished with fried garlic-rubbed bread. The name of the sauce, including the bread garnish, was codified by the chef and food writer Auguste Escoffier in 1928. The name's origin is debatable: among other possibilities, it may derive from the Latin *moretum*, a Roman sauce mentioned by Ovid (only quite different), or from the archaic adjective *moret*, meaning "dark." The eggs can be poached in the wine before the sauce is made, and kept warm in a bowl of salted warm water. Select a Mâcon red or Beaujolais wine to make the sauce and accompany the dish.

For the eggs
6 eggs
3 tablespoons white wine vinegar
   (optional, if poaching the eggs)
salt and pepper

For the meurette sauce
3 cups/25 fl oz (750 ml) red wine
1 small onion, finely chopped
1 shallot, finely chopped
1 sprig of thyme
1 bay leaf
2 sprigs flat-leaf parsley
5 tablespoons/2½ oz (70 g) butter
2 tablespoons/½ oz (15 g) all-purpose
   (plain) flour
salt and pepper

For the fried bread
6 slices bread
butter, for frying
½ clove garlic

Make the eggs: Bring a small pan of water to a boil and add a pinch of salt. Gently lower the eggs into the boiling water and boil for 10 minutes to hard-boil, or for 5 minutes to soft-boil. Remove the eggs with a slotted spoon and plunge into cold water. Peel and discard the shells. Alternatively, poach the eggs: pour 12 cups/ 5¼ pints (3 liters) of water and the vinegar into a pan and bring to a boil, then reduce to a gentle simmer. Crack each egg into a cup or ramekin, then let it slide into the water so that it is just covered. If necessary, spoon the white back over the yolk. Simmer gently for 3½ minutes. Meanwhile, prepare a bowl of salted warm water. Remove the eggs with a slotted spoon and keep warm in the salted water.

Make the meurette sauce: Put the wine, onion, shallot, thyme, bay leaf, and parsley in a pan. Bring to a boil, then reduce the heat and simmer until reduced by half.

Place the flour and 2 tablespoons/1 oz (25 g) of the butter into a small bowl. Work the butter into the flour to make a smooth paste, called a "beurre manié." Whisk this into the wine and then boil for 1 minute to thicken. Whisk in the remaining butter. Strain the sauce through a sieve into a fresh bowl. Discard the solids. Season the sauce with salt and pepper.

Make the fried bread: Melt a little butter in a skillet or frying pan and place one or two slices of the bread in the pan. Fry on both sides for a few minutes, then rub the slices with the garlic. Repeat for the remaining slices of bread.

Place the eggs on top of the fried bread, coat with the sauce and sprinkle with black pepper.

EGGS IN JELLY

ŒUFS EN GELÉE

Preparation time: 20 minutes,
    plus setting time
Cooking time: 4 hours 15 minutes
Serves 6

1 quantity aspic jelly (see page 58)
3 tablespoons white wine vinegar
6 eggs
6 tarragon leaves
1 small truffle, cut into 6 slices (optional)
1 cup/4½ oz (125 g) cooked peeled shrimp
    (prawns) (optional)
2 tablespoons chopped mixed herbs,
    such as flat-leaf parsley, chives, tarragon
    and chervil

In France, if you visit a *charcutier-traiteur*, which is a kind of French deli, the refrigerated counters will probably display rows of pretty, transparent jelly cylinders revealing ingredients imprisoned within. To older generations of French people, these feel a little nostalgic, since they have largely disappeared from menus. You can make them at home for guests who will be impressed. The truffle and shrimp (prawns) in this recipe are not obligatory. Make your own aspic if you have the patience and ingredients, or use a ready-made sachet of powder.

Spoon a layer of the aspic into the bottom of each of 6 small round molds or ramekins while it is still slightly warm. Set the remaining aspic aside. Put the molds in the refrigerator to set.

Meanwhile, pour 12 cups/5¼ pints (3 liters) water and the vinegar into a pan and bring to a boil, then reduce to a gentle simmer. Crack each egg into a cup or ramekin, then let it slide into the water so that it is just covered. If necessary, spoon the white back over the yolk. Simmer gently for 3½ minutes. Remove the eggs with a slotted spoon and drain on a clean tea towel.

When the aspic in the molds has set, garnish each layer with a tarragon leaf and a slice of truffle, if using. Carefully put a poached egg into each mold and spoon in some of the reserved aspic to fill it. Chill the molds and the remaining aspic in the refrigerator for 3 hours, or until set.

Run the blade of a knife around the edge of each mold and turn out on a serving dish. Chop the remaining aspic. Garnish the molded jellies with the chopped aspic, shrimp (prawns), if desired, and herbs.

EGGS IN COCOTTES   ŒUFS COCOTTE

Preparation time: 5 minutes
Cooking time: 10 minutes
Serves 6

Eggs baked in cream turn out lovely and luscious.
It's important to cook them in a water bath as explained
below, which prevents the temperature from rising
too much inside the oven. The recipe is a basic one that
you can adapt; try adding herbs, sautéed mushrooms,
or bacon. Serve with lots of good, fresh bread to mop
up the yolks and creamy whites. Eggs in cocottes make
an easy starter for a dinner party or a main course for
a light family meal, perhaps followed by a green salad.

boiling water, for bain-marie
½ cup/4 fl oz (125 ml) crème fraîche
6 eggs
salt and pepper

Preheat the oven to 425°F/220°C/Gas Mark 7.
  Half-fill a roasting pan with boiling water. Put 2 teaspoons of the crème fraîche into each of 6 ceramic
cocottes or ramekins. Put the ramekins into the roasting
pan and heat in the oven for 2 minutes.
  Removed from the oven, then break 1 egg into each
cocotte. Divide the remaining crème fraîche between
them and season with salt and pepper. Return the
roasting pan to the oven and bake for 6–8 minutes or
until set, then serve.

HERB OMELET

OMELETTE AUX FINES
HERBES

Preparation time: 5 minutes
Cooking time: 5 minutes
Serves 6

6 eggs
2 tablespoons/1 oz (30 g) butter
1–2 tablespoons chopped fresh herbs,
    such as flat-leaf parsley, chervil, chives,
    and tarragon, plus extra to serve
salt and pepper

Knowing how to make a good omelet will save many hungry situations. To produce something really satisfying with barely anything but three basic ingredients—eggs, butter, and salt—is truly in the spirit of cooking the French way. The trick lies in shaking the pan when the sides and bottom start to set, and to use a pan of the appropriate size. Purists like their omelet *"baveuse"*—a little runny in the center—but you can cook it a little more if you prefer.

Season the eggs with salt and pepper in a bowl, and mix in the chopped herbs.

Heat a skillet, frying pan, or omelet pan over medium heat and melt the butter in it. When the butter is very hot and nut-colored, pour the eggs into the pan.

When the eggs start to set and small bubbles have formed around the edge, bring the edges of the omelet toward the center with a fork while shaking the pan. Fold the omelet in half, folding the side of the omelet nearest to the handle of the pan toward the outside edge, and then quickly slide on to a hot dish. Sprinkle with the remaining chopped herbs. A good omelet should be slightly runny in the center.

PIPERADE

PIPERADE

Preparation time: 25 minutes
Cooking time: 30 minutes
Serves 6

4 tablespoons olive oil, plus extra for frying
1 onion, chopped
2¼ lb (1 kg) green bell peppers, seeded
  and chopped
2¼ lb (1 kg) tomatoes, skinned and chopped
1 clove garlic, crushed
3 slices cured ham
6 eggs
salt and pepper

Piperade is a vegetable stew that originates from Basque country and Gascogne, usually containing tomatoes, bell peppers, and onions cooked with olive oil in a terra-cotta dish. The colors of this dish are supposed to replicate those of the *ikurrina*, the Basque flag: red, green, and white. It is often served with cured ham from the same region, as well as eggs, as in this version, where the eggs are scrambled in the sauce and fried cured ham is used as a garnish. You will want some good bread to go with this.

Heat the oil in a large pan over medium–low heat and then add the onion, peppers, and tomatoes. Fry for about 10 minutes until the onions have softened. Add the garlic and season with salt and pepper. Simmer over low heat for a few minutes to thicken and reduce the liquid.

Meanwhile, heat a small pan over medium and add a little oil. Add the ham and fry for a few minutes, then keep hot.

Beat the eggs in a bowl and then stir them into the vegetables. Continue to gently cook over low heat, stirring occasionally, until the eggs are scrambled and cooked through.

Season with salt and pepper. Serve in a hot dish garnished with the ham.

POACHED EGGS
WITH ASPARAGUS

Preparation time: 15 minutes
Cooking time: 20 minutes
Serves 6

3 tablespoons white wine vinegar
6 eggs
18 asparagus spears, trimmed to 4 inches
   (10 cm) if green or 2 inches (5 cm) if white
4 tablespoons crème fraîche
1½ tablespoons/¾ oz (20 g) butter
salt and pepper

Asparagus has a short season, so its unique taste should be showcased with simple preparations. Eggs are a perfect match. If using green asparagus, you simply need to wash them and trim the hard woody end. If using white, you will have to peel them to remove the tough outer skin, and trim them shorter. Adjust their cooking time in the boiling water to their size: thicker ones may take up to ten minutes to become tender.

———————

Pour 12 cups/5¼ pints (3 liters) water and the vinegar into a large pan and bring to a boil, then reduce to a gentle simmer. Crack each egg into a cup or ramekin, then let it slide into the water so that it is just covered. If necessary, spoon the white back over the yolk. Simmer gently for 3½ minutes. Meanwhile, prepare a bowl of salted warm water. Remove the eggs with a slotted spoon and keep warm in the salted water.

Bring another large pan of salted water to a boil. Add the asparagus and cook for 5–10 minutes, or until just tender, then drain.

Return the asparagus to the pan with the crème fraîche and butter and cook over low heat for 10 minutes.

Season with salt and pepper. Drain the eggs, put them on a dish, and spoon the asparagus mixture over them.

PÂTÉ IN PASTRY

PÂTÉ EN CROUTE

Preparation time: 1½ hours,
    plus resting time
Cooking time: 1½ hours
Serves 6

Pâté en croûte—or *pâté-croûte* in Lyon and the Champagne region—is meat and stuffing encased in pie dough (shortcrust pastry). It's a glorious addition to a buffet spread or picnic. A generous slice can also be served at lunch with a green salad. The dish probably originates from medieval times, when a then-nonedible crust simply helped cook and preserve the meat. It was later that scrumptious pastry started to be eaten, blending the traditional arts of charcuterie and pâtisserie. Cooks often take pride in pinching the edges in pretty patterns and shaping decorations with the cuttings.

For the pie dough (shortcrust pastry)
4¼ cups/18 oz (500 g) all-purpose (plain)
    flour, plus extra for dusting
scant 1 cup/7 oz (200 g) chilled butter,
    diced, plus extra for greasing
2 teaspoons salt
about ⅔ cup/5 fl oz (150 ml) ice-cold water,
    to bind the dough

For the filling
7 oz (200 g) thin bacon slices (rashers)
1½–2½ cups/14 oz (400 g) stuffing of your
    choice (see pages 166 and 168)
11 oz (300 g) ham, sliced
11 oz (300 g) veal, cut into strips
1 egg yolk, whisked, to glaze
salt and pepper

Preheat the oven to 400°F/200°C/Gas Mark 6.

First, make the pie dough (shortcrust pastry): Place the flour in a bowl, make a well in the center, and add the butter and salt. Rub together with your fingers until the mixture has a breadcrumb-like texture. Add enough ice-cold water to just bring the dough together, mixing with your hands. Turn out onto a floured counter and knead well for 5 minutes until the dough is smooth. Form the dough into a ball shape, then place in a clean bowl. Cover and allow it to rest for 12 hours in the refrigerator.

Grease a 12 x 3½ x 3½-inch (32 x 8.5 x 8.5 cm) pâté dish or terrine with butter. Roll out two-thirds of the dough and use it to line the dish, leaving ¾ inch (2 cm) of dough above the rim.

Assemble the filling: Place a layer of bacon slices (rashers) at the bottom, then a layer of stuffing, a little of the ham, then a layer of the veal, seasoning each layer well with pepper. Continue making layers until you have used all the ingredients.

Roll out the remaining dough to create a lid slightly larger than the dish, and use to cover the filling. Pinch the edges of the dough together to seal. Brush with the whisked egg yolk to glaze, and make a hole in the center of the lid, keep it open during cooking with a small funnel made of cardboard. Bake in the oven for 1½ hours, or until deep golden brown.

Remove from the oven and cool completely before serving.

LIVER PÂTÉ

PÂTÉ DE FOIE

Preparation time: 25 minutes,
  plus marinating time
Cooking time: 2–3 hours
Serves 6

11 oz (300 g) calves' and chicken livers
scant 1 cup/7 fl oz (200 ml) Madeira
11 oz (300 g) fatty bacon
2 eggs
1 shallot, finely chopped
½ handful flat-leaf parsley, chopped
pinch of freshly grated nutmeg
butter, for greasing
bread, for serving (optional)
salt and pepper

This pâté may look like it has come from a real charcuterie, but it is truly simple to put together and bake.
For this dish, it's best to use a porcelain or terracotta
terrine, which is an oblong cooking vessel with a lid.
If you don't have one, try using a loaf pan lined with
parchment (baking) paper and tightly cover it with foil
before baking. Bring the terrine (which by extension,
is the name given to the pâté itself) to picnics, along
with pickles (gherkins). Or serve it as part as a *buffet
campagnard*—a country-style buffet spread.

The day before serving, place the livers in a bowl and
pour over the Madeira. Cover and let marinate in the
refrigerator for 24 hours.

Preheat the oven to 300°F/150°C/Gas Mark 2 and
grease a 7¾ x 5¾ x 3-inch (17 x 12 x 7.5 cm) terrine
with butter.

Remove and finely chop the marinated livers, along
with the bacon. Place both in a bowl and then stir in
the eggs, shallot, and parsley. Season with salt, pepper,
and the nutmeg. Press the mixture into the mold and
place in a roasting pan. Half-fill the pan with hot water.
Cover with aluminum foil, or the lid of the terrine, and
bake for 2–3 hours, until the blade of a knife inserted
into the middle comes out clean.

Remove from the oven, then let cool before serving
with bread, if desired.

FRESH DUCK
FOIE GRAS

FOIE GRAS FRAIS
DE CANARD

Preparation time: 30 minutes,
   plus standing and chilling times
Cooking time: 25 minutes
Serves 6

1 × 1 lb 2-oz (500-g) fresh foie gras,
   at room temperature
1 tablespoon truffle essence
4 tablespoons/2 fl oz (50 ml) port
toast, for serving (optional)
salt and pepper

The idea of over-feeding duck or geese to consume their fat-rich meat or liver has probably existed for more than four thousand years, according to Egyptian engravings. Written mentions also abound in Roman literature, including in Apicius' *De re coquinaria*, a culinary treaty dating back to the first century BCE. In France, the tradition developed in the seventeenth century in Alsace and the southwest, which are today still the two main areas where it is produced. Foie gras is iconic of classic French cuisine, and should be bought from trusted, small-scale, good-quality producers. Outside France, the traditional production and consumption of foie gras is a contentious subject, and is not permitted in some areas of the world. This recipe sits here as a reference as to how the French cook and eat it.

Begin preparing 3 days ahead. Remove the thin outer membrane, blood vessels (gently pull these out with a blunt knife), and gallbladder from the foie gras. Be careful not to rupture the gallbladder when removing it from the liver, as it will taint the flavor of the meat.

Reshape the foie gras and place it on a large piece of plastic wrap (clingfilm). Season with salt and pepper and pour the truffle essence and port over it. Wrap the plastic wrap around the foie gras and chill in the refrigerator for 12 hours or overnight.

The next day, take the foie gras out of its wrapping. Let it stand at room temperature for 1 hour, then preheat the oven to 250°F/120°C/Gas Mark ½.

Put the foie gras in an oval 7¾ x 5¾ x 3-inch (17 x 12 x 7.5 cm) terrine, pressing it down carefully with your fingers to get rid of any air. Put the terrine in a roasting pan, then half-fill the pan with hot water (about 175°F/80°C) and cook for 20 minutes. To check that it is properly cooked, place a metal skewer into the center of the foie gras and remove: it should feel warm.

Take the terrine out of the oven (and out of the bain-marie), and pour off the fat into a bowl of water; it will solidify in the water. Set the terrine aside to cool. Using a spoon or your fingers, remove the solidified fat from the water and place in a small pan. Set over low heat until the fat melts, then pour it over the surface of the foie gras and let set.

Using the terrine as a template, cut a piece of cardboad slightly smaller than the dish. Cover it in plastic wrap. When the fat has set, cover the foie gras with aluminum foil and place a the cardboard template and weigh it down, then chill in the refrigerator for 24 hours before serving with toast.

DUCK TERRINE WITH PRUNES

TERRINE DE CANARD AUX PRUNEAUX

Preparation time: 2 days and 45 minutes,
 plus marinating time
Cooking time: 1½ hours
Serves 12

The process of making this terrine may stretch over three days, but there is nothing complicated about it. This is a handy recipe for a dinner party because you can prepare it in advance and serve it as an appetizer, or as a starter with a nice green salad. Autumn and winter are the best seasons for this dish, with a touch of warm spice and the sweet note of dried prunes playing in contrast with the richly flavored meats. Make sure to include the duck liver, which brings a lot of taste.

1¼ cups/10 fl oz (300 ml) red wine
¼ cup/1¾ oz (50 g) superfine (caster) sugar
scant 1 cup/7 oz (200 g) prunes
1 × 1½–1¾-lb (700–800-g) duck
7 oz (200 g) pork side (belly)
3½ oz (100 g) breast of veal
1 duck liver
3½ tablespoons/1¾ oz (50 g) butter
4 tablespoons/1¾ oz (50 g) chopped onion
⅓ cup/3½ fl oz (100 ml) dry white wine
pinch of crushed juniper berries
2 sprigs thyme
2 bay leaves
9 oz (250 g) pork fat
2 eggs
7 oz (200 g) bacon slices (rashers)
salt

Begin preparing 3 days ahead. In a medium pan, bring the red wine and sugar to a boil, then reduce the heat and simmer until the sugar has dissolved.

Put the prunes in a bowl and pour the wine marinade over. Allow the prunes to soak for 12 hours.

Meanwhile, bone the duck and cut the meat, and the pork and veal, into large pieces. Cut the liver into two and put in a bowl along with the rest of the meat and set aside.

Melt the butter in a pan over medium heat and add the onion. Cook for about 10 minutes until softened.

Add the white wine and stir, scraping any sediment from the bottom, then add the juniper berries, 1 sprig of thyme, and 1 bay leaf. Season with salt, then remove from the heat and let cool. Pour this liquid over the meat, cover, and then let marinate in the refrigerator for 24 hours.

Preheat the oven to 350°F/180°C/Gas Mark 4.

Remove the meat and strain the marinade into a bowl. Put the meat and pork fat through a meat grinder (mincer) into a large bowl. Add the eggs and half the reserved marinade, then mix thoroughly.

Line a 7¾ x 5¾ x 3-inch (17 x 12 x 7.5 cm) terrine with the bacon slices (rashers), letting them hang over the edge. Drain the prunes, then pit (stone) them. Arrange alternate layers of the meat mixture and prunes in the terrine, finishing with a layer of meat. Fold the bacon over to cover. Put the remaining sprig of thyme and bay leaf on top. Cover with aluminum foil and place the terrine in a roasting pan. Half-fill the pan with hot water, then cook in the oven for 30 minutes. Lower the temperature to 250°F/120°C/Gas Mark 1 and cook for another 1 hour.

Remove from the oven and let cool at room temperature, then refrigerate for 48 hours before serving.

PORK RILLETTES

RILLETTES DE PORC

Preparation time: 40 minutes
Cooking time: 5¼ hours
Serves 6

1 cup/7 oz (200 g) lard or clarified butter
1 lb 2 oz (500 g) pork fillet, cut into 1¼-inch
   (3-cm) pieces
1 lb 2 oz (500 g) fatty unsmoked bacon,
   cut into 1¼-inch (3-cm) pieces
1 bouquet garni
bread or toast, for serving (optional)
salt and pepper

Rillettes were originally developed to preserve pork or other meat (duck, rabbit, goose, etc.) during the winter, by cooking it slow and low, mincing it, stirring in some fat, and packing it into jars. The result is a delicious paste, which sixteenth-century author Rabelais described as a "brune confiture de cochon"—a "dark pork jam." Indeed, rillettes spread on baguette make a great sandwich with pickles (gherkins). "Rillettes du Mans" (Le Mans is a town between Paris and Britany) are the most famous, but they can be made anywhere, including Tours, their town of origin in the Loire Valley.

Melt 4 tablespoons/1¾ oz (50 g) of the lard or butter in a large skillet or frying pan over medium–low heat. In batches, add the pork and bacon and cook, turning occasionally, for 10–15 minutes until golden brown.

Pour off the fat and set aside. Add enough salted water to cover the meat in the pan and bring just to a boil. Add the bouquet garni, reduce the heat to very low, and simmer for 5 hours, stirring the mixture occasionally once the water has evaporated, so that the meat is lightly browned all over.

Working in batches, transfer to a meat grinder (mincer) or a food processor and process to make a paste, adding a little water if necessary to make a looser mixture. Stir in the reserved fat, and then season with salt and pepper. Pack the meat into 6 small pots or ramekins. Melt the remaining ¾ cup/5½ oz (150 g) lard or butter, let cool, then cover the ramekins with a layer of the cooled lard or butter. Store in the refrigerator and serve cold, with bread or toast, if desired.

ONION SOUP GRATIN

SOUPE À L'OIGNON GRATINÉE

Preparation time: 10 minutes
Cooking time: 30–35 minutes
Serves 6

This gratinée version of onion soup is considered a Parisian classic, to be eaten at very late (or very early) hours after a night out in town. It's really quite marvelous how just a few ingredients, including the humble onion, can become such a delicious, restorative broth. Although it conquered the big city, this recipe is evidently a typical example of rustic yet ingenious cooking. Day-old bread is fine to use (to avoid waste), as it will be moistened by the liquid.

---

4 tablespoons/2 oz (60 g) butter
1 cup/9 oz (250 g) finely chopped onions
⅔ cup/2¾ oz (80 g) all-purpose (plain) flour
6¼ cups/2½ pints (1.5 liters) any broth
   (stock), hot
6 slices bread or 1¾ oz (50 g) vermicelli
grated Gruyère cheese, for sprinkling
salt and pepper

Preheat the oven to 475°F/240°C/Gas Mark 8.

Melt the butter in a large pot over low heat. Add the onions and cook, stirring occasionally, for 10 minutes until golden brown. Sprinkle with the flour and cook, stirring constantly, for a few minutes until browned. Pour in the broth (stock) and simmer for 10 minutes. Season with salt and pepper.

Place the bread, if using, in an ovenproof tureen, then strain the soup to remove the onion and pour it over the bread. Alternatively, return the strained soup to the pot, add the vermicelli, and cook for a few minutes until the pasta is tender, then pour into an ovenproof tureen.

Sprinkle with grated cheese and brown in the oven for 10 minutes. Remove from the oven and serve warm.

PISTOU SOUP

SOUPE AU PISTOU

Preparation time: 25 minutes
Cooking time: 40 minutes
Serves 6

A specialty from Provence, this can be served as a starter or a light main for lunch or supper. The vegetables may be changed according to season, so it can be made all year round. Sometimes, beans are added to make it more substantial. The word pistou comes from the Latin verb *pisto*, which means to pound, and refers to a ground paste of basil and garlic. In this recipe, the basil leaves are simply added at the end, highlighting their freshness and vivacity, rather than the pungency of classic pistou. Ginette Mathiot suggests serving with Gruyère but Parmesan or a sheep *tomme* would be a more contemporary choice.

---

4 tablespoons/2 fl oz (50 ml) olive oil
⅔ cup/5½ oz (150 g) diced carrots
⅔ cup/5½ oz (150 g) diced turnips
¼ cup/2 oz (60 g) diced onions
3½ oz (100 g) very ripe tomatoes,
  cut into wedges
1 clove garlic, crushed
1 good sprig fresh basil, finely chopped
grated Gruyère cheese, to serve (optional)
salt and pepper

Heat half the oil in a large pot over low heat and add the diced vegetables. Cook for 10 minutes, then add 7½ cups/ 3 pints (1.75 liters) water. Add salt and pepper to taste, bring to a simmer, and gently cook for 10 minutes.

Meanwhile, heat the rest of the oil in a large skillet or frying pan. Add the tomato wedges and garlic and gently fry for a few minutes to soften. Add to the vegetable broth (stock) and simmer for another 20 minutes.

Stir in the basil, and simmer for another 10 minutes. Serve very hot, sprinkled with grated cheese, if desired.

LOBSTER BISQUE

POTAGE À LA BISQUE DE HOMARD

Preparation time: 1½ hours
Cooking time: 55 minutes
Serves 6

1 quantity Court-Bouillon with Salt
   or Vinegar (page 27)
1 x 1 lb 2-oz (500 g) lobster
⅓ cup/3½ fl oz (100 ml) crème fraîche
6 tablespoons/3¼ oz (90 g) butter
⅓ cup/1¾ oz (50 g) rice flour or 1 tablespoon
   cornstarch (corn flour)
6¼ cups/2½ pints (1.5 liters) any broth (stock)
2 egg yolks
pepper (optional)

This recipe illustrates several techniques representative of French cooking: making a roux with the butter and flour before adding broth (stock) to make a sauce base for the soup; binding it at the end with yolks and butter as a *liaison;* then pounding the shells through a sieve to extract the last drop of flavor without wasting anything. The result—a coral-colored, velvety soup—is a most refined way to start a meal, and worth all the hard work.

Put the court-bouillon in a large pot and bring to the boil. Add the lobster and boil for about 10 minutes. Remove the lobster and allow it to cool slightly. When it is cool enough to handle, remove the tail and claw meat and reserve the head and shell.

Dice half the lobster meat and set aside, then finely chop the remainder. Put the reserved head and shell into a chinois (conical sieve) or other fine-mesh strainer, and pound with a pestle over a bowl. Mix the resulting paste with the finely chopped lobster flesh.

Pour the crème fraîche in a small pan and place over low heat. Gently heat but do not allow it to boil.

Meanwhile, melt 4 tablespoons/2 oz (60 g) of the butter in a large pan over low heat. Stir in the rice flour or cornstarch (corn flour) and cook, stirring constantly, for a few minutes, then gradually stir in the broth (stock), a little at a time. Cook, stirring constantly, until thickened—about 10–15 minutes.

Stir in the warm crème fraîche and the lobster paste. Beat the egg yolks with the remaining butter in a bowl and then stir into the soup. Just before serving, add the diced lobster meat, and some pepper, if desired.

LEEK SOUP

SOUPE AUX POIREAUX

Preparation time: 20 minutes
Cooking time: 45 minutes
Serves 6

This country soup would typically be found in nineteenth- and early-twentieth-century cookery manuals under the name "Bonne femme" (which literally translates as "good woman" but implies a modest, homely woman), suggesting its household simplicity. It's definitely a winter staple in many French homes, being so straightforward to make, healthy, and nourishing. It's often considered a good way to draw children to vegetables, the sweetness of the leeks perfectly complementing the starch of the potatoes.

---

4 cups/1 lb 2 oz (500 g) diced leeks
scant 2 cups/1 lb 2 oz (500 g) diced potatoes
2 cups plus 1 tablespoon/17 fl oz (500 ml)
  milk, heated
2 tablespoons/1 oz (30 g) butter
salt and pepper

Put the leeks and potatoes in a large pot, pour in 5 cups/ 2 pints (1.25 liters) water, and season with salt and pepper. Bring to a boil. Reduce the heat, cover, and simmer gently for 30 minutes, or until tender.

Transfer the mixture to a food processor or blender and process until smooth. Add the hot milk and briefly process to mix. Put the butter in a tureen, pour the soup over it, and serve.

Note
As a variation, replace the potatoes with ½ cup/3½ oz (100 g) long-grain rice.

JULIENNE SOUP

POTAGE JULIENNE

Preparation time: 45 minutes
Cooking time: 45 minutes
Serves 6

Most of the work here resides in the cutting. To julienne, chop the root vegetables into 1½–2-inch (4–5-cm) chunks, then cut into thin slices (about 1/16 inch/1 mm) and finally into thin strips of the same width. Shred the cabbage in strips of the same size. For the celery and leeks, start with chunks, then cut the strips lengthwise. Not only is this recipe good practice for honing knife skills, but it yields a delightfully light and interestingly textured soup, perfect to showcase good vegetables from the market.

5½ oz (150 g) carrots, cut into julienne strips
5½ oz (150 g) turnips, cut into julienne strips
2 leeks, cut into julienne strips
3½ oz (100 g) celery, cut into julienne strips
3½ oz (100 g) cabbage, cut into julienne strips
7 oz (200 g) potatoes, cut into julienne strips
¾ cup/3½ oz (100 g) shelled peas
2 sprigs chervil, finely chopped
1 head lettuce (greens), finely chopped
2 tablespoons/1 oz (30 g) butter
salt and pepper

Put the carrots, turnips, leeks, celery, cabbage, and potatoes into a large pot. Pour in 8 cups/3½ pints (2 liters) water and bring to a boil, then reduce the heat, cover, and simmer for 30 minutes.

Season with salt and pepper, add the peas, chervil, and lettuce (greens), and simmer for another 15 minutes.

Ladle into a tureen, stir in the butter, and serve immediately.

STARTERS / ENTRÉES

FISH SOUP

SOUPE DE POISSONS

Preparation time: 25 minutes
Cooking time: 40 minutes
Serves 6

fish heads from white fish, such as whiting
   (silver hake), sea bream, or red mullet
   (goatfish) (serve the rest as the main course)
¼ cup/2 oz (60 g) chopped onion
1 teaspoon chopped garlic
2 tablespoons/1 oz (30 g) butter
⅓ cup/1½ oz (40 g) all-purpose (plain) flour
2 cups plus 1 tablespoon/17 fl oz (500 ml) milk
6 slices bread
1 clove garlic, halved
scant 1 cup/7 fl oz (200 ml) crème fraîche
salt and pepper

When cooking fish for a main course, save the heads to make this soup as a starter (and the rest of the trimmings for broth). Or you can freeze them until you have a small batch. This means it is best to fillet the fish yourself or buy it from a fishmonger and ask if they will give you the trimmings. This recipe is a basic version, but fish soups in France come in many regional varieties (*cotriade*, bourride, *chaudrée*, bouillabaisse, etc.) incorporating different types of fish and shellfish, all made following the same elementary method.

Cut out and discard the gills from the fish heads. Put the heads in a large pan, add the onion, garlic, and 4 cups/1¾ pints (1 liter) of water. Bring to a boil, then reduce the heat, cover, and simmer for 20 minutes. Drain, pressing the fish heads to extract as much flavor as possible, and reserving the broth (stock).

Melt the butter in another pan over low heat. Stir in the flour and cook, stirring constantly, for 1–2 minutes, but do not allow the flour to brown. Gradually stir in the reserved broth, a little at a time, and then the milk and bring to a boil, stirring constantly. Season with salt and pepper and simmer, stirring frequently, for 20 minutes.

Meanwhile, preheat the broiler (grill) to medium, then toast each slice of bread on one side for a couple of minutes. Rub the untoasted side with the cut side of the halved garlic, and then return to the broiler to toast for 1–2 minutes.

Put the garlic toasts into 6 serving dishes. Stir the crème fraîche into the soup and pour the soup over the garlic toasts. Serve immediately.

Note
If desired, omit the garlic toasts and poach 12 shucked oysters in boiling water for 2 minutes, then add them to the soup just before serving.

GARBURE

GARBURE

Preparation time: 40 minutes
Cooking time: 3–3½ hours
Serves 6

Emblematic of the region of Gascogne in the southwest of France, garbure is strongly evocative of hearty peasant food. A healthy vegetable soup, it gets its bulk from beans and lots of character from the generous addition of garlic. Of course, recipes vary from one household to another, and are often enriched with local goose confit, which is meat slowly cooked in fat and preserved in jars. As shown in the two options below, it makes use of seasonal vegetables, often including cabbage when available. In all cases, it's substantial enough to play the role of a full meal all on its own.

Select the vegetables according to the time of year. Bring 12 cups/5¼ pints (3 liters) water to a boil in a large pot. Add the summer or winter ingredients, apart from the cabbage, along with the herbs and garlic from the soup base, and season with salt and pepper. Simmer gently for 1–1½ hours, topping up with boiling water if necessary during cooking.

Add the cabbage, if using summer vegetables, and continue simmering for 30 minutes. Add the goose confit and continue simmering for another 30 minutes.

Put the bread in a tureen. Reserving the goose, pour in the soup: it should be very thick—the spoon should stand upright in the tureen. If the soup is too liquid, thicken it with a purée of cooked navy (haricot) beans. Serve immediately with the goose.

In summer
9 oz (250 g) green beans
1¾ cups/9 oz (250 g) fava (broad)
    beans, shelled
scant 2 cups/9 oz (250 g) peas
11 oz (300 g) potatoes, cut into pieces
1 small green cabbage, shredded

In winter
scant 1½ cups/9 oz (250 g) chopped carrots
1 onion, chopped
½ cup/3½ oz (100 g) chopped turnips
2½ cups/1 lb 2 oz (500 g) dried navy (haricot)
    beans, soaked overnight

For the soup base
1 handful of chopped herbs, such as flat-leaf
    parsley, marjoram, or thyme
3 cloves garlic, crushed
1 piece goose confit
6 slices bread
cooked navy (haricot) beans, puréed,
    to thicken (if needed)
salt and pepper

CAULIFLOWER SOUP

POTAGE AU CHOU-FLEUR OU CRÈME DUBARRY

Preparation time: 30 minutes
Cooking time: 30 minutes
Serves 6

The humble cauliflower makes for a surprisingly elegant soup, a good starter for a dinner party. It was created by the cook of Madame du Barry, a commoner who became a countess and one of Louis XV's mistresses, and was very much appreciated at the royal court. The "crème" part of the name allegedly refers to its milky whiteness, reminiscent of the countess's pale complexion. If it's made with only water or broth (stock), it's called a "potage" (soup) and if bound with egg yolks, it becomes a crème.

1 medium cauliflower, separated into florets
⅓ cup/1 oz (30 g) cornstarch (corn flour)
2 egg yolks
2 tablespoons/1 oz (30 g) butter
salt and pepper

Bring 6¼ cups/2½ pints (1.5 liters) salted water to a boil in a large pot. Add the cauliflower and cook for 15 minutes, or until tender.

Drain well, reserving the cooking liquid. Set aside a few very small florets to be added to the soup just before serving. Purée the rest in a food processor or blender and mix with the cornstarch (corn flour). Add enough of the cooking liquid to thin it out until you have a good soup consistency. Return to the pot and simmer for 10 minutes.

Just before serving, stir in the egg yolks to thicken, then add the butter and reserved cauliflower florets. Season with salt and pepper, if necessary.

CELERY ROOT SALAD

CÉLERI-RAVE EN SALADE

Preparation time: 20 minutes,
 plus chilling time
Cooking time: 10 minutes
Serves 6

     ✳

2 tablespoons Dijon mustard
scant 1 cup/7 fl oz (200 ml) olive, peanut
 (groundnut), or sunflower oil,
 or a combination
1 shallot, finely chopped
1 celery root (celeriac)
salt and pepper

Often named *céleri rémoulade*, this hors d'oeuvre (part of a set of starters) is a school lunch and railroad station buffet classic. Commissaire Maigret, the famous fictional police detective of Georges Simenon's novels, is described as a man who enjoys simple working-class food, and this celery root (celeriac) salad is a representative example of what he would eat. Rémoulade is a version of mayonnaise flavored with mustard and shallots (and sometimes pickles/gherkins, herbs, and anchovies). The strong flavors play well against the slight aniseed taste of the celery root and its somewhat bland texture.

Begin preparing 6 to 8 hours in advance. Make sure all the ingredients and utensils to be used are at room temperature. Put the mustard in a bowl and gradually stir in the oil in a thin steady stream as if making mayonnaise (see page 35). Season with salt and pepper, and stir in the shallot. Set aside.

Bring a pot of salted water to a boil. Meanwhile, peel the celery root (celeriac) and cut it into wedges. Blanch it in the boiling water for 4–5 minutes. Drain and let cool.

When cool enough to handle, cut the celery root into fine strips or coarsely grate it. Place in a bowl and cover with the rémoulade sauce, then cover and chill in the refrigerator for 6–8 hours before serving.

MACÉDOINE

MACÉDOINE

Preparation time: 10 minutes
Cooking time: 10–15 minutes
Serves 6

1 lb 5 oz (600 g) mixed vegetables
   (carrots, beans, and small potatoes)
6 hard-boiled eggs, halved
Vinaigrette (page 32), to taste
Mayonnaise (page 35), to taste (optional)
salt

A macédoine is a mixture of diced or sliced vegetables or meats decoratively arranged and seasoned with a vinaigrette or mayonnaise. The version below is the most classic. You can also make macédoine with boiled and diced potatoes arranged in a pyramid, with a ring of cooked sliced beets (beetroot) garnished with chopped meat, and seasoned with sliced onions and a herby vinaigrette. Alternatively, layer slices of tomatoes and hard-boiled eggs with peeled shrimp (prawns) and dot with mayonnaise. For a green macédoine, combine strips of cabbage, celery, and small onions with grated carrots and cubes of avocado, all seasoned with either mayonnaise or vinaigrette.

Bring a pot of salted water to a boil. Add the mixed vegetables and boil for 10–15 minutes until tender. Drain and let cool.

Cut the vegetables into small dice and put into a bowl. Dress with vinaigrette, if using. Divide among plates and top with halved hard-boiled eggs and dress with mayonnaise, if using.

STUFFED MUSHROOMS

CHAMPIGNONS FARCIS

Preparation time: 30 minutes
Cooking time: 30 minutes
Serves 6

v

These mushrooms are stuffed with duxelles, which is a finely chopped mixture of mushrooms and flavorings and used as a filling or to boost texture and taste. It was created by La Varenne, a famous seventeenth-century cook and author who served the marquis d'Uxelles, hence the name. In this recipe, it is made with the mushroom stems (stalks) to reduce waste. These mushrooms may be served as a starter or as an accompaniment for meats. They could even be turned into a vegetarian main, perhaps with the addition of finely chopped vegetables in the filling such as carrots, Swiss chard, or spinach.

12 large white (button) mushrooms
6½ tablespoons/3¼ oz (90 g) butter, melted, or 3 tablespoons olive oil
¼ cup/2 oz (60 g) finely chopped onion
1 shallot, finely chopped
freshly grated nutmeg
6 tablespoons dried breadcrumbs
salt and pepper

Preheat the oven to 400°F/200°C/Gas Mark 6.

Clean the mushrooms, cut the stems (stalks) off, and set aside. Sprinkle the caps with a little of the melted butter or oil. Put the mushrooms on a baking sheet, gills upward, and bake for 7–8 minutes.

Remove from the oven, turn them over, and let cool.

Heat 2 tablespoons/1 oz (30 g) of the butter or oil in a pan over low heat. Add the onion, shallot, and mushroom stems, then fry for about 10 minutes until the onion is translucent. Add the nutmeg and gently cook over low heat until the mixture thickens. Season with salt and pepper.

Heap the duxelles into the mushrooms and sprinkle with the breadcrumbs. Arrange on a baking sheet, drizzle with the remaining butter or oil, and bake for 12–15 minutes, until heated through and topping is golden brown.

MAIN DISHES
PLATS PRINCIPAUX

In France, the main course—or *le plat principal*—is traditionally a dish of meat, poultry, fish, or sometimes shellfish served with a side but is nowadays frequently replaced by a vegetarian dish. Many recipes in this chapter give serving suggestions or recommend particular sides to go with the dish, though some regional recipes like Cassoulet (page 170) or Alsace Choucroute (page 172) are substantial enough to be meals in themselves. Keep in mind that many egg, cheese, or vegetable-based dishes from other chapters may be served as a main or single dish for everyday meals.

When shopping for meat and poultry, find out about the way the animals are raised, ideally in small-scale farms where animals have enough space to roam free. It might be a little more expensive, but the meat will have a significantly better taste, a more satisfying texture, and will be healthier and more nutritious. If you eat less meat, you can favor good-quality over quantity.

Select beef cuts according to your budget and the dish you intend to make. On the whole, the upper section of the animal provides the most tender cuts, suitable for rapid cooking, whereas the cuts from the lower section are tougher and best for braising or slow boiling. Both taste delicious. On average, 4 oz (120 g) meat off the bone, or 5½ oz (160 g) on the bone, should be enough for one person, but you can serve more or less depending on the meal as a whole.

Grilled meats are usually served plated with Sautéed Potatoes (page 232) or Fries (page 228) and steamed green beans or a green salad, with the sauce on the side.

Roast meat or poultry is carved and arranged on a serving dish with one or more garnishes of vegetables and the sauce or roasting juices on the side, in a sauce boat. They are good with Mashed Potatoes (page 229), Pommes Dauphine (page 222), and Duchess Potatoes (page 224), and ideally a seasonal vegetable: Ratatouille (page 260), Vichy Carrots (page 250), or Peas à la Française (page 242) would be good choices. Simmered meats in sauce—such as Beef Bourguignon (page 126), Daube of Beef (page 128), and Veal Blanquette (page 142) —can be brought to the table in their cooking vessels. They usually pair well with boiled potatoes or another starch that will absorb the sauce, such as rice or fresh pasta.

Always buy fresh-looking fish, with shiny skin, a firm belly, undamaged, bright eyes, and a fresh sea smell. Find out about seasons and endangered species, and shop responsibly.

The fishmonger can prepare the fish according to how you intend to cook it, but it is useful to know how to do it yourself, for example if you buy fish from fish markets by the sea where they don't usually fillet or clean the fish for you.

Scallops are associated with Brittany and Normandy, while mussels are primarily cultivated along the English Channel coast, up to Belgium, but also along the Mediterranean, where larger ones might be served stuffed or in fish soups. Sardines are sold in fishing harbors from Basque Country up to Brittany, as well as all along the Mediterranean. Cod is mostly fished in the Northern part of the Atlantic; you can also buy it salted, which is common in Provençal cuisine. Bass is seasonally fished in the English Channel and the Atlantic under the name "bar," or the Mediterranean, where it's called "loup." The region around Lyon has a strong tradition of freshwater fish recipes. Flat fishes tend to be represented mostly in regions neighboring the northern coasts of France.

In France, fish recipes are abundant and regionally varied, as the country has a very long and diverse coastline. In Normandy and Brittany, fish and shellfish are often cooked with cream or butter sauces (like Sole Meunière, page 180). Small mussels from the Northern coastline are enjoyed with local *frites*. Along the Mediterranean, fish are often cooked with local vegetables, for example *à la provençale*. Every coastal region has a version of a fish soup that includes local fish and ingredients.

Arrange large poached fish on a long dish, garnished with flat-leaf parsley, anchovies, capers, sliced tomatoes, or lemons, if you like. To serve, skin the fish first, then cut the fillets diagonally into portions. Serve the sauce separately, in a sauce boat. Grilled fish can be served on a dish garnished with lemon slices or quarters, with the sauce in a sauce boat or bowl. Serve fish meunière on a dish, coated with the sauce in which it was cooked, garnished with lemon slices or quarters.

Shellfish dishes are usually lighter but spectacular enough to be served as main dishes, so they could be preceded by a more substantial starter, or followed by something starchy that works on its own, like a potato salad.

BOILED BEEF (POT-AU-FEU)

BŒUF BOUILLI (POT-AU-FEU)

Preparation time: 25 minutes
Cooking time: 3½ hours
Serves 6

Although its principle is universal, the specific combination of vegetables and accompanying condiments make pot-au-feu unmistakably French, so much so that it has become a symbol of French cooking and a winter favorite in many households. It takes time and must be cooked very slowly, but it does not require much attention. It is comforting but light and vegetable rich. Ideally, choose a mixture of on-the-bone and gelatinous stewing cuts of beef.

2½ tablespoons/1 oz (30 g) fine salt
1¾ lb (800 g) stewing beef on the bone
1⅓ cups/7 oz (200 g) roughly chopped carrots
scant 1 cup/4½ oz (125 g) roughly
    chopped turnips
¾ cup/3½ oz (100 g) roughly chopped leeks
⅓ cup/2 oz (60 g) chopped parsnips
1 celery stalk, chopped
coarse salt, to serve
pickles (gherkins), to serve
Dijon or other mustard, to serve (optional)

Put 12 cups/5¼ pints (3 liters) water and the fine salt in a large Dutch oven (casserole) over high heat and bring to a boil. Carefully put the meat and bones into the boiling water, then reduce the heat and simmer for 15 minutes.

Skim off the fat, and add the vegetables. Bring back to a boil, then lower the heat and simmer for 3 hours.

Just before serving, skim off the fat again and transfer the beef to a serving platter. Pour the soup into a tureen, leaving the vegetables in the pot. Serve the beef in a separate dish, surrounded by its vegetables, with coarse salt, pickles (gherkins), and mustard, if desired.

BEEF BOURGUIGNON BŒUF BOURGUIGNON

Preparation time: 20 minutes
Cooking time: 2½ hours
Serves 6

1 tablespoon oil
2 oz (60 g) pearl (baby) onions or shallots
generous ½ cup/3½ oz (100 g) bacon lardons
5 cups/1 lb 8½ oz (700 g) stewing beef,
   cut into pieces
¼ cup/1 oz (30 g) all-purpose (plain) flour
1¼ cups/10 fl oz (300 ml) any broth
   (stock), heated
1¼ cups/10 fl oz (300 ml) red wine
1 bouquet garni
1 cup/3½ oz (100 g) peeled and
   chopped mushrooms
salt and pepper

According to the 1867 edition of the French reference dictionary by Pierre Larousse, "bourguignon" describes dishes prepared with wine, including bœuf bourguignon, which is perhaps the most classic French stewed dish. When cooking, the collagen in the meat slowly transforms into gelatin, which dissolves in the hot liquid, creating a thick sauce that coats the tender meat. Do not pick an expensive wine for this but one you would definitely enjoy drinking, and not too light either. Serve as a weekend lunch with potatoes or fresh pasta.

Heat the oil in a heavy Dutch oven (casserole) over medium–high heat. Add the onions and fry for a couple of minutes, then add the lardons and cook for another 5 minutes until browned. Remove them from the pot and set aside.

Add the meat and fry on all sides for 5 minutes to brown. Sprinkle with the flour, then stir for 1 minute until browned. Add the hot broth (stock), fried onions and lardons, wine, and bouquet garni, and season with salt and pepper. Gently simmer over low heat for 2 hours.

Add the mushrooms and continue simmering for another 30 minutes.

Remove from the stove and serve.

DAUBE OF BEEF

BŒUF EN DAUBE

Preparation time: 15 minutes,
  plus marinating time
Cooking time: 3¼ hours
Serves 6

1 quantity Basic or Sweet Marinade (page 25)
2 lb (900 g) stewing beef, cut into 1¼-inch
  (3-cm) slices
2 tablespoons/1 oz (30 g) butter
scant 1 cup/7 fl oz (200 ml) any broth (stock)
1 onion, chopped
1 bouquet garni
salt and pepper

Daube is the southern and more aromatic version of bœuf bourguignon, a stewed dish of beef in wine. Red would be more appropriate here for the marinade. The recipe has many variations in the southeastern corner of France, from Nice to Avignon. It can also be prepared with other meats such as boar or Camargue bull, in which case it becomes a *gardianne*, and is often served with boiled or mashed potatoes. Often, a dried-out piece of orange zest is added to the marinade.

Begin preparing 12 hours in advance. Make the marinade. Place the beef in a bowl and pour over the marinade, cover, then let marinate in the refrigerator for 12 hours.

Remove the slices of meat, reserving half of the marinade, and pat dry with paper towels. In a heavy Dutch oven (casserole), heat the butter on medium–high heat. Add the meat slices and fry them on both sides for a few minutes to brown, then lower the heat and cook gently for 15 minutes.

Add the reserved marinade, the broth (stock), onion, bouquet garni, and salt and pepper, to taste. Cover and cook on low heat for 3 hours.

Serve warm.

SHEPHERD'S PIE

HACHIS PARMENTIER

Preparation time: 30 minutes
Cooking time: 25 minutes
Serves 6

Leftover meat from Pot-au-Feu (page 124) is ideal for this, as it will have been cooked to a tender, shreddable consistency and is full of flavor. Shepherd's pie is called Parmentier in France in honor of the eighteenth-century scientist who promoted the consumption of the American potato in France. Hachis parmentier is a perfect family dish, very popular with children. It can also be made with blood sausage (black pudding) or duck confit instead of the meat. It's also a good example of how a dish originally created to use up leftovers can become a much-loved classic. As it's a filling dish, you can just serve it with a good green salad seasoned with vinaigrette.

For the beef mixture
1½ tablespoons/¾ oz (20 g) butter
¼ cup/2 oz (60 g) chopped onion
2 cups/3½ oz (100 g) fresh breadcrumbs
⅓ cup/3½ fl oz (100 ml) milk, hot
2¼ cups/11 oz (300 g) chopped leftover
   cooked beef
generous ½ cup/3½ oz (100 g) chopped
   smoked bacon
1 tablespoon chopped flat-leaf parsley

For assembling
1 quantity Mashed Potatoes (page 229)
¾ cup/2 oz (60 g) dried breadcrumbs or
   ½ cup/2 oz (60 g) grated Gruyère cheese
butter, cut into small pieces, for dotting

Preheat the oven to 400°F/200°C/Gas Mark 6.
  Make the beef mixture: Heat the butter in a pan over medium–high heat, add the onion, and cook for 5 minutes until softened. Soak the breadcrumbs in the hot milk, then squeeze out the excess liquid. In a bowl, mix together the beef, bacon, onion, breadcrumbs, and chopped parsley. Season with salt and pepper.
  For asssembling: Using half of the mashed potatoes, cover the bottom of a large ovenproof dish. Spread the beef mixture on top, and layer with the rest of the potatoes. Sprinkle with the breadcrumbs or cheese.
Dot with the butter and cook in the oven for 20 minutes until brown.
  Remove from the oven and serve hot.

TOURNEDOS ROSSINI

TOURNEDOS ROSSINI

Preparation time: 15 minutes
Cooking time: 15 minutes
Serves 6

6½ tablespoons/3¼ oz (90 g) butter
6 slices day-old bread
6 tournedos steaks
6 slices foie gras
1 truffle, sliced
salt and pepper

A seared steak topped with foie gras and truffle and served on fried bread, this dish was created sometime in the nineteenth century to satisfy the decadent culinary desire of Italian composer Gioachino Rossini. It's not really clear which of Casimir Moisson, Antonin Carême, or Modeste Magny, three famous Parisian cooks of the time, prepared it for the first time. In any case, it quickly made it into the bourgeois culinary pantheon. Tournedos is a round, tender, and lean cut of beef, thickly sliced in the fillet and barded with fat. Outside France, the traditional production and consumption of foie gras is a contentious subject, and is not permitted in some areas of the world. This recipe sits here as a reference as to how the French cook and eat it.

Heat half the butter in a large skillet or frying pan over medium heat. Add the bread slices and fry on both sides for a few minutes to brown. Transfer to plates and set aside.

Heat the remaining butter in the pan and add the tournedos; cook for about 3 minutes on each side for medium-rare. Season with salt and pepper and place each tournedos on a slice of fried bread.

Heat the pan over high heat again and, when it is very hot, sear the foie gras slices for 1–2 minutes on each side until deep golden brown. Arrange them on top of the tournedos and put a slice of truffle on each one. Season with salt and pepper, if desired, and then serve.

Note
The foie gras needs to be seared only if it is raw. Slices of Fresh Duck Foie Gras (page 94) can also be used, in which case no further cooking is necessary.

ENTRECÔTE STEAK

ENTRECÔTE

Preparation time: 5 minutes
Cooking time: 9 minutes
Serves 6

6 × 3½ oz (100 g) entrecôte steaks
oil, for brushing
1 quantity Béarnaise Sauce (page 39), Maître
    d'Hôtel Butter (page 28), Poivrade Sauce
    (page 31), or Roquefort Sauce (page 33),
    warmed, to serve
Fries (page 228), to serve (optional)
salt and pepper

"Steak frites" is almost an emblem of Frenchness. It's the quintessential brasserie main course and a favorite of all generations, usually served with a béarnaise (a tarragon-flavored sauce, page 39), a blue cheese sauce, or a flavored butter. You could also serve the entrecôte with green beans. Reduce the cooking time if you like your meat rare or medium–rare. If you have chosen a béarnaise to go with the steak, cook the sauce first, and keep it warm in a water bath while you take care of the steaks. If you are going with the compound butter, you can make it well in advance.

Heat a grill pan over high heat and brush the steaks with oil. As entrecôtes are thicker than other steaks, they need to be cooked longer. When the pan is hot, put on the steaks and cook for 4 minutes on the first side until brown, rotating the meat halfway through to make cross-hatch marks; then flip and cook for 5 minutes until the other side is browned, again rotating to achieve the desired grill marks.

Season with salt and pepper and serve with the chosen sauce and fries, if desired.

Note
Entrecôte steaks are cut from just behind the shoulder, between the ribs. Ask your butcher to cut these. Alternatively, porterhouse (sirloin) and sirloin (rump) steaks can be cooked in the same way.

TRIPE À LA MODE

TRIPES À LA MODE

Preparation time: 35 minutes,
  plus soaking time
Cooking time: 13 hours
Serves 6

2¼ lb (1 kg) tripe
scant 1 cup/7 oz (200 g) chopped onions
1 shallot, chopped
2 tablespoons chopped chives
2 tablespoons chopped flat-leaf parsley
1¾ cup/3½ oz (100 g) fresh white breadcrumbs
1⅔ cups/14 fl oz (400 ml) white wine
3 tablespoons/1½ oz (40 g) butter, cut into
  small pieces
salt and pepper

Tripe can be quite polarizing, but several popular regional dishes are based on it, such as tripe cooked in cider in Normandy or tripe parcels in Provence. All recipes rely on strong flavorings to match the pungent taste and smell of tripe. Originally a simple way of using every part of an animal, it has reached the status of valued delicacy for some gourmets. The following recipe offers a straightforward way to prepare it. Remember that offal should be absolutely fresh and it's important to be sure of its origin. Ask your butcher if you're not sure.

Wash, brush, and scrape the tripe, and soak it for about 4 hours in water.

To cook, place in a large pot filled with plenty of salted water. Cover and bring to a simmer, then cook for at least 5 hours.

Preheat the oven to 300°F/150°C/Gas Mark 2.

Cut cooked tripe into strips. Mix together the onions, shallot, chives, parsley, and breadcrumbs. Arrange a layer of the tripe and a layer of the onion and breadcrumb mixture in an ovenproof dish. Season with salt and pepper and continue to add alternate layers until all the tripe is used up. Pour in the wine, dot with the butter, cover, and cook for 6–8 hours.

KIDNEYS WITH MUSHROOMS

ROGNONS AUX CHAMPIGNONS

Preparation time: 25 minutes
Cooking time: 40 minutes
Serves 6

4 tablespoons/2 oz (60 g) butter, plus extra
  for frying
7 oz (200 g) mushrooms
1 lb 8½ oz (700 g) kidneys
¼ cup/1 oz (30 g) all-purpose (plain) flour
scant 1 cup/7 fl oz (200 ml) Madeira
⅓ cup/3½ fl oz (100 ml) tomato paste (purée)
6 slices day-old bread, cubed
1 tablespoon chopped flat-leaf parsley
salt and pepper

Beef kidneys require special care. Once prepared and blanched to remove their strong smell of ammonia, their taste is not aggressive at all, and along with their slightly bouncy texture, plays well against a richly flavored sauce of mushrooms and Madeira. *Rognons aux champignons* is somewhat old-school, reminiscent of the France seen in 1950s films. But it definitely still has its fans, and very justifiably so.

Melt 1½ tablespoons/¾ oz (20 g) of the butter in a large pan over medium heat, add the mushrooms, and cook for 10 minutes. Set aside, reserving both the mushrooms and the pan juices.

Taking special care, split the kidneys into two and remove the thin outer membrane, the fat, and the small internal membranes. Dry with paper towels (kitchen paper), then cut the kidneys into diagonal slices ½ inch (1 cm) thick. Bring a medium saucepan of water to a boil and cook the sliced kidneys for 5 minutes.

Melt 1½ tablespoons/¾ oz (20 g) of the butter in the pan over medium heat, add the blanched kidneys, and fry for 4 minutes, then remove them.

Mix the flour with the reserved mushroom pan juices and add to the pan juices from the kidneys, along with the Madeira and tomato paste (purée). Bring to a boil, then reduce the heat and simmer until the sauce has thickened and reduces—about 10 minutes. Add the kidneys and cook for 20 minutes more.

Meanwhile, heat the remaining 1 tablespoon of butter in another pan, add the bread cubes, and fry for a few minutes until golden brown and crisp.

Shortly before serving, add the mushrooms to the kidneys and heat until warmed through. Season with salt and pepper and sprinkle with the parsley. Serve with the croutons.

VEAL PAUPIETTES

PAUPIETTES DE VEAU

Preparation time: 35 minutes
Cooking time: 1¾ hours
Serves 6

⅔ cup/1 oz (30 g) fresh breadcrumbs
1 tablespoon milk, heated
3½ tablespoons/1¾ oz (50 g) butter
1 onion, chopped
⅓ cup/2 oz (60 g) diced bacon
1 cup/3½ oz (100 g) chopped mushrooms
1 handful of flat-leaf parsley, chopped
6 large veal scallops (escallops)
⅓ cup/3½ fl oz (100 ml) any broth
  (stock), heated
greens (salad leaves), to serve (optional)
salt and pepper

In France, veal paupiettes are most often bought ready to cook from the butcher. But these parcels of veal meat wrapped around a stuffing of mushrooms, bacon, and breadcrumbs can also be made at home. Recipes for paupiettes can be found in eighteenth-century household cookbooks such as the Belgian 1746 *La Cuisinière bourgeoise*, which is considered one of the ancestors of Ginette Mathiot's book. Paupiettes are good for a special but simple lunch but could also be served as main course for guests.

In a small bowl, soak the breadcrumbs in the hot milk.

Heat half the butter in a large, heavy pan over medium–low heat, add the onion and bacon, and cook for about 10 minutes until the onion is lightly browned. Remove from the heat and stir in the mushrooms, parsley, and soaked breadcrumbs. Season with salt and pepper.

Flatten the veal scallops (escallops) by placing them between 2 pieces of plastic wrap (clingfilm) and beating them with a meat mallet to about ¼ inch (5 mm) thick. Put 1 teaspoon of the mushroom mixture on each scallop, roll it up, and tie it with kitchen twine (string) to keep the stuffing in.

Melt the remaining butter in the pan over high heat, add the paupiettes, and fry on all sides for a few minutes until browned, then pour in the hot broth (stock). Cover and bring to a boil, then reduce the heat and simmer gently for 1½ hours.

Remove the twine to serve and strain the cooking juices. Serve the paupiettes with their cooking juices, and greens (salad leaves), if desired.

MAIN DISHES / PLATS PRINCIPAUX

VEAL BLANQUETTE

BLANQUETTE

Preparation time: 15 minutes
Cooking time: 2½ hours
Serves 6

1 lb 2 oz (500 g) breast of veal, cut into pieces
1 lb 2 oz (500 g) veal shoulder, cut into pieces
scant 1 cup/7 fl oz (200 ml) dry white wine
2 oz (60 g) carrot
1 onion, sliced
1 bouquet garni
3 tablespoons/1½ oz (40 g) butter
⅓ cup/1½ oz (40 g) all-purpose (plain) flour
1 egg yolk
1 tablespoon chopped flat-leaf parsley
   (optional)
salt and pepper

"Blanquette" refers to the creamy color of the sauce in this white stew, which is one of French people's favorite dishes. The recipe was first written and codified in Vincent La Chapelle's *Le Cuisinier moderne,* published in 1735, and it has since made multiple apparitions in cookbooks, novels, and films. Traditionally served with rice, it's usually pictured as a nostalgic and comforting dish giving a sense of home and tradition.

Put the veal pieces in a heavy Dutch oven (casserole) and pour in enough water to just cover the meat. Add the wine, carrot, onion, and bouquet garni. Season with salt and pepper, then bring to a boil. Skim, then reduce the heat and gently simmer for 1½–2 hours until tender. Drain the meat and keep it warm, and strain the broth (stock) in which it was cooked.

Melt the butter in a heavy pan over medium heat. When it is hot, on the point of smoking, add the flour and cook for a couple of minutes, stirring with a wooden spoon, until the roux is light fawn in color and still sandy in texture.

Take the roux off the heat and gradually add the strained broth, stirring constantly to avoid lumps. Return to the heat and slowly bring to a simmer, stirring all the time. Simmer for 10 minutes, stirring frequently.

Just before serving, whisk the egg yolk into the sauce over low heat until it thickens. Pour the sauce over the veal, sprinkle with flat-leaf parsley, if desired, and serve.

FRIED CALVES' SWEETBREADS

Preparation time: 10 minutes, plus soaking
 and chilling times
Cooking time: 15 minutes
Serves 6

1 calf's sweetbreads
4 tablespoons/2 oz (60 g) butter
½ handful flat-leaf parsley, chopped

Sweetbreads come from the thymus, a gland present in young animals near the throat. They have a melt-in-the-mouth texture and a refined taste, which makes them perhaps the most elegant pieces of offal. These rare delicacies have their aficionados and are sometimes found on the menu of classic or neo-classic bistros, having recently enjoyed a renewed interest. They are usually braised or fried, or used to fill vol-au-vents (page 62). They are not complicated to cook but demand a little preparation beforehand.

To clean the sweetbreads, soak them in water for 5 hours, changing the water several times.

Put the sweetbreads in a large saucepan and cover with salted water. Slowly bring to a boil, simmer gently for 3–5 minutes, and then drain. Rinse in water and pat dry with paper towels. Remove the thin membrane that covers them, and the gristle. Wrap them in a kitchen cloth, cover with a cutting (chopping) board, and place a 4½-pound (2-kg) weight on top. Let stand for 1 hour in the refrigerator.

Cut the sweetbreads into slices. Heat the butter in a large sauté or frying pan with high sides over high heat. Add the sliced sweetbreads and cook for 5 minutes on each side until brown, basting the meat by pouring on the fat tilting the pan to collect it in a spoon.

Transfer to plates, sprinkle with the parsley, and pour the butter from the pan over the sweetbreads to serve.

VEAL IN BREADCRUMBS

ESCALOPES PANÉES

Preparation time: 10 minutes
Cooking time: 10 minutes
Serves 6

This is a crowdpleasing family meal, and quick to make. Try not to buy breadcrumbs: when you have leftover bread, just cut it into pieces and let it dry in an aired box or cupboard, then process it or grate it into crumbs. This is a good way to avoid waste. The breadcrumbs can be used on Shepherd's Pie (page 130), in fillings, or for breaded scallops (escalopes), as in this recipe. The veal can be swapped for turkey or chicken, if you prefer. The scallops can be served with a tomato sauce in a sauce-boat or a mixed green salad, including bitter leaves, seasoned with a vinaigrette made of olive oil, lemon juice, and perhaps a crushed anchovy.

6 veal scallops (escallops)
2 eggs
2 cups/5½ oz (150 g) dried breadcrumbs
4 tablespoons/2 oz (60 g) butter
½ handful of flat-leaf parsley, chopped
sea salt
pepper

Flatten the veal scallops (escalopes) by placing them between 2 pieces of plastic wrap (clingfilm) and beating them with a meat mallet to about ¼ inch (5 mm) thick.

Beat the eggs in a small bowl and place the bread-crumbs in a shallow bowl or on a plate. Heat the butter in a large skillet or frying pan over high heat. Dip each scallop in the beaten eggs, then dredge in the bread-crumbs and place in the hot pan. Cook for 5 minutes on each side, or until golden.

Season with sea salt, pepper, and sprinkle with the parsley, then serve.

NAVARIN

NAVARIN

Preparation time: 15 minutes
Cooking time: 2¼ hours
Serves 6

4 tablespoons/2 oz (60 g) butter
2¼ lb (1 kg) mutton, cut into pieces
4½ oz (125 g) onions
5½ oz (150 g) carrots, quartered
2½ lb (1.25 kg) turnips, cut into pieces
¼ cup/1 oz (30 g) all-purpose (plain) flour
2 cups plus 1 tablespoon/17 fl oz (500 ml)
   any broth (stock), heated
1 bouquet garni
salt and pepper

The name is supposed to refer both to the recipe's *navet*, which means turnip, and to the town of Navarin in Greece where a battle was won against the Turks in 1827. A colorful, vegetable-rich dish was allegedly created for this occasion, then later reinterpreted by the famous chef Auguste Escoffier. It's a simple mutton (or if you prefer, lamb) stew ideally cooked with young spring vegetables. You can serve it with potatoes, if you like; add them to the simmering pan 30 minutes before the end of the cooking time.

Heat the butter in a heavy Dutch oven (casserole) over medium–high heat. Add the mutton, onions, carrots, and turnips, and cook for 10–15 minutes until golden brown.

Sprinkle with the flour and cook, stirring, for a few minutes until the flour turns golden. Pour in the hot broth (stock), season with salt and pepper, and add the bouquet garni. Cover and cook over very gentle heat for 2 hours. Serve warm.

ROASTED LEG
OF LAMB

Preparation time: 10 minutes
Cooking time: 1–1½ hours
Serves 6

1 × 4½-lb (2-kg) leg of lamb
1 clove garlic

Lamb meat has so much flavor that it does not need complicated embellishments—just a waft of garlic. Serve this roast with with flageolet beans, Sautéed Potatoes (page 232), or Ratatouille (page 260), depending on the season. Lamb is the traditional meat of choice in France for an Easter lunch, and it's very nice too in the summer and autumn, when the animals have had time to graze on richly aromatic grass. Their taste varies according to their terroir of origin and the type of plants they have eaten, from saltmarshes to robust mountain flora.

Preheat the oven to 425°F/220°C/Gas Mark 7.

Trim the leg of lamb, removing a layer of fat if it is too thick. Insert the garlic into the thick end.

Put the lamb in an ovenproof dish and cook it in the oven: 10 minutes per 1 lb 2 oz (500 g) for very rare meat; 15 minutes per 1 lb 2 oz (500 g) for medium-rare meat.

Note
Shoulder, saddle, or loin of lamb can be roasted in the same way. For shoulder, leave the bone in or ask for boneless shoulder, which is easier to carve.

ROASTED RABBIT WITH MUSTARD

LAPIN RÔTI À LA MOUTARDE

Preparation time: 10 minutes
Cooking time: about 45 minutes, depending
   on the size of the rabbit
Serves 6

1 small rabbit, cleaned, or the saddle of a
   large rabbit, rolled and tied
3½ tablespoons/2 oz (60 g) strong mustard,
   such as Dijon
lean (streaky) bacon, for larding or barding
boiled potatoes, to serve (optional)

In the French countryside, rabbits used to be bred
as small family livestock or were hunted as a source
of food. Their taste is not very strong and not all that
different from chicken, so it benefits from the piquancy
of mustard and black pepper. As always for meat, it's
good to buy it from a trusted seller, to make sure the
animals have been raised in good conditions. You can
use strong classic mustard or grainy mustard; either
way, the mustard has a good kick, so you need only
serve with simple boiled potatoes or rice.

Preheat the oven to 475°F/240°C/Gas Mark 8.
   Spread the rabbit with the mustard, then lard the
fleshy parts of the rabbit with the bacon using a larding
needle, or wrap the piece in the bacon slices (rashers).
Tie with kitchen twine (string) and place in a roasting
pan. Roast, allowing 20 minutes per 1 lb 2 oz (500 g).
   Untie and serve with the cooking juices, along with
the bacon, and boiled potatoes, if desired.

BASQUE CHICKEN

POULET BASQUAISE

Preparation time: 25 minutes
Cooking time: 50 minutes
Serves 6

1 × 2½-lb (1.2-kg) chicken
3 tablespoons olive oil
9 oz (250 g) tomatoes, seeded and chopped
6 sweet green bell peppers, quartered
   and seeded
2 cups/4½ oz (125 g) sliced mushrooms
scant 1 cup/5½ oz (150 g) diced smoked ham
⅔ cup/5 fl oz (150 ml) white wine
2 tablespoons flat-leaf parsley, chopped
   hot Spanish peppers, chopped, to garnish
   (optional)
salt and pepper

Technically, Basque chicken is the combination of piperade, a stew of tomatoes and peppers (page 56), and casseroled chicken. The marriage works so well that the dish has become a favorite far out of its region of origin. The local ham adds a nice smoked touch. Basque country is the home of piment d'Espelette, a relatively hot and nicely aromatic red pepper, which is traditionally used in the dish, though the French are not used to hot food, which explains why Ginette Mathiot suggested making it with or without the hot peppers. Serve with rice or potatoes.

Cut (joint) the chicken into pieces: Stick a fork in the leg, apply pressure to lift it, and slide a knife along the carcass to detach the meat. Cut off at the joint. Stick a fork under the wing, find the joint with a knife, and cut through it. Press down on the fork to remove the wing, using the knife to hold the chicken steady. Divide the legs and wings into two, then cut the chicken carcass down the middle, lengthways, to remove the meat. Keep the carcass for another use.

Heat the oil in a large, heavy pan over high heat. In batches if necessary, add the chicken pieces and fry for 5–10 minutes until golden. Add the tomatoes, bell peppers, and mushrooms to the pan with the chicken. Stir in the ham and season with salt and pepper. Pour in the wine, reduce the heat, then cover and cook over medium heat for 40 minutes.

Remove the chicken pieces and arrange on a serving dish. If necessary, simmer the cooking liquid to reduce it to the desired consistency. Pour it over the chicken. Sprinkle with the parsley and garnish, if using, with chopped hot Spanish peppers.

COQ AU VIN

COQ AU VIN

Preparation time: 25 minutes,
    plus chilling time
Cooking time: 1½ hour
Serves 6

3 tablespoons oil
6½ tablespoons/3¼ oz (90 g) butter
1 × 3¼-lb (1.5-kg) capon or chicken,
    cut into pieces (jointed, see page 154)
2½ tablespoons/1¼ oz (30 g) chopped onion
⅓ cup/1½ oz (40 g) all-purpose (plain) flour
4 tablespoons/2 fl oz (50 ml) Cognac
2 cups plus 1 tablespoon/17 fl oz (500 ml)
    red Burgundy wine
2 cloves garlic, crushed or finely chopped
6½ oz (185 g) white (button) mushrooms
3½ oz (100 g) pearl (baby) onions or shallots
generous ½ cup/3½ oz (100 g) diced
    smoked bacon
salt and pepper
potato straws (see Fries, page 228, but cut
    the potatoes into ⅛-inch (3-mm) straws
    and cook for only 1 minute, then a further
    10 seconds), to serve

Legend has it that the Gaul leader Vercingétorix sent a live rooster to his assailant Julius Caesar as a symbol of how combative he was. The Roman general ironically invited the Gauls to a feast and served them the animal, cooked *au vin*. The next day, the Gauls were victorious. However symbolic, this dish is not difficult to make. The marinating and long stewing was initially intended to tenderize the flesh of an older rooster, but it works equally well on chicken or even capon.

Begin preparing the day before serving. Heat the oil and 3½ tablespoons/1¾ oz (50 g) of the butter in a heavy Dutch oven (casserole) over medium–high heat. Add the capon or chicken pieces and the onion and cook for 10 minutes until browned on all sides. Sprinkle with the flour and continue to cook, stirring.

Pour in the Cognac and bring to a boil, then simmer vigorously to evaporate the alcohol. Pour in the wine, season with salt and pepper, and add the garlic. Cook for 1 hour. Let cool and store, covered, in the refrigerator until the next day.

The next day, slowly reheat over low heat.

Shortly before serving, heat 1½ tablespoons/¾ oz (20 g) butter in a large skillet or frying pan over medium–low heat. Add the mushrooms and fry for 10–15 minutes until softened. Meanwhile, heat the remaining 1½ tablespoons/¾ oz (20 g) butter in another skillet or frying pan over low heat, add the pearl (baby) onions or shallots and bacon, and fry for about 10 minutes until browned. Add the bacon, onions or shallots, and mushrooms to the capon or chicken and serve with the potato straws.

CHICKEN WITH TARRAGON

Preparation time: 25 minutes
Cooking time: 1 hour
Serves 6

1 × 2¼-lb (1-kg) prepared chicken,
   plus its liver, chopped
2¼ cups/9 oz (250 g) ground (minced) pork
generous 1 cup/4½ oz (125 g) ground
   (minced) veal
1½ cups/9 oz (250 g) diced smoked bacon
1½ tablespoons (20 ml) Cognac
¾ cup/1½ oz (40 g) chopped tarragon
   (about 1½ bunches), plus 1 sprig
4 tablespoons/2 oz (60 g) butter
4 tablespoons/2 oz (60 g) chopped onion
salt and pepper

Brillat-Savarin, the celebrated food critic who died in
1826, wrote in his *L'Art du bien manger* that chicken
with tarragon was the national dish of his "good, dear,
and voluptuous town of Bourg-en-Bresse" (a region
near Lyon that is famous for its excellent poultry).
Tarragon has a unique taste: warm and fresh, with a hint
of aniseed and a woody depth, which is best released
when bathed in sauces or cooking juices. So it is only fit
that it would be the real star of this luxurious dish of
meat-stuffed chicken. Serve as lunch for a special occasion.

Combine the liver, pork, veal, and half of the bacon in
a bowl to make a stuffing. Stir in the Cognac and ⅔ cup/
1¼ oz (30 g) of the chopped tarragon. Season with salt
and pepper. Fill the inside of the chicken with this mixture.
   Truss the chicken: Fasten the feet and wings to the
body in such a way that the bird retains its shape when
being cooked, using a trussing needle and a piece of
thin kitchen twine (string). Stick the needle into the right
drumstick, under the bone, go through the inside of the
body, come out through the other drumstick, and make
a knot. Stick the needle into the left wing and go through
the inside of the body, coming out through the right
wing, then pick up the flap of skin hanging from the neck.
Tie a fairly tight knot.
   Melt the butter in a heavy Dutch oven (casserole) over
high heat, add the remaining bacon and the onion, and
cook for about 5–10 minutes until browned, then remove
them with a slotted spoon and set aside. Add the chicken
and cook on all sides over high heat for about 10 minutes
to brown.
   Return the bacon and onion to the pot, season with
salt and pepper, and add the tarragon sprig. Reduce
the heat, pour in a little water, and cook, covered, over
gentle heat for 40 minutes, or until cooked through.
   When ready to serve, add the remaining 2 tablespoons
chopped tarragon to the cooking juices. Place the
chicken on a serving dish and serve the cooking juices
in a sauceboat.

DUCK À L'ORANGE

CANARD À L'ORANGE

Preparation time: 15 minutes
Cooking time: 40 minutes, depending on the
   size of the duck
Serves 6

This dish probably originates from medieval Spain and Italy, which explains its sweet and sour style not common in classic French cuisine. It may have arrived at the French royal court via Catherine of Medici and her Italian cooks. There are many versions of this recipe, which became quite fashionable in the 1960s. Ginette Mathiot's method is easy and straightforward. It uses fresh orange and bitter orange liqueur to make the sauce. It's fancy enough for a fancy lunch, served with boiled potatoes or bulgur. But it's also fancy enough to be served as a dinner party main dish, with Pommes Dauphine (page 222) and some greens such as Provençale Swiss chard (page 262).

1 prepared duck, plus its liver
1 orange, zest sliced off and finely chopped,
   then peeled and flesh chopped
⅓ cup/3½ fl oz (100 ml) veal broth (stock)
4 tablespoons/2 fl oz (50 ml) Curaçao
3½ tablespoons/1¾ oz (50 g) butter
1 orange, cut into wedges, for serving
salt and pepper

Preheat the oven to 425°F/220°C/Gas Mark 7.
   Put the chopped orange flesh inside the duck, then truss the duck: Fasten the feet and wings to the body in such a way that the bird retains its shape when being cooked, using a trussing needle and a piece of thin kitchen twine (string). Stick the needle into the right drumstick, under the bone, go through the inside of the body, come out through the other drumstick, and make a knot. Stick the needle into the left wing and go through the inside of the body, coming out through the right wing, then pick up the flap of skin hanging from the neck. Tie a fairly tight knot.
   Place the duck in a roasting pan. Roast for 20 minutes per 1 lb 2 oz (500 g).
   Meanwhile, bring a small saucepan of water to a boil, add the orange chopped zest and boil for 10 minutes to blanch. Drain and mash it in a small bowl along with the duck liver.
   Remove the duck from the roasting pan, then carve it (page 15). Arrange the pieces on a serving dish and garnish with the orange wedges.
   Pour off the cooking juices from the roasting pan and strain them into a pitcher. Pour the broth (stock) into a pan, bring to a boil, then pour in the strained juices, the zest and liver mixture, and the Curaçao. Bring back to a boil, then immediately remove from the heat. Season with salt and pepper, stir in the butter, and pour into a sauceboat to serve.

STUFFED PIGEONS

PIGEONS FARCIS

Preparation time: 30 minutes
Cooking time: 30 minutes
Serves 6

3 pigeons
4 slices white bread
milk, for soaking
3½ oz (100 g) sausage meat
½ cup/3½ oz (100 g) chopped bacon
½ cup/3½ oz (100 g) finely chopped onions
1 egg (optional)
bacon slices (rashers), for barding
salt

Pigeons have a dark, tasty meat. Serve them stuffed and give any dinner party the flair of a medieval banquet. It's necessary to truss the bird so it retains its shape. Stick the trussing needle into the right drumstick, under the bone, go through the inside of the body, come out through the other drumstick, and make a knot. Stick the needle into the left wing and go through the inside of the body, coming out through the right wing, then pick up the flap of skin hanging from the neck. Tie a fairly tight knot.

Preheat the oven to 425°F/220°C/Gas Mark 7.

Prepare the pigeons for cooking: Pluck the feathers, cut off the ring of muscle around the rump. Make a cut along the neck and pull the upper part of the digestive tract and the crop through this opening. Press down on the breast and push the intestines toward the rump. Remove the liver, lungs, heart, and gizzard. Remove the gallbladder from the liver. Open the gizzard, clean out its contents, remove the skin covering the inside, wash it, and set aside. Holding the head in one hand and the feet in the other, pass the bird over a clear flame, until all the down and small feathers have disappeared. After singeing, use the point of a small knife to remove all the small quills that remain in the skin. Finally, cut off the head and neck, pinions and feet.

Put the bread in a bowl and add enough milk to cover; let soak. In another bowl combine the sausage meat, chopped bacon, soaked bread, and chopped onions, and the pigeons' livers and gizzards, if desired, to make a stuffing. Bind with the egg, if using the livers and gizzards.

Season the insides of the pigeons with salt, then spoon in the stuffing. Cover them with the bacon slices (rashers), tie with kitchen twine (string) to truss it (see headnote), place in a roasting pan, and roast for 25–30 minutes.

Note
If you do not wish to prepare the pigeons yourself, you can ask your butcher to do it.

QUAIL CASSEROLE

CAILLES EN COCOTTE

Preparation time: 10 minutes
Cooking time: 50 minutes
Serves 6

Quails are migrating birds that have raised interest as food for several millennia. They are a hieroglyph in ancient Egypt, and biblical food, quoted several times in the Old Testament as a gift from God to save the Hebrews from famine. Initially hunted as game, they have long been bred for their meat. Their taste is quite delicate and cannot support too many embellishments, so a simple side of Pommes Anna (page 234) and a green salad will do. They are a bit fiddly to eat, so feel free to use your fingers.

3 tablespoons/1½ oz (40 g) butter
¾ cup/4½ oz (125 g) diced lean (streaky) bacon
¼ cup/2 oz (60 g) chopped onion
6 prepared quails
⅓ cup/3½ fl oz (100 ml) white wine
1½ cups/4½ oz (125 g) chopped mushrooms
salt and pepper

Preheat the oven to 400°F/200°C/Gas Mark 6.

Melt the butter in a heavy Dutch oven (casserole) over medium–high heat. Add the bacon and onion and cook for 5–10 minutes until browned. Remove with a slotted spoon and set aside.

Put the quails in the pot and cook on all sides for about 10 minutes to brown.

Return the bacon and onion to the pot, and pour in the wine. Season with salt and pepper. Cover with a tight-fitting lid and cook in the oven for 15 minutes.

Remove from the oven and add the mushrooms to the pot. Return to the oven and cook for 15 minutes more.

Serve warm.

TURKEY WITH CHESTNUT STUFFING

DINDE FARCIE AUX MARRONS

Preparation time: 45 minutes
Cooking time: 3¼ hours, depending on the
  size of the turkey
Serves 6

For the chestnut stuffing
1 lb 10 oz (750 g) chestnuts
1½ cups/12 fl oz (350 ml) any broth (stock)
2 tablespoons/1 oz (25 g) butter
1½ teaspoons chopped shallots
reserved turkey liver, finely chopped
scant 1 cup/3½ oz (100 g) ground
  (minced) veal
scant 1 cup/3½ oz (100 g) ground
  (minced) pork
generous ½ cup/3½ oz (100 g) diced bacon
a few truffle peelings (optional)

For the turkey
1 × 6½-lb (3-kg) prepared turkey, plus its liver
bacon slices (rashers), for barding
butter, softened, for foil (if needed)
watercress, to garnish (optional)
scant 1 cup/7 fl oz (200 ml) wine or chicken
  broth (stock), to deglaze

As in several other countries, turkey is a classic Christmas food in France. Imported from America in the sixteenth century, it tends to replace goose as a festive bird. The French tradition is to cook it with chestnuts, either as an accompaniment or, better still, included in a rich meat stuffing. "Marrons" is normally the word for inedible horse chestnuts (conkers) but is in certain cases colloquially used instead of *châtaignes*, the real name of the edible fruit. Chestnuts represent rusticity and frugality, acting as a culinary and symbolic counterpart to all the luxurious fare involved.

Preheat the oven to 425°F/220°C/Gas Mark 7.

Make the chestnut stuffing: Carefully cut a cross in the rounded part of the shell of each chestnut with a sharp knife. Bring a large saucepan of water to a boil and blanch the chestnuts in the water for 2 minutes. Drain, let cool slightly, and remove the shells. Cook the shelled chestnuts for another 10 minutes in fresh boiling water.

Remove them from the water in batches and rub off the inner skins while they are still hot (the skin sticks to the nuts as they cool). Bring the broth (stock) to a boil in the same saucepan and cook the chestnuts for 30 minutes until softened, then pass through a fine-mesh sieve.

Meanwhile, melt the butter in a large skillet or frying pan over low heat, add the chopped shallots, and cook for 5–10 minutes until softened.

Mix together the turkey liver, veal, pork, bacon, cooked shallots, and chestnut purée, and, if desired, add a few truffle peelings. Stuff the mixture into the turkey.

Cook the turkey: Cover the turkey breast with the bacon slices (rashers) and truss the turkey (see page 160). Place in a roasting pan and roast, allowing 20 minutes per pound (450 g). If necessary, cover the turkey with a piece of well-buttered aluminum foil to prevent it browning too quickly.

Remove from the oven when cooked through, untie the turkey, and arrange on a serving dish. Garnish with watercress, if desired.

Add the wine or broth to the roasting pan, bring to a boil, reduce the heat, and simmer for 5 minutes, scraping the bottom of the pan to release any sediment. Serve the juices in a sauceboat.

STUFFED CABBAGE CHOU FARCI

Preparation time: 45 minutes
Cooking time: 2¼ hours
Serves 6

For the cabbage
1 × 3¼-lb (1.5-kg) head of cabbage
4½ oz (125 g) bacon slices (rashers)
1 onion, sliced
1 carrot, sliced
scant 1 cup/7 fl oz (200 ml) any broth (stock)
⅓ cup/3½ fl oz (100 ml) white wine
salt and pepper

For the stuffing
¾ cup/4½ oz (125 g) finely chopped
   unsmoked bacon
¾ cup/4½ oz (125 g) finely chopped pork
1 handful flat-leaf parsley, finely chopped
1½ tablespoons Cognac
salt and pepper

Stuffed cabbage is an example of rustic yet substantial sophistication. Making it requires some time and care, and the result is truly a beauty. Stuffed cabbage leaves exist in many culinary traditions, but in France, the whole cabbage is used. Once ready, it is cut into slices and shared among guests. You could serve it as a family meal but also at a dinner party, accompanied with some simple rice and a red wine from the Loire Valley or Beaujolais. Begin the meal with a light vegetable starter and perhaps Pears in Wine (page 270) for dessert.

Begin preparing the cabbge: Trim the cabbage, removing any wilted or damaged leaves. Cut a deep cross in the bottom. Bring a large saucepan of salted water to a boil and blanch the cabbage in boiling water for 10 minutes. Drain the cabbage, remove some of the core to expose the ends of the leaves, and drain again with the bottom facing downward.

Prepare the stuffing: Mix all the ingredients, seasoning with salt and pepper.

Stuff the cabbage: Beginning in the center of the cabbage, slip a little stuffing into the bottom of each leaf without pulling the cabbage completely apart. Wrap the bacon slices (rashers) around the cabbage and tie with kitchen twine (string). Put it in a heavy Dutch oven (casserole) with the onion and carrot, and pour on the broth (stock) and wine. Season with salt and pepper, cover with a lid, and bring to a boil, then reduce the heat and simmer gently for 2 hours.

Serve warm.

CASSOULET

CASSOULET

Preparation time: 1 hour, plus soaking time
Cooking time: 4¾ hours
Serves 6

2½ cups/1 lb 2 oz (500 g) dried navy (haricot)
   beans, soaked overnight
1 carrot
1 onion, studded with cloves
1 × 5-oz (150-g) piece of lean (streaky) bacon
1 bouquet garni
2 oz (60 g) goose fat
1 lb 10 oz (750 g) pork or mutton, cut into
   5-cm (2-inch) pieces
scant 1 cup/7 oz (200 g) chopped onions
1 oz (25 g) garlic, crushed
1 cup/5½ oz (150 g) tomato paste (purée)
5½ oz (150 g) raw garlic sausage or
   Toulouse sausage
1 lb 5 oz (600 g) goose or duck confit
salt and pepper

A robust meat and bean stew, cassoulet is a south-western specialty from the towns of Castelnaudary, Toulouse, and Carcassonne, all three having slightly differing recipes (so there will always be a purist to say that it's not done right or that such-and-such ingredient does not belong). But you can't really go wrong if you stick to regional produce. Cassoulet is a notoriously long dish to make, and starts the day before with the beans. It's better to use bacon with its rind as it releases collagen, which will bind the cooking juices. Serve with a red wine from Fronton.

Rinse and drain the beans, and place them in a large, heavy Dutch oven (casserole) with the carrot, clove-studded onion, bacon, bouquet garni, and enough water to ensure everything is covered, about a gallon/7 pints (4 liters). Bring to a boil, reduce the heat, and simmer for 1 hour, skimming off any scum. Remove and discard the carrot and onion.

In a separate pot, melt the goose fat over low heat, then increase the heat and, working in batches, fry the pork or mutton for 5–10 minutes until browned. Add the chopped onions, garlic, tomato paste (purée), and 2 cups plus 1 tablespoon/17 fl oz (500 ml) of the bean cooking juices. Bring to a boil, then reduce the heat and simmer for 10 minutes.

Transfer to the pot with the beans and bacon and add the sausage and goose or duck confit. Draw off some of the liquid, leaving just enough to cover the meat. Bring to a boil, cover, then simmer over low heat for 1 hour.

Preheat the oven to 350°F/180°C/Gas Mark 4.

Remove the sausage and bacon and cut them into pieces. Arrange alternate layers of beans, cooking juices, pork or mutton, confit, and bacon and sausage pieces in the Dutch oven. Season carefully with salt and pepper. Finish with a layer of bacon and sausage.

Cover the dish and cook in the oven for 2 hours, then remove the lid and cook for another 15 minutes before serving.

ALSACE CHOUCROUTE

CHOUCROUTE À L'ALSACIENNE

Preparation time: 10 minutes
Cooking time: 3½ hours
Serves 6

11 cups/2¼ lb (1 kg) sauerkraut
4 tablespoons/1¾ oz (50 g) lard or oil
1 cup/3½ oz (100 g) chopped onion
1 cup/8 fl oz (250 ml) white wine
1 × 11-oz (300-g) piece of smoked bacon
1 × 9-oz (250-g) piece of cured sausage
1 lb 2 oz (500 g) potatoes
6 slices ham
sweet mustard, for serving (optional)
salt and pepper

Meet the most famous Alsatian dish, based on lacto-fermented cabbage. The word *choucroute* is a phonetic and semantic derivation of the German *sauerkraut*, which means sour cabbage. This means the shredded cabbage has undergone a process in which it is mixed with salt and spice and left to ferment, making it an excellent source of probiotics. It's usually bought ready-soured, raw, in jars or buckets, and is cooked as below in white wine and garnished with potatoes and ideally a variety of regional pork products, smoked and unsmoked. Serve with sweet mustard on the side and a chilled Riesling.

Rinse the sauerkraut in a colander and let drain.

Melt the lard or oil in a large Dutch oven (casserole) over low heat. Add the onion and sauerkraut and fry for 5 minutes to soften. Pour in the wine, then season with salt and pepper. Cover and cook for 2½ hours over low heat.

Add the bacon and cook, covered, for another 30 minutes.

Add the sausage, potatoes, and ham and cook, covered, for a final 30 minutes.

Carefully remove the bacon and sausage from the pot. Slice the bacon and sausage and then return to the pot. Stir and then serve on a warmed serving dish, with sweet mustard, if desired.

GRILLED BLOOD SAUSAGE

Preparation time: 5 minutes
Cooking time: 15 minutes
Serves 6

1 lb 2 oz (500 g) blood sausage (black pudding)
Dijon or other mustard, to taste
Mashed Potatoes (page 229), to serve
   (optional)
sea salt

Boudin—blood sausage (black pudding)—is the kind of food that people either hate or love. The texture is unique, a little gritty and melt-in-the-mouth at the same time. The taste is not very strong and varies slightly depending on the flavorings, such as onions or herbs, inside. Blood sausage was traditionally made fresh, as soon as a pig was slaughtered, and consumed within a few days, so serious *charcutiers* will not stock it outside of the cold season. In France, it's very common to serve it with mashed potatoes and *aux pommes*—with thick slices of pan-fried tart apples.

Prick the skin of the sausage with a fork and cut it into as many slices as there are guests. Heat a grill pan over medium heat, add the sausage slices, and cook for 12–15 minutes, turning several times. Season with sea salt, and serve hot, with mustard, and mashed potatoes, if desired.

FRIED BLOOD SAUSAGE / BOUDIN POÊLÉ
Prepare the blood sausage (black pudding) as above. Melt 3 tablespoons/1½ oz (40 g) butter in a skillet or frying pan over medium heat, add the sausage slices, and cook for about 12 minutes, turning several times. Serve hot with mustard.

BOUILLABAISSE

BOUILLABAISSE

Preparation time: 25 minutes
Cooking time: 20 minutes
Serves 6

A generously flavored fisherman soup from the town of Marseille, bouillabaisse makes the most of the local catch. It was originally a pauper's broth, and the langoustine (Norwegian lobster) or spiny lobster suggested here is not obligatory; it just shows that you can make a fancy dish out of it, fit for a dinner party. The selection of fish, crustaceans, and shellfish may vary, but it's good to achieve a balance between robust rock fish and delicate varieties (always be careful not to overcook the latter). It is usually served as a main dish with toast and rouille, a kind of garlicky red pepper mayonnaise.

For the soup
5 tablespoons olive oil
¾ cup/3½ oz (100 g) chopped leeks
    (white part only)
scant ½ cup/3½ oz (100 g) chopped onions
9 oz (250 g) tomatoes, skinned, seeded,
    and chopped
3 cloves garlic, 2 crushed, 1 halved
1 handful mixed herbs, such as flat-leaf
    parsley and fennel fronds
1 bay leaf
pinch of saffron threads
4½ lb (2.5 kg) fish fillets, such as whiting
    (silver hake), weever, conger eel, monkfish,
    red scorpion fish, sea robin (gurnard),
    red mullet (goatfish), or John Dory
2¼ lb (1 kg) crustaceans, such as spiny lobsters
    and langoustines (Norwegian lobster)
1¾ lb (800 g) mussels, cleaned
slices of bread, for toasting
salt and pepper

For the rouille
2 cloves garlic
3 small hot peppers, seeded
2 egg yolks
1¼ cups/10 fl oz (300 ml) olive oil
salt

Make the soup: Heat the oil in a large pot over medium–low heat, add the leeks, onions, tomatoes, and crushed garlic, and fry for 5 minutes. Season with salt and pepper, and add the herbs, bay leaf, and saffron.

Slice the thicker fish (such as conger eel, weever, and monkfish) and add to the pan along with the crustaceans. Cover with 6¼ cups/2½ pints (1.5 liters) water. Rapidly bring to a boil and cook for 7 minutes. Add the more delicate fish. Continue to cook over high heat for another 5 minutes, then add the mussels and cook for 3 minutes.

Meanwhile, make the rouille: Pound the garlic and hot peppers to a paste with a mortar and pestle, then add the egg yolks and season with salt. Gradually add the olive oil, stirring constantly, until thick and smooth. Add 1 tablespoon of the fish cooking liquid and set aside.

Check the seasoning of the bouillabaisse and add more salt and pepper if necessary. Toast the bread and rub it with the halved clove of garlic. Put the garlic toast in a soup tureen, and pour the fish cooking juices over. Serve the fish, crustaceans, and mussels separately on a serving dish, accompanied by the rouille.

PIKE WITH BEURRE BLANC

Preparation time: 20 minutes
Cooking time: 35 minutes
Serves 6

  ✳

Freshwater fish have become quite rare on French tables, even in regions far from the coasts, with their habitat increasingly destroyed and refrigerated transport carrying sea fish everywhere. Yet the French repertoire is rich with recipes for them. Pike is a carnivorous fish that lives in lakes or brackish waters. If you're lucky enough to happen upon a specimen, perhaps thanks to an angler friend, cook it simply, as below, poached in a court-bouillon. Creamy and delicately balanced, this simple beurre blanc below is the perfect sauce to serve with it, but it could also be served with a more traditional Beurre Blanc (page 29).

For the pike
1 × approx. 2¼-lb (1-kg) pike
1 quantity Court-Bouillon with Vinegar
   (page 27)

For the beurre blanc
2 oz (60 g) shallots
⅓ cup/3½ fl oz (100 ml) Muscadet wine
⅔ cup/5½ oz (150 g) butter, diced
salt and pepper

Prepare the pike: Place the pike in a fish kettle or large pan and cover with the court-bouillon. Bring to a boil, reduce the heat, and simmer very gently for 25 minutes.

Meanwhile prepare the beurre blanc: Finely chop the shallots and place in a small saucepan with the wine. Bring to a boil, reduce the heat, and simmer for 20–25 minutes, or until the liquid has reduced by three-quarters.

Gradually whisk in the butter and season with salt and pepper. The reduction should emulsify with the butter, and turn creamy and white. Serve immediately in a sauceboat with the fish.

SOLE MEUNIÈRE

Preparation time: 15 minutes
Cooking time: 15 minutes
Serves 6

½ cup/4 fl oz (120 ml) milk
⅓ cup/1½ oz (40 g) all-purpose (plain) flour
3 Dover or lemon sole, skinned
scant ½ cup/3½ oz (100 g) butter
2 tablespoons chopped flat-leaf parsley
salt and pepper

"Meunière" refers to a type of preparation where the fish is dredged in flour before frying: a *meunier* is a miller. Sole is one of the most delicately fleshed fish. Tastes have evolved and nowadays, it may be cooked for a slightly shorter time—8–10 minutes in total—than prescribed in Ginette Mathiot's original recipe, below. A little lemon juice is a good addition at the end. Once it is cooked, bone the fish and share it between guests. Serve with boiled potatoes and green beans on the side.

Pour the milk into a shallow bowl and place the flour on a plate. Season each sole with salt and pepper, dip it in the milk, then roll in the flour. Melt 4 tablespoons/2 oz (60 g) of the butter in a large skillet or frying pan. Add the fish and cook over high heat, turning once, for 10–15 minutes until browned.

Transfer the fish to a serving dish and sprinkle with the parsley. Heat the remaining butter in another pan over medium heat until it is nut-brown, stir it into the skillet, then pour the mixture over the fish. Serve immediately.

SEA BREAM WITH HERBS

Preparation time: 20 minutes
Cooking time: 30 minutes
Serves 6

oil, for brushing
1 × 2½-lb (1.2-kg) sea bream
½ cup/2 oz (60 g) sliced onion
12 oz (350 g) tomatoes, quartered
1 sprig fennel fronds, chopped
1½ teaspoons chopped chives
1 sprig of flat-leaf parsley, chopped
1 sprig of thyme
1 bay leaf
scant 1 cup/7 fl oz (200 ml) white wine
3 tablespoons/1½ oz (40 g) butter
freshly grated nutmeg
boiled potatoes, to serve (optional)
salt and pepper

Sea bream can be found all year round in markets, but it does have a peak season (in France, from September to November; ask your fish supplier when peak season is in your area) and it's best to try and respect that. When shopping for fish, choose to buy from small-scale fisheries who use non-destructive fishing methods within a local perimeter. Bream's white, tasty, and lean flesh benefits from baking, during which the ingredients placed around it will impart their flavors while keeping it nicely moist, and at the same time, acting as a sauce. Serve with potatoes and a late summer Ratatouille (page 260) or further along in the season, with steamed broccoli.

Preheat the oven to 375°F/190°C/Gas Mark 5 and brush a gratin dish with oil.

Make 3–4 slashes on each side of the bream and put it into the prepared dish. Sprinkle the onion over the bream. Put the tomatoes around the fish, sprinkle it with the fennel, chives, and parsley, and add the thyme and bay leaf. Pour the wine over the fish and dot with the butter. Season with nutmeg, salt, and pepper. Bake for 30 minutes.

Remove from the oven and discard the thyme and bay leaf. Serve immediately, with boiled potatoes, if desired.

SALT COD À LA PROVENÇALE

Preparation time: 20 minutes,
   plus soaking time
Cooking time: 20 minutes
Serves 6

Morue is French for salt cod, while the fresh fish is called *cabillaud*. As early as the sixteenth century it started to be fished abundantly by the French in the North Atlantic, off the coasts of Saint-Pierre-et-Miquelon. Its salted version became an inexpensive nourishing, and handy resource. The prestigious chef Auguste Escoffier even wrote a whole book of recipes for it in 1929, *La Vie à bon marché. La Morue.* Once so humble, this now-endangered species should be enjoyed only as a delicacy. As below, it is paradoxically well suited to Mediterranean-style embellishments.

---

1 lb 2 oz (500 g) salt cod
Court-Bouillon with White Wine (page 27),
   or water
2 tablespoons olive oil
scant ½ cup/3½ oz (100 g) chopped onions
5 cloves garlic, chopped
1 lb 2 oz (500 g) tomatoes, coarsely chopped
1 cup/4½ oz (125 g) black olives
2 tablespoons chopped flat-leaf parsley
sliced baguette, for serving (optional)
pepper

Put the fish, skin side up (to allow the salt to fall to the bottom), into a colander in a bowl of water and let soak for 12–24 hours, changing the water 2–3 times.

Put the fillets into a large saucepan, and cover with the court-bouillon or water. Bring just to a boil over high heat, then immediately remove the pan from the heat, without allowing the salt cod to boil. Cover and let stand for 10–15 minutes. Drain the fish, remove any skin and bones, and flake the flesh.

Heat the oil in a pan. Add the onions, garlic, and tomatoes and cook over low heat, stirring occasionally, for 5 minutes. Add the olives and parsley, season with pepper, and cook for another 5 minutes. Add the flaked salt cod to the pan and simmer gently for 10 minutes, then serve with baguette, if desired.

BRANDADE

BRANDADE

Preparation time: 25 minutes,
  plus soaking time
Cooking time: 10 minutes
Serves 6

1 lb 2 oz (500 g) salt cod
2 cloves garlic, peeled
1 cup/8 fl oz (250 ml) olive oil
5 tablespoons (75 ml) crème fraîche
juice of 1 lemon
pepper
toasted bread, for serving (optional)

Brandade happens when you beat (*brandar*, in Provençal language) poached salt cod with garlic and olive oil, resulting in a rich and textured spread. The addition of warmed cream makes it even more luscious. Serve as such on sourdough toast, seasoned with lemon and black pepper, or mix with an equal part of mashed potato before flashing under a hot broiler (grill) to make *brandade Parmentier.* In both cases, prepare to be transported to the south of France.

Put the fish, skin side up (to allow the salt to fall to the bottom), into a colander in a bowl of water and let soak for 12–24 hours, changing the water 2–3 times.

Bring a large saucepan of water to just a simmer, and poach the fish for about 8 minutes, ensuring the water does not boil. Drain the fish, remove any skin and bones, and flake the flesh. Transfer to a mortar, along with the garlic, and crush, adding the oil a little at a time, until the mixture becomes creamy.

Place in another saucepan over very low heat, and, stirring constantly, add the crème fraîche a little at a time until fully incorporated. Season with pepper and the lemon juice, then let cool. Chill in the refrigerator and then serve cold with toasted bread, if desired.

SARDINES WITH HERBS

SARDINES AUX FINES HERBES

Preparation time: 10 minutes
Cooking time: 20 minutes
Serves 6

12–18 sardines
⅔ cup/1½ oz (40 g) dried breadcrumbs
½–1 cup/2 oz (60 g) finely chopped mixed
    herbs, such as flat-leaf parsley, chives,
    and tarragon
4 tablespoons/2 fl oz (50 ml) olive oil
salt and pepper

Sardines are abundant, inexpensive fish. Their oily flesh is a good match for a bouquet of flavorful fresh herbs. When shopping for this summer fish, check that they are firm, with glistening skin and a pleasant sea smell. To scale, hold a fish by the tail on a cutting (chopping) board, its head facing away from you, and run the blade of a knife (not one of your best ones) from tail to head. Rinse and pat dry.

Preheat the oven to 400°F/200°C/Gas Mark 6.

Put the sardines into an ovenproof dish, sprinkle with the breadcrumbs and herbs, season with salt and pepper, and pour the oil over them. Bake for 20 minutes.

Remove from the oven and serve warm.

MARINATED HERRING FILLETS

FILETS DE HARENGS MARINÉS

Preparation time: 20 minutes,
   plus marinating time
Serves 6

The fishing, salting, and smoking of herring has been done since medieval times, becoming a trade that played a capital role in the European economy. After risking extinction in the 1970s due to industrial methods, its population has now partly grown back thanks to regulations. For this recipe, choose shiny fresh fish with a bright eye, best in the late winter months. If served with boiled potatoes it becomes *Harengs pommes à l'huile*, a common Parisian bistro starter.

---

6 herrings with soft roe, filleted
1 quantity Court-Bouillon (page 27)
⅓ cup/3½ fl oz (100 ml) white wine vinegar
⅓ cup/3½ fl oz (100 ml) oil
chervil or flat-leaf parsley, chopped
1 bouquet garni (optional)
1 carrot, sliced
1 lemon, sliced
1 small onion, sliced
pepper

Prepare 4 days in advance. Bring the court-bouillon to a boil in a large pan, add the herring fillets, and poach for 8 minutes per 1 lb 2 oz (500 g).

There are 2 alternative ways to prepare the roe: either mash it well, mix with the vinegar and oil, season with pepper, and add the chervil or parsley; or place the vinegar, bouquet garni, and pepper in a pan, bring to a boil, and cook for 2 minutes, then remove the bouquet garni, let the vinegar cool slightly and add to the roe, mashing well, and add the oil and the chervil or parsley.

Put the herring fillets on a dish and cover with the carrot, lemon, and onion slices. Pour the roe mixture over them. Let marinate in the refrigerator for 4 days, then serve.

MACKEREL IN
WHITE WINE

MAQUEREAUX
AU VIN BLANC

Preparation time: 15 minutes,
   plus marinating time
Cooking time: 30 minutes
Serves 6

⅓ cup/3½ fl oz (100 ml) white wine vinegar
scant 1 cup/7 fl oz (200 ml) white wine
4 tablespoons/2 fl oz (50 ml) oil, plus extra
   for brushing
1 sprig of thyme
1 sprig of flat-leaf parsley
1 bay leaf
1 teaspoon ground coriander
1 carrot, sliced
1 onion, sliced
6 mackerel
1 lemon, sliced
baguette, for serving (optional)
salt and pepper

Mackerel are best caught and eaten during the spring. Their white, oily flesh is a good backdrop for robust herbs and spice. Mackerel in white wine can be bought tinned, like sardines, but of course the fresh, homemade version is more authentic and delicious. The recipe below yields well-cooked flesh. You may, if you prefer, follow the same method at first but pour a warm, but not hot, marinade on the fish, and let it marinate for a day without baking. Either way, eat with a good baguette.

———————————

Begin preparing 2–3 days ahead. Pour the vinegar, wine, and oil into a large saucepan. Add the thyme, parsley, bay leaf, ground coriander, carrot, and onion, season with salt and pepper, and bring to a boil. Reduce the heat, cover, and simmer for 10 minutes.

Meanwhile, preheat the oven to 375°F/190°C/Gas Mark 5 and brush an heavy skillet or frying pan with oil.

Put the mackerel into the prepared pan in a single layer and pour in the marinade. Garnish each fish with a slice of lemon. Cover with parchment (baking) paper and bring to a boil over medium heat. Transfer the pan to the oven and bake for 15 minutes.

Transfer the fish to a serving dish and let cool, then store in the refrigerator for 2–3 days before serving.

RED MULLET
WITH TOMATOES

ROUGETS AUX TOMATES

Preparation time: 20 minutes
Cooking time: 30 minutes
Serves 6

2 tablespoons olive oil
1 onion, chopped
1 clove garlic, chopped
1 shallot, chopped
1 lb 2 oz (500 g) tomatoes, quartered
1 bouquet garni
scant 1 cup/7 fl oz (200 ml) dry white wine
2½ lb (1.2 kg) red mullet (goatfish),
2 tablespoons chopped flat-leaf parsley
cooked rice, for serving (optional)
salt and pepper

Buy red mullet (goatfish) when they are at their best, during the warm months—they conveniently pair well with summer vegetables and Mediterranean flavors. Try to pick specimens caught in the Atlantic though, as the Mediterranean and North Sea resources tend to be over-exploited. Their flesh and skin are very delicate so any brutal exposure to high temperature should be avoided. They may be cooked wrapped in parcels of parchment (baking) paper or as below, in a gently simmering sauce of tomatoes and wine. Serve with some rice as a starter or a light main course.

Heat the oil in a large saucepan over low heat. Add the onion, garlic, shallot, and tomatoes and cook over low heat, stirring occasionally, for 5 minutes. Add the bouquet garni, season with salt and pepper, and pour in the wine. Cover and simmer for 15 minutes.

Add the red mullet (goatfish), cover again, and simmer for another 15 minutes. Remove the bouquet garni and add the parsley. Cut the fish into pieces and serve in the sauce.

FLAKED SKATE WITH HERBS

EFFILOCHÉE DE RAIE AUX AROMATES

Preparation time: 45 minutes
Cooking time: 15 minutes
Serves 6

The "wings" of a skate are actually its edible, bat-like pectoral fins. Skate, which is better consumed in the winter, is covered in mucus and tends to smell of ammonia, which are both normal signs of freshness and can be removed by thorough rinsing in water and vinegar. The recipe below is like a salad where the shreds of cooked flesh mingle with a warm mayonnaise-based sauce enhanced with a robust mixture of flavorings and acidic ingredients (souring agents). It can be served with potatoes, as suggested, as a substantial starter or a main dish.

1 quantity Court-Bouillon with Salt
  (page 27), warmed
3 lb (1.4 kg) skate wings
2¾ oz (80 g) garlic, separated into cloves
1 egg
⅓ cup/3½ fl oz (100 ml) oil
4 tablespoons/2 fl oz (50 ml) sherry vinegar
1 tablespoon Dijon mustard
1 lb 8½ oz (700 g) tomatoes, skinned,
  seeded and diced
1 cup/1¾ oz (50 g) chopped chervil
½ cup/2 oz (60 g) snipped chives
3 tablespoons/3½ oz (100 g) very finely
  chopped shallots
scant ½ cup/2 oz (60 g) capers
boiled potatoes, sliced, to serve (optional)
1 quantity Vinaigrette made with sherry
  vinegar (page 32), to serve (optional)
salt and pepper

Pour the court-bouillon into a large saucepan and add the skate. Bring to a simmer and poach gently for 20 minutes. Remove from the heat and keep warm.

Bring a small saucepan of water to a boil. Add the garlic and blanch in the boiling water for 2 minutes, then drain. Repeat, blanching in fresh boiling water, twice more, then drain and thinly slice.

Make a mayonnaise (see page 35) with the egg, oil, vinegar, and mustard in a large heatproof bowl and season with salt and pepper. Set the bowl over a pan of simmering water and heat until warm.

Drain the skate. Remove and discard the skin and flake the flesh, taking care to remove all the cartilage. Transfer the fish to a serving dish. Remove the mayonnaise from the heat and stir in the sliced garlic, tomatoes, chervil, chives, shallots, and capers, then pour it over the fish. Serve immediately. If desired, serve with sliced boiled potatoes, seasoned with a sherry vinaigrette dressing.

MOULES MARINIÈRES

Preparation time: 20 minutes
Cooking time: 10 minutes
Serves 6

6½ lb (3 kg) mussels
5½ tablespoons/2¾ oz (80 g) butter
¼ cup/1¾ oz (50 g) chopped carrot
⅓ cup/3¼ oz (90 g) chopped onion
2 tablespoons chopped flat-leaf parsley
1 sprig thyme
1 bay leaf
scant 1 cup/7 fl oz (200 ml) dry white wine
1 shallot, chopped
Fries (page 228), for serving (optional)
pepper

Mussels can be foraged, but those that are sold are cultivated. There are two principal methods used regionally. The first is *moules de bouchot*, where they are grown on posts planted in the sand, alternatively covered and uncovered by the tide. In the Mediterranean, mussels of a different variety grow on hanging ropes and are constantly submerged, usually yielding larger specimens. The first kind tends to be more appropriate for the classic, basic *moules marinières*, which are ideally served with Fries (page 228). Try to buy mussels when they are in season (this will change depending on where they come from).

Discard any mussels that are cracked or that remain open when tapped. Remove the beards, scrape and wash the mussels in several changes of water, then drain.

Put the mussels in a large pot with 2 tablespoons/1 oz (30 g) of the butter, the carrot, 2 tablespoons of the onion, half the parsley, the thyme, and the bay leaf. Season with pepper. Cover and cook over low heat for about 6 minutes, shaking the pan to mix the mussels when they begin to open.

Discard any that remain closed, and discard the empty half-shells. Transfer the mussels to a warm serving dish and set aside. Strain the cooking liquid and pour it back into the pan, along with the wine, remaining butter, parsley, shallot, and remaining onion. Cook over high heat for 3 minutes. Pour the sauce over the mussels and serve hot.

SEA SCALLOP GRATIN

SAINT-JACQUES EN GRATIN

Preparation time: 50 minutes
Cooking time: 15 minutes
Serves 6

18 sea scallops
5 tablespoons/2½ oz (70 g) butter
1 shallot, chopped
small handful flat-leaf parsley, chopped
1½ cups/4½ oz (125 g) chopped mushrooms
¼ cup/1 oz (30 g) all-purpose (plain) flour
⅓ cup/3½ fl oz (100 ml) white wine
scant 1 cup/7 fl oz (200 ml) any broth (stock)
1 egg yolk
dried breadcrumbs, for sprinkling
salt

For the French, scallops are a seasonal treat. They can be enjoyed in many ways, for example, simply seared in butter and served with sautéed leeks and potato mash. They are also considered festive food, and look especially pretty when baked in their shells as in the recipe below. Scallops are not hard to open: Place one in your hand, curved-side down. Wedge the blade of a regular, rounded knife between the shells, force the opening to a gap wide enough for your thumb to maintain it while you slide the knife further along the inner upper shell and cut the muscle. The shells will release from each other, then you can prepare as desired. The recipe below is also a deliciously old-fashioned starter.

Preheat the oven to 425°F/220°C/Gas Mark 7.

Take the scallops out of their shells, remove the black muscle, and wash the meat and corals in water. Scrub 6 of the shells to clean them. Bring a medium saucepan of water to a boil and blanch the cleaned shells for a few minutes. Let cool and then dry them. Arrange the cleaned shells in a baking dish.

Bring scant 1 cup/7 fl oz (200 ml) salted water to a boil; add the scallops and poach for 1 minute. Drain and thoroughly dry with paper towels, then set aside.

Heat 1½ tablespoons/¾ oz (20 g) of the butter in a skillet or frying pan over medium–high heat, add the shallot, parsley, and mushrooms, and cook for about 5 minutes until the shallot has softened.

Melt 2 tablespoons/1 oz (30 g) of the remaining butter in a pan over medium–high heat, and when it is on the point of smoking, add the flour and stir until the roux is golden in color. Gradually add the wine and broth (stock), a little at a time, stirring constantly. Bring to a boil and let boil for 2 minutes. Reduce the heat to low, then whisk in the egg yolk to bind everything together.

Add the scallops and the shallot, parsley, and mushroom mixture. Spoon the mixture into the shells, with 3 scallops per shell. Sprinkle with the breadcrumbs, dot each shell with some of the remaining butter, and bake for 10 minutes.

Remove from the oven and serve hot.

STUFFED OYSTERS

COQUILLES D'HUÎTRES FARCIES

Preparation time: 15 minutes
Cooking time: 15 minutes
Makes 9 stuffed oysters

18 Pacific or rock oysters
juice of ½ lemon
2 tablespoons/1 oz (30 g) butter, plus extra
    for dotting
1 cup/3½ oz (100 g) chopped mushrooms
½ cup/4 fl oz (120 ml) milk
½ cup/1 oz (25 g) fresh breadcrumbs
1 hard-boiled egg yolk
⅓ cup/1 oz (25 g) dried breadcrumbs, plus
    extra for sprinkling
salt and pepper

To eat oysters *chaudes*, which in this case means "cooked," and stuffed can be a less intimidating introduction to the shellfish, as opposed to trying them raw. Choose the larger, fleshier ones for this recipe and serve immediately after baking, as a starter. If you wish to serve oysters raw, do so at the very beginning of a meal: once open, leave the oysters and their liquor in the half-shell and serve with a slice of lemon or chopped shallots in vinegar, rye bread, and butter.

Preheat the oven to 475°F/240°C/Gas Mark 8.

To open the oysters, wrap a tea towel around the hand that will hold the oyster to protect it. Place an oyster curved side down in the palm of your hand. Wedge a wide-bladed oyster-shucking knife into the hinge that connects the top and bottom shells. Run the knife all the way around the oyster and, using a twisting motion, prize the shells apart, taking care not to spill the liquid inside. Slide the knife under the oyster to sever its base and release the meat. Put them on a plate and sprinkle with the lemon juice. Wash and dry 9 of the bottom shells, arrange them in an ovenproof dish, and put the oysters back in (2 per shell).

Melt the butter in a small skillet or frying pan over medium heat, add the mushrooms, and cook for a few minutes until softened. In a separate pan over medium heat, warm the milk, taking care not to let it boil, then add the fresh breadcrumbs and let soak. Mash the egg yolk and add it to the breadcrumb and milk mixture, along with the mushrooms and dried breadcrumbs. Season with salt and pepper.

Cover the oysters with the stuffing, sprinkle with more dried breadcrumbs and dot each one with butter. Bake for 10 minutes, or until golden brown, then serve.

LOBSTER THERMIDOR

Preparation time: 1 hour
Cooking time: 30 minutes
Serves 6

1 quantity Court-Bouillon with Salt
   or with Vinegar (page 27)
3 × 1 lb 2-oz (500-g) lobsters
¾ cup/6½ oz (185 g) butter
1¼ cups/10 fl oz (300 ml) crème fraîche
⅔ cup/5 fl oz (150 ml) Madeira
⅔ cup/5 fl oz (150 ml) Cognac
cayenne pepper, to taste
salt and pepper

Needless to say, the lobster should be bought alive. Freeze it for 30–60 minutes before you plunge it in the boiling court-bouillon. This recipe was one of many classics created by Escoffier, the celebrated chef and author. Thermidor is a month in the French revolutionary calendar, the hottest of the year (the name comes from the Greek *thermos*); it is often when lobster is abundant and inexpensive. Though the recipe was actually named after a controversial yet successful play that was staged near Escoffier's Parisian restaurant. It dealt with political events that had occurred about a hundred years earlier, during the month of Thermidor 1794, which had led to a new, less radically revolutionary governance.

Preheat the oven to 425°F/220°C/Gas Mark 7.
   Put the court-bouillon in a large saucepan and bring to a boil. Add the lobsters and boil for about 10 minutes. Remove the lobster and let cool slightly. When it is cool enough to handle, remove the meat from the shell and chop into small dice.
   Melt the butter in a large skillet or frying pan over medium heat, add the diced lobster, and cook for 5 minutes. Pour in the crème fraîche, then add the Madeira and Cognac. Season with cayenne pepper and salt. Put the mixture into an ovenproof dish and bake for 5 minutes before serving, sprinkled with black pepper.

LANGOUSTINE SALAD

SALADE DE LANGOUSTINES

Preparation time: 30–40 minutes
Cooking time: 10 minutes
Serves 6

In France, the langoustine (Norwegian lobster) season starts in spring and ends in summer, so it makes perfect sense to combine their delicate flesh with equally delicious and fresh new vegetables and greens, such as asparagus and purslane. This salad will make a beautiful impression on a spring table. Langoustines (known as *scampi* in Italy) are consumed in France as a seasonal and regional delicacy, particularly in the coastal areas of Brittany and the Atlantic. They are best bought alive.

2 oz (60 g) green beans, trimmed
7 oz (200 g) asparagus (about ½ bunch), trimmed
11 oz (300 g) curly endive, peeled
7 oz (200 g) lamb's lettuce
3½ oz (100 g) purslane
50 small langoustines (Norwegian lobster)
1 oz (25 g) mushrooms
1 quantity Vinaigrette (page 32)
4 tablespoons/2 fl oz (50 ml) oil
scant ½ cup/1¾ oz (50 g) chopped chives
salt and pepper

Bring a large saucepan of salted water to a boil. Add the beans, and asparagus, and blanch for 5–8 minutes, or until tender, then drain. Wash and drain all the greens.

Peel the langoustine (Norwegian lobster) tails and discard the claws. If desired, keep some lobsters whole and unpeeled to garnish the salad. Remove the stems (stalks) from the mushrooms and wipe them with a damp cloth, then cut into strips.

Dress the greens with some of the vinaigrette, mix thoroughly, and arrange on a dish. Cut the asparagus into slices and the beans into julienne strips.

Heat the oil in a large skillet or frying pan over high heat, add the langoustines, and fry for about 5 minutes. Add the asparagus, beans, and mushrooms, then moisten with a little vinaigrette, season with salt and pepper, and sprinkle with the chives. Arrange the contents of the skillet or frying pan on top of the bed of salad and top with the reserved whole langoustines. Serve immediately.

CRAYFISH NANTUA

ÉCREVISSES À LA NANTUA

Preparation time: 1½ hours
Cooking time: 1 hour 10 minutes
Serves 6

40 crayfish
1 quantity Court-Bouillon with Salt
  or Vinegar (page 27)
3 tablespoons/1½ oz (40 g) butter
2 cups/6½ oz (185 g) chopped mushrooms
scant 1 cup/7 fl oz (200 ml) crème fraîche
4 egg yolks

This freshwater crustacean has become less common because of the pollution of rivers and streams. Louisiana crayfish, intentionally imported for farming in Europe during the 1970s, acts as an invasive species, which tends to replace the endemic wild populations. That said, it is also perfectly edible and can be used in traditional recipes. Nantua is a town not far from Lyon, a city that has a high gastronomic reputation itself, in an area rich with waterways and marshes. It's only natural that Nantua sauce be a match for the crustacean.

Bring the court-bouillon to a boil in a large saucepan, add the crayfish, and poach for 8–10 minutes. Let cool in the court-bouillon. Remove the crayfish, reserving 4 cups/1¾ pints (1 liter) of the court-bouillon. Make a small incision in the crayfish shells to allow the court-bouillon to drain out, then devein: Snap off the fin in the center of the tail, and the black tube will come away whole. Peel, and set the tail meat aside.

Carefully crush all the shells thoroughly, add them to the pan with the reserved court-bouillon, and cook over low heat for 1 hour until the liquid has reduced by half. Pass the reduction through a sieve to make a sauce.

Meanwhile, melt half the butter in a large skillet or frying pan over medium heat and cook the mushrooms for 10 minutes. Remove the mushrooms and set aside. Add the remaining butter to the pan and cook the crayfish tail meat over medium heat for 10 minutes.

Add the sauce and stir in the crème fraîche and the mushrooms. Just before serving, reduce the heat to low and whisk in the egg yolks to thicken the sauce.

SIDES AND VEGETABLES

ACCOMPAGNEMENTS ET LÉGUMES

In the classic French menu organization, vegetable, pasta, and rice are primarily considered sides for meat or fish, and rarely the main show. Nevertheless, they are not to be neglected, as eating them is the key to a balanced diet. And indeed the French culinary repertoire has many sophisticated ways to prepare vegetables that enhance their flavors and textures. These dishes are not complicated to make but require real care. Great attention should be given to cooking times and seasonings. Modern tastes tend to favor vegetables that retain a certain firmness, so do adjust cooking times accordingly.

When planning a meal, choose one or two recipes in this chapter—one starchy, or potato-based, the other vegetable-based—that will go well with your main course. But some of these sides can also be made as starters, such as Leeks Served Like Asparagus (page 238). Many could also act as a vegetarian main course or as a meal in itself, for example Tomatoes Stuffed with Rice (page 258), Knepfles (page 218), Zucchini Gratin (page 246), or Lentil Salad (page 212). Most recipes would also complement a simple egg or cheese dish perfectly—try Ratatouille (page 260) or Provençale Swiss Chard (page 262) with an omelet, for instance.

French cuisine offers a rather impressive range of potato recipes to choose from, often playing with textures and shapes, which can make them suitable for any type of meal. The fluffier ones like Mashed Potatoes (page 229) or Pommes Dauphine (page 222) are good with dishes that have sauces or juices to absorb. Sautéed Potatoes (page 232) and mash are quick to make and well-suited to impromptu meals, for example, served with eggs and ham. Fries (page 228) are an emblematic classic, perfect with steak (page 134) or mussels (page 198). Duchess Potatoes (page 224) can be piped in pretty ways, and are lovely when matched with a festive roast bird alongside other accompaniments; while Potatoes Anna (page 234) will surely impress guests at a fancy dinner party.

Vegetable dishes are seasonal, and should be made accordingly. Don't attempt ratatouille in the winter or Belgian Endive with Cheese (page 244) in the summer. Peas à la Française (page 242) are nothing but a celebration of spring. These recipes are often embedded in regional traditions: Artichokes à la Barigoule (page 256) is originally a Provençale recipe reinterpreted by chefs, while the endive recipe comes from the north of France where this vegetable is mostly grown. Aside from the recipes in this chapter, you can of course cook seasonal vegetables in simple ways, for example, steamed or boiled in salted water (measure about one teaspoon salt per liter of water), as sides. Buy local, organic vegetables, ideally from the farmer's market and use them quickly to avoid losing too many of their vitamins and nutrients.

Pulses are usually eaten as starters—it's common to find a lentil salad as a starter in a French bistro—or as sides, often for pork dishes, for example, Fresh Navy Beans with Tomatoes (page 254) served with sausage. These dishes may also be served as vegetarian mains, ideally accompanied with another vegetable such as leeks, carrots, or asparagus.

The French have also incorporated Italian-style pasta in their everyday diet, though no such recipes are included in this book as they're not representative of French heritage. Nevertheless, there is a typically French pasta-like tradition, especially in Alsace (with knepfle, and *spätzle*) and the Alps, with *crosets* (page 216). They are often eaten as sides, in soups, or as main dishes with cheese and butter.

LENTIL SALAD

Preparation time: 5 minutes
Cooking time: 45 minutes
Serves 6

2¼ cups/1 lb 2 oz (500 g) lentils
1 quantity Vinaigrette (page 32)
parsley, for sprinkling (optional)

This tasty and nourishing lentil salad can often be found as an entrée (starter) in bistros. Try a mustardy vinaigrette, if you like; you can also enliven it with chopped herbs and shallots. Choose a variety of lentil that stays firm during cooking: the *lentille verte du Puy*, a small bronze-colored lentil from Auvergne, or the beluga, named after its caviar-like black color. Modern tastes would command a shorter cooking time of around 20 minutes.

———————

Put the lentils in a large saucepan and cover with water. Bring to a boil, reduce the heat, and simmer very gently until tender, 25–45 minutes. Exact timing will depend on the size and type of lentil chosen (consult the package directions).

Drain the lentils and, when cool, dress with the vinaigrette. Sprinkle with parsley, if using, and serve.

LENTILS WITH MUSTARD

Preparation time: 10 minutes
Cooking time: 35 minutes
Serves 6

2¼ cups/1 lb 2 oz (500 g) lentils
2 tablespoons/1 oz (30 g) butter
1 onion, chopped
scant 1 cup/5½ oz (150 g) chopped
    cured ham
⅓ cup/3½ fl oz (100 ml) broth (stock), heated
2½ tablespoons/1¼ oz (30 g) Dijon mustard
parsley, for sprinkling (optional)
salt and pepper

The humble, biblical lentil is quite present in French cooking. This dish will turn out different but equally delicious whether it's cooked with a firm variety (see examples in the Lentil Salad headnote, page 212) or one that turns mushy like the brown or green varieties. It can be served as an accompaniment for sausages or as a warming winter main course for a family meal, maybe with a dish of raw vegetables on the side. Lentils have many qualities: they are filling, inexpensive, quick and easy to cook (no soaking is required), and rich with protein, fiber, iron, and vitamins.

Put the lentils in a heavy Dutch oven (casserole) or saucepan and cover with water. Bring to a boil, reduce the heat, and simmer very gently until tender, 25–45 minutes, then drain. The exact timing will depend on the size and type of lentil chosen (consult the package directions).

Meanwhile, melt the butter in a small skillet or frying pan over low heat. Add the onion and ham and fry for 10 minutes until golden brown. Add the hot broth (stock) and the mustard, season with salt and pepper. Stir this sauce into the drained lentils, sprinkle with parsley, if desired, and serve.

CROSETS SAVOYARDS

Preparation time: 30 minutes
Cooking time: 5 minutes
Serves 6

 ✳

4½ cups/1 lb 2 oz (500 g) all-purpose (plain)
    flour, plus extra for dusting
4 eggs
1 cup/8 fl oz (250 ml) milk
1 teaspoon salt
scant 1 cup/3½ oz (100 g) grated Gruyère
    cheese, to serve
⅓ cup/3½ fl oz (100 ml) melted butter or meat
    juices, to serve

Crosets (or crozets) are a kind of pasta from Savoie, in the Northern Alps. They come in tiny, thin squares about ¼ inch (5 mm) wide and made of a mixture of common wheat and durum wheat or buckwheat. Several other regions in France have a pasta tradition: Alsace and its egg pasta, its spätzle, and its Knepfles (page 218); the Dauphiné and its ravioles (tiny cheese ravioli); Corsican gnocchi... There is a special tool for making perfectly square homemade crosets, but they will be equally good cut with a knife. They are served in soups or, as below, with cheese and butter.

Put the flour in a bowl, add the eggs, milk, and salt, and mix to make a firm dough.

Tip onto a floured work counter and roll the dough out to a thickness of about 1/8 inch (3 mm), and then cut into small dice.

Bring a large pot of salted water to a boil, add the diced dough, and cook for about 5 minutes, or until al dente. Drain.

Sprinkle with the cheese and serve with the butter or meat juices.

KNEPFLES

KNEPFLES

Preparation time 25 minutes, plus resting
   time
Cooking time: 5 minutes
Serves 6

v

2½ cups/11 oz (300 g) all-purpose (plain)
   flour, plus extra for dusting
2 eggs
⅓ cup/3½ fl oz (100 ml) milk
3½ tablespoons/1¾ oz (50 g) butter, melted
1 tablespoon flat-leaf parsley (optional)
salt and pepper

Knepfles are a kind of Eastern European gnocchi or
dumpling eaten in Alsace and in the Vosges mountains,
where a variant called *kneff* is traditional. The Alsatians
also eat *spätzle*, which are made in a similar way but are
closer to pasta, finer and longer, while knepfles are more
dumpling-like. The egg dough is shaped into cylinders
that can be cut into disks either on your counter or
directly over the pot of boiling water, if you like. They are
usually served with stewed meat dishes, absorbing the
rich sauce, or on their own, with butter.

Begin preparing 2 hours in advance. Put the flour in a
bowl and add the eggs and milk, a little at a time, seasoning with salt and pepper as you go. Mix with your hands
until you have a dough and knead until smooth. Cover and
set aside for 2 hours.

Bring 12 cups/5¼ pints (3 liters) salted water to a boil
in a large pot.

Shape the dough into cylinders 1½ inches (4 cm) long,
then cut them into disks ¾ inch (2 cm) in diameter.
Cook in the boiling water for a few minutes until they
float to the surface, then continue to cook for 5 minutes
more until cooked through. Drain, then transfer to
a serving dish and pour the butter over them, and sprinkle
with parsley, if desired. Serve immediately.

Note
Herbs such as chives, parsley, or chervil can be added
to the dough for these dumplings from Alsace.

COUNTRY-STYLE RICE RIZ À LA PAYSANNE

Preparation time: 10 minutes
Cooking time: 20 minutes
Serves 6

Rice is not very French but does appear in many traditional recipes. Attempts had been made as early as the sixteenth century to grow rice in Camargue, a wetland area between the two arms of the Rhône Delta, but the first rice fields weren't really planted until the nineteenth century, originally as an effort to dry out the wetlands. It was only fairly recently—after 1945—that it became a successful crop. Short-grain rice is used in desserts, while long-grain varieties are often cooked *à la Créole*—boiled in water—as an accompaniment. The recipe below is also a main course for a family-style meal.

1½ tablespoons/¾ oz (20 g) butter
scant ½ cup/2½ oz (75 g) diced lean bacon
scant ½ cup/2½ oz (75 g) diced fatty bacon
1 onion, sliced
1½ cups/11 oz (300 g) long-grain white
    or brown rice
3¾ cups/30 fl oz (900 ml) any broth
    (stock), heated
1 sprig parsley
1 sprig thyme
1 sprig chervil
1 small bunch chives
⅔ cup/2¾ oz (80 g) finely grated
    Gruyère cheese
salt and pepper

Melt the butter in a large skillet or frying pan over low heat. Add the bacon and onion and fry for 5 minutes until softened. Add the rice. Fry, stirring, for 2–3 minutes to coat the rice in fat, then add the hot broth (stock).

Tie the herbs in a bunch with kitchen twine (string) and add to the pan, then season with salt and pepper. Cook for 15 minutes, or until the rice is tender (which will take longer if using brown rice).

Discard the herbs, then stir in the cheese and serve.

POMMES DAUPHINE

POMMES DE TERRE DAUPHINE

Preparation time: 40 minutes
Cooking time: 30 minutes
Serves 6

v

1 lb 2 oz (500 g) potatoes
3 egg yolks
3 whole eggs
3 tablespoons/1½ oz (40 g) butter
½ quantity Choux Pastry (page 42)
freshly grated nutmeg, to taste
1½ cups/3½ oz (100 g) dried breadcrumbs
vegetable oil, for deep-frying
salt and pepper

Crunchy as fries (chips) on the outside and fluffy like mash on the inside, *dauphine* are the best of both worlds. The first written recipes date back to the late nineteenth century. Their name refers to the *dauphine*, or wife of the *dauphin*, the king's male firstborn and heir to the throne in the pre-revolutionary period, but it's not totally clear why. They do require a lot of work—you need to make choux pastry and mashed potato first—but they are a wonderful accompaniment for grilled meats and roast poultry.

Put the potatoes in a large saucepan and cover with cold salted water. Bring to a boil, then reduce the heat and simmer for 20 minutes, or until tender. Drain thoroughly and pass through a food mill or potato ricer into a bowl while the potatoes are still hot. Mix with the egg yolks, 1 of the whole eggs, and the butter.

Mix the choux pastry with the potatoes. Season well with salt, pepper, and nutmeg.

Beat the remaining 2 whole eggs in a small bowl and place the breadcrumbs on a plate or in a shallow bowl. Form the dough mixture into small egg shapes. Dip in the beaten eggs, then roll in the breadcrumbs.

Heat the oil in a deep-fryer to 350°F/180°C, or until a cube of bread browns in 30 seconds. Working in batches, fry the potatoes for a few minutes until golden brown. Serve hot.

Note
The ratio of mashed potatoes to choux pastry should be 2:3.

DUCHESS POTATOES

POMMES DE TERRE DUCHESSE

Preparation time: 30 minutes,
   plus chilling time
Cooking time: 35 minutes
Serves 6

v ✱

2¼ lb (1 kg) potatoes
5 tablespoons/2½ oz (70 g) butter,
   plus extra for greasing
3 egg yolks
3 whole eggs
freshly grated nutmeg, to taste
all-purpose (plain) flour, for dipping
salt and pepper

Duchesse are derived from basic mashed potatoes, elevated to rich, golden, crunchy nuggets. They can be shaped in any elegant way, making them suitable for a chic dinner party. Cut the refrigerated mixture as below, or pipe with a fluted nozzle for an even fancier look, as pictured. They are quicker to make than *dauphine* (page 222), and easier to manage as they can be prepared in advance and baked in the last 15 minutes before the main course (roast or stewed meat) is served, not requiring further attention.

Put the potatoes in a large saucepan and cover with cold salted water. Bring to a boil, then reduce the heat and simmer for 20 minutes, or until tender. Drain thoroughly and pass through a food mill or potato ricer into a bowl while the potatoes are still hot. Beat in the egg yolks, 1 of the whole eggs, and the butter, then season with salt, pepper and nutmeg.

Preheat the oven to 425°F/220°C/Gas Mark 7 and grease a baking sheet with butter.

Spread out the potato mixture to a thickness of ½ inch (1 cm) on another sheet. Let cool, then chill in the refrigerator until firm.

Place the flour on a plate or in a shallow bowl. Beat the remaining 2 whole eggs in a bowl. Cut the potatoes into squares, diamonds, rectangles, or bun shapes as desired. Dip in the flour, brush with more beaten egg, and place on the prepared sheet. Bake for 15 minutes until well browned. Serve hot.

DAUPHINOIS POTATOES

GRATIN DAUPHINOIS

Preparation time: 20 minutes
Cooking time: 1½ hours
Serves 6

Dauphinois comes from Dauphiné, the area around the town of Grenoble, with the Alps to the east, Lyon to the north, and Provence to the south. This garlic-infused gratin contains no cheese nor eggs, but the potatoes will absorb the milk or cream they are cooked in, browning at the top and acquiring a deliciously sweet taste from the reduced dairy. The peeled potatoes, once cut in slices, need not be rinsed, or the starch they contain will be lost and the dish will lose its cohesion. Gratin Dauphinois is a hearty and luxurious accompaniment for grilled meats.

3½ tablespoons/1¾ oz (50 g) butter,
  plus extra for greasing
2¼ lb (1 kg) potatoes
1 clove garlic, peeled (optional)
1 cup/8 fl oz (250 ml) crème fraîche
salt and pepper

Preheat the oven to 350°F/180°C/Gas Mark 4 and grease an ovenproof dish with butter.

Cut the potatoes into thin slices. Pat dry with paper towels, and then season with salt and pepper.

Rub the prepared dish with a clove of garlic, if desired. Layer the potatoes in the dish to within ½ inch (1 cm) of the rim. Cover with the crème fraîche. Dot with the butter and bake for 1½ hours, or until the potatoes are tender and browned on top.

FRIES

Preparation time: 20 minutes
Cooking time: 10 minutes
Serves 6

Fries (chips) do seem to be a French invention, with written mentions appearing in the second half of the eighteenth century. In French they are sometimes called *"Pont-Neuf"* because they would be served on the Pont-Neuf, Paris' most famous bridge on the Seine, during the French revolution. Curnonsky, a celebrated food critic who died in 1956, wrote that fried potatoes were "one of the most intelligent creations of the Parisian spirit." Choose baking (floury) potatoes, as they are twice-cooked in hot oil, though duck fat is sometimes used in southwest France and beef drippings in the north, particularly in regions close to Belgium, the other land of fries. They go well with with Moules Marinières (page 198) or Entrecôte Steak (page 134).

2½ lb (1.2 kg) potatoes
vegetable oil, for deep-frying
salt

Cut the potatoes into ½-inch (1-cm) thick fingers. Dry on paper towels (kitchen paper).

Heat the oil in a deep-fryer to 350°F/180°C, or until a cube of bread browns in 30 seconds.

Carefully lower the potatoes into the hot oil and cook for about 5 minutes until softened but not colored. Using a slotted spoon, carefully remove the fries from the oil and drain on paper towels.

Heat the oil to 375°F/190°C. Put the fries back in the oil and cook until brown, about 5 minutes. Serve hot, sprinkled with salt.

MASHED POTATOES

PURÉE DE POMMES DE TERRE

Preparation time: 15 minutes
Cooking time: 20 minutes
Serves 6

2¼ lb (1 kg) potatoes, peeled
4 tablespoons/2 oz (60 g) butter
2 cups plus 1 tablespoon/17 fl oz (500 ml)
 milk, heated
salt

In France, mashed potatoes served with ham—or *jambon-purée*—is a children's favorite and a regressive pleasure for many adults. You need a baking (floury) variety of potatoes for your potatoes to turn out really fluffy and lovely. Avoid using any electric appliance to reduce them to a purée or they will turn elastic and sticky. A generous quantity of butter is essential, but feel free to adjust the quantity of milk to reach your desired consistency. Serve with roast poultry, Grilled Blood Sausages (page 174) or Daube of Beef (page 128).

Put the potatoes in a large saucepan and cover with cold salted water. Bring to a boil, then reduce the heat and simmer for 20 minutes, or until tender. Drain thoroughly and pass through a food mill or potato ricer into a bowl while the potatoes are still hot. Beat in the butter and hot milk with a wooden spoon. Season with salt. Do not cook or beat the purée after adding the butter and milk.

POTATO PUFFS

POMMES DE TERRE SOUFFLÉES

Preparation time: 15 minutes
Cooking time: 10 minutes
Serves 6

1¾ lb (800 g) waxy potatoes
vegetable oil, for deep-frying
salt

These beauties most often appear at the table of chic and classic restaurants. Although not easy, they can be made at home if you take care to cut the slices quite precisely and are willing to organize a double fryer on your stove. The surfaces on each side of the slices puff up slightly, and an air bubble forms inside. They are most likely an accidental nineteenth-century creation: The story goes that an important client of a restaurant sent back his fried potatoes because they were not sliced the usual way. The chef threw them back into the fryer, and they miraculously puffed. Potato Puffs can be served with a baked sea bream (page 182) or even on their own, as a little appetizer to snack on.

Cut the potatoes into 1/8-inch (3-mm) slices. Dry the slices on paper towels.

Heat the oil in 2 deep-fryers to 350°F/180°C, or until a cube of bread browns in 30 seconds. Increase the heat in the second fryer to 375°F/190°C. This will be used to puff the potatoes.

Lower the slices into the hot oil in the first fryer and cook for 7 minutes. Using a slotted spoon, carefully remove from the oil and drain on paper towels (kitchen paper). The oil in the second fryer should be very hot. Immediately add the slices to this fryer and carefully stir. The potato slices will puff up. When they are golden brown and firm, after a few minutes, remove with a slotted spoon, drain well, and sprinkle with salt to serve.

SAUTÉED POTATOES

POMMES DE TERRE SAUTÉES

Preparation time: 10 minutes
Cooking time: 25 minutes
Serves 6

1 lb 10 oz (750 g) potatoes
4 tablespoons/2 oz (60 g) butter
½ teaspoon salt
1 tablespoon flat-leaf parsley, finely chopped

This is the perfect dish to make on a whim, when you are short of ideas but want something delicious for an informal meal. Sautéed Potatoes can be served as a side or with just a fried egg for a filling meal. Methods and ingredients may vary from one household to another: some use oil; some use duck fat, which is especially good and, with the addition of garlic, turns the dish into potatoes *sarladaises*, from the town of Sarlat in the southwest; some don't boil the potatoes first. Firm potatoes are best but baking (floury) ones will work, too.

Bring a large saucepan of water to a boil, add the potatoes, then reduce the heat and simmer for 15 minutes, or until almost cooked. Drain. Let cool, then slice.

Heat the butter in a large skillet or frying pan over medium heat and fry the potatoes for 5–10 minutes until golden, shaking the pan frequently so that they brown evenly. Sprinkle with salt and the parsley and serve.

SIDES AND VEGETABLES / ACCOMPAGNEMENTS ET LÉGUMES   233

POTATOES ANNA

POMMES DE TERRE ANNA

Preparation time: 30 minutes
Cooking time: 1¼ hours
Serves 6

2¼ lb (1 kg) waxy potatoes
1 tablespoon goose fat or oil
scant ½ cup/3½ oz (100 g) butter, melted
salt and pepper

Chef Adolphe Dugléré invented these around 1870 at the Café Anglais, a restaurant not far from the Paris opera, and named them after the courtesan Anna Deslions, a regular, who inspired the main character of Zola's novel *Nana*. Pommes Anna is perhaps one of the most refined ways to enjoy potatoes. The potato slices are molded into a kind of cake, crunchy outside and soft inside. You can also make individual potatoes Anna if you have little molds, instead of a large one to share.

Peel or scrub the potatoes. Cut one-third of them into 1/16-inch (2-mm) slices and place in a bowl of salted water for 10 minutes.

Meanwhile, heat the goose fat or oil in a solid-bottom round cake pan or shallow ovenproof pan until very hot.

Drain the potato slices and dry with paper towels. Protecting your hands with oven mitts, carefully tilt the hot fat in the pan to coat the sides and bottom, then pour any surplus out. Arrange the potato slices neatly around the bottom and sides of the pan, overlapping them.

Preheat the oven to 400°F/200°C/Gas Mark 6.

Cut the remaining potatoes into ½-inch (1-cm) slices. Heat some of the butter in a large skillet or frying pan over high heat, add the potatoes, in batches if needed, and fry them for a few minutes until they start to brown.

Arrange in the prepared cake pan in layers, pressing each layer down, seasoning them with salt and pepper, and brushing with the remaining butter. Continue until the pan is full. Cover and cook for about 1 hour.

Turn out and serve hot. The potatoes should form a golden-brown cake.

POTATO SALAD

POMMES DE TERRE EN SALADE

Preparation time: 20 minutes
Cooking time: 20 minutes
Serves 6

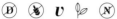

2¼ lb (1 kg) waxy potatoes, unpeeled
1 quantity Vinaigrette (page 32)
1 onion, finely chopped
1 tablespoon finely chopped flat-leaf parsley,
   plus extra to garnish
2 hard-boiled eggs, sliced (optional)
1 beet (beetroot), cooked and sliced (optional)
salt

Make potato salad for a picnic or serve as part of a buffet for a party. It's also a good accompaniment for Marinated Herring Fillets (page 190) or leftover roast meats. It is important to dress the salad while the potatoes are still warm, so they will absorb the flavors of the vinaigrette better.

Bring a large saucepan of salted water to a boil. Add the potatoes, then reduce the heat and simmer for 20 minutes, or until tender.

Let cool slightly, then peel and thinly slice into a salad bowl. Dress with the vinaigrette, then gently stir in the onion and parsley, along with hard-boiled eggs and beet (beetroot), if using. Garnish with parsley and serve.

Note
To prevent the salad from being too dry, a little broth (stock) or milk can be placed in the bottom of the salad bowl, before the salad ingredients are combined.

LEEKS SERVED LIKE ASPARAGUS

POIREAUX EN ASPERGES

Preparation time: 10 minutes
Cooking time: 20 minutes
Serves 6

The version with vinaigrette, aptly named *Poireaux vinaigrette*, is a classic bistro starter and always sure to please, as much as with the other sauces. If using vinaigrette or mayonnaise, make a lightly mustardy sauce and use vegetable oil such as sunflower or peanut (groundnut) rather than olive. When preparing the leeks, trim the tops, leaving a little of the tender green middle area along with the white, which is the sweetest and most tender part. Save the tougher green tops for broth (stocks) as they are full of flavor.

---

24 medium leeks
1 quantity Mousseline Sauce (page 38),
  white sauce (page 248), Vinaigrette
  (page 32), or Mayonnaise (page 35)
salt

To prepare the leeks, remove the roots, cut out any damaged leaves, and wash very carefully to remove any soil trapped between the layers. Bring a pot of salted water to a boil. Add the whole leeks and boil, uncovered, for around 20 minutes.

Drain well and serve with mousseline, white sauce, vinaigrette, or mayonnaise in a sauce boat.

JARDINIÈRE OF VEGETABLES

JARDINIÈRE DE LÉGUMES

Preparation time: 30 minutes
Cooking time: 1½ hours
Serves 6

1 cup/5½ oz (150 g) flageolet beans
5½ oz (150 g) carrots, julienned
5½ oz (150 g) turnips, julienned
1 small cauliflower, separated into florets
7 oz (200 g) green beans
1½ cups/7 oz (200 g) shelled peas
4 tablespoons/2 oz (60 g) butter
salt

This is the most basic way to elevate new-season produce to perfection. The secret lies in choosing only very fresh vegetables, cutting them evenly, and boiling each variety separately to respect their specific cooking times. The name *jardinière* is evocative of a colorful, well-kept vegetable garden: a promise of gorgeous spring-time flavor, especially with the final addition of a good knob of butter, and served with poached bream or roast veal.

Bring a medium saucepan of salted water to the boil. Add the flageolet beans and boil for 1 hour until tender, then drain. Meanwhile, bring another saucepan of salt water to a boil. Working in batches, boil the vegetables separately until tender, then drain: cook the carrots, turnips, and cauliflower for 5–10 minutes each; cook the green beans and peas for around 5 minutes. Cut the green beans into dice after cooking.

Arrange the vegetables separately on a platter, or mix them together. Top with the butter, and serve.

PEAS À LA FRANÇAISE

PETITS POIS À LA FRANÇAISE

Preparation time: 15 minutes
Cooking time: 45 minutes
Serves 6

This classic remains fully suited to modern tastes, and is a wonderful way to enjoy new-season peas, which appear in the springtime. The sugar is there to accentuate the natural sweetness of the peas, onions, and lettuce. Peas appeared in France for the first time in 1660 at the royal table, and became so popular with Louis XIV and his court that he commanded they be grown in his vegetable garden in Versailles. In 1828, writer Grimod de La Reynière deemed them "without contradiction, the best vegetable to be eaten in Paris." If you shell the peas yourself, keep the pods to make broth (stock).

---

3 tablespoons/1½ oz (40 g) butter
1¾ oz (50 g) pearl (baby) onions
7½ cups/2¼ lb (1 kg) shelled peas
2 heads lettuce, shredded
1 teaspoon superfine (caster) sugar
salt

Heat the butter in a large, high-sided skillet or frying pan over low heat. Add the onions, cover, and braise over very low heat for 10 minutes.

Add the peas, shredded lettuce, and sugar and season with salt. Cover with 1¼ cups/10fl oz (300 ml) water and simmer over very low heat for 30 minutes, or until peas are tender.

Note
If using frozen peas, add them to the pan 10 minutes before the end of cooking time.

BELGIAN ENDIVE WITH CHEESE

Preparation time: 20 minutes
Cooking time: 40 minutes
Serves 6

 ✳

4 tablespoons/2 oz (60 g) butter, plus extra
    for greasing
2¼ lb (1 kg) Belgian endive (chicory)
juice of 1 lemon
1 quantity Béchamel Sauce (page 30)
⅓ cup/1½ oz (40 g) grated Gruyère cheese
salt and pepper

Modern endives were created from wild chicory in 1850 by the Belgians, and their production then developed in the north of France. They are partly grown in the dark, which yields a pale yellow, crunchy, and slightly bitter bunch of tight leaves. Endive can be enjoyed raw in a salad, with blue cheese, firm pears, walnuts, and a vinaigrette (page 32). But some prefer it cooked and drowned in béchamel and cheese, as below, which offers a rich counterpart to the endives' bitterness. Ham is sometimes added to this dish, creating *endives au jambon*, the terror of French schoolchildren—but in fact quite delicious when made at home with love.

Preheat the oven to 425°F/220°C/Gas Mark 7 and grease an ovenproof dish with butter.

Cut the root end off each endive (chicory) head. Remove any withered leaves and rinse quickly but carefully under cold running water to remove earth or sand. Drain and wipe dry.

Melt the butter in a high-sided skillet or frying pan over low heat. Add the endive, season with salt and pepper, and pour over the lemon juice. Cover tightly and cook over very low heat for 30 minutes until soft.

Place the endive in the prepared dish, coat with the béchamel sauce, and sprinkle with the cheese. Bake for 10 minutes until golden brown.

ZUCCHINI GRATIN

COURGETTES EN GRATIN

Preparation time: 15 minutes
Cooking time: 15 minutes
Serves 6

 ✳

Zucchini (courgettes) have a fairly long season, from June to September. They are inexpensive, easy to come by, and not complicated to prepare, but also not exceptionally flavorsome, so they make a good backdrop for béchamel and cheese. Serve as an accompaniment to grilled meats or a homely main dish on its own. Alternatively, you can dredge chunks of zucchini in seasoned flour and sauté in butter or olive oil before scattering with chopped parsley, chervil, and tarragon. In the winter, cauliflower make a good gratin base, as in the variation below.

---

3 tablespoons/1½ oz (40 g) butter or oil
4 large zucchini (courgettes), unpeeled,
   cut into ¾-inch (1.5-cm) slices
1 quantity Béchamel Sauce (page 30)
⅓ cup/1½ oz (40 g) grated Gruyère cheese
salt and pepper

Preheat the oven to 475°F/240°C/Gas Mark 8 and grease an ovenproof dish with a little of the butter or oil.
   Heat the remaining butter or oil in a large skillet or frying pan over low heat. Add the zucchini (courgettes) and cook gently for 10 minutes. Season with salt and pepper.
   Arrange the zucchini slices in the prepared dish. Coat with the béchamel sauce, sprinkle with the cheese, and bake for 5–10 minutes until golden brown.
   Remove from the oven and serve warm.

CAULIFLOWER EN GRATIN / CHOU-FLEUR EN GRATIN
For a cauliflower gratin, separate 1 large cauliflower in florets and boil in salted water for 15 minutes. Drain and place in a buttered dish. Add a scant 1 cup/3½ oz (100 g) grated Gruyère cheese to the warm béchamel sauce to make a cheese sauce. Coat the cauliflower with the béchamel sauce, sprinkle with ⅓ cup/1½ oz (40 g) grated Gruyère cheese and bake for 5–10 minutes, until golden brown.

SALSIFY IN WHITE SAUCE

SALSIFIS EN SAUCE BLANCHE

Preparation time: 30 minutes
Cooking time: 30–40 minutes
Serves 6

v Ⓝ ✲

For the salsify
30 stems of salsify
distilled white vinegar
salt and pepper
sliced baguette, for serving (optional)

For the white sauce
2 tablespoons/1 oz (30 g) butter
⅓ cup/1½ oz (40 g) all-purpose (plain) flour

Salsify tends to suffer from a terrible reputation, but if not overcooked, it is really tasty and interesting. Once peeled, it needs to be put in vinegar water or it will oxidate and turn black. Serve with grilled or roast beef, or as part of a set of starters. Salsify may also be generously drizzled with olive oil, sprinkled with salt, and roasted in a 350°F/180°C/Gas Mark 4 oven for about 40 minutes.

Cook the salsify: Cut the end off each piece of salsify, then scrape and rinse in water with a little vinegar added to it. Slice it into 2-inch (5-cm) pieces. Bring a large saucepan of salted water to a boil. Boil the salsify for 30 minutes, or until tender, then drain.

Make the white sauce: Melt the butter in a medium saucepan over medium–low heat. Stir in the flour and cook for 2–3 minutes to form a roux. Gradually add 2 cups plus 1 tablespoon/17 fl oz (500 ml) hot water, a little at a time, stirring all the time to prevent lumps forming, until you have a smooth sauce. You may not need all the water. Simmer for 10 minutes over low heat, stirring constantly, until it coats the back of the spoon. Season with salt and pepper.

Mix with the salsify and serve warm with baguette, if desired.

VICHY CARROTS

CAROTTES À LA VICHY

Preparation time: 10 minutes
Cooking time: 20 minutes
Serves 6

This method of cooking yields melt-in-the mouth, deliciously caramelized carrots. The town of Vichy, in Auvergne, is famous for its highly mineralized water, and people have been travelling there to enjoy its benefits for several centuries. Carrots have been cooked in Vichy water probably since as early as the sixteenth or seventeenth century, as the mineral-rich water helps produce deliciously flavored and highly digestible carrots. The baking soda (bicarbonate) in the recipe below helps reproduce the same effect. Serve alongside braised poultry or roast meats, or enjoy as a starter on its own.

1 lb 5 oz (600 g) carrots, evenly sliced
3 tablespoons/1½ oz (40 g) butter
1 teaspoon salt
1 tablespoon superfine (caster) sugar
pinch of baking soda (bicarbonate of soda)
1 handful flat-leaf parsley, chopped

Put the carrots in a large saucepan. Add the butter, salt, sugar, baking soda (bicarbonate of soda), and 1⅔ cups/14 fl oz (400 ml) water. Bring to a boil, then reduce the heat and gently cook until tender, about 15 minutes.

Continue cooking, shaking the pan every few minutes, until the cooking liquid is completely reduced, and the carrots are coated in a shiny glaze. Sprinkle with the parsley and serve.

PORCINI WITH HERBS

CÈPES AUX FINES HERBES

Preparation time: 15 minutes, plus
  marinating time
Cooking time: 20 minutes
Serves 6

6 large, firm porcini mushrooms (ceps)
⅓ cup/3½ fl oz (100 ml) oil
2 shallots
2 tablespoons/1 oz (25 g) butter
1 tablespoon chopped mixed herbs,
  such as flat-leaf parsley, chives, chervil,
  and tarragon
salt and pepper

Porcinis (ceps) can be found at markets from late summer to early autumn. You can forage them in the woods, but take care to learn from an experienced forager—and if ever in doubt, don't eat them. They should always be chosen very firm, with beautiful fresh caps. Prepare them as soon as possible, in simple ways. Sautéed as in following recipe, they can be served with roast and grilled meats or game, or simply as a beautiful side to fried eggs with a nicely runny yolk.

Begin preparing 3 hours in advance. Clean the porcinis (ceps) with a damp cloth and cut off and reserve their stems (stalks). Place the caps in a bowl and toss with the oil, then season with salt and pepper. Set aside to marinate for 3 hours.

Finely chop the shallots and the stems from the porcinis. Melt the butter in a large skillet or frying pan over low heat. Add the shallots, stems, and herbs and gently cook for 15 minutes.

In a separate pan over high heat, brown the mushroom caps in their oil for 5 minutes. Add the chopped mushroom mixture to the pan and cook for another 5 minutes. Season with more salt and pepper if necessary and serve very hot.

FRESH NAVY BEANS WITH TOMATOES

HARICOTS BLANCS FRAIS AUX TOMATES

Preparation time: 40 minutes
Cooking time: 1 hour 10 minutes
Serves 6

Beans were brought to Europe from the Andes by the conquistadors and quickly became a country staple and precious source of protein during the winter. The word *haricot* used to refer to a stew, and beans became so common in this type of dish that, in France, they took its name. Many regional varieties of beans are grown in France. The following recipe calls for fresh ones that appear on market stalls in the summer. But it could also be made with dried beans; just soak them in water for 24 hours beforehand.

---

12 cups/4½ lb (2 kg) fresh navy (haricot)
   beans, shelled
1 clove garlic
1 bouquet garni
a few slices carrot
4 tablespoons/2 oz (60 g) butter
scant ½ cup/3½ oz (100 g) chopped onions
1 lb 2 oz (500 g) tomatoes, skinned, seeded,
   and diced
salt and pepper

Bring a large saucepan of salted water to a boil. Add the beans along with the garlic, bouquet garni, and carrot. Reduce the heat and gently simmer for 30–40 minutes until tender, then drain, discarding the bouquet garni, garlic, and carrot slices.

Heat the butter in a high-sided skillet or frying pan over medium–low heat and add the onions. Fry for 10 minutes until golden.

Stir in the tomatoes, then the beans, and season with salt and pepper. Simmer over low heat, uncovered, for 20 minutes, then serve.

ARTICHOKES
À LA BARIGOULE

ARTICHAUTS
À LA BARIGOULE

Preparation time: 1 hour
Cooking time: 30 minutes
Serves 6

6 globe artichokes
1 tablespoon lemon juice
2 cups/7 oz (200 g) finely chopped mushrooms
¾ cup/4½ oz (125 g) diced bacon
1 handful flat-leaf parsley, finely chopped
12 bacon slices (rashers)
2 tablespoons/1 oz (30 g) butter
2 tablespoons olive oil
scant 1 cup/4½ oz (125 g) roughly
   chopped carrots
scant ½ cup/3½ oz (100 g) roughly
   chopped onions
a few raw bacon rinds
1¼ cups/10 fl oz (300 ml) white wine
2 cups plus 1 tablespoon/17 fl oz (500 ml)
   any broth (stock)
salt and pepper

This Provençale recipe from the Alpilles, a small chain of mountains, used to be a kind of peasant's stew prepared with small local wild mushrooms called *barigoules*. This version is a restaurant-style interpretation, where the artichokes are stuffed with an aromatic filling and simmered in white wine and broth (stock). It can be served as a side, a starter, or even as a vegetarian main, if you leave out the bacon.

To prepare the artichokes, break off the stem (stalk) and, using a very sharp knife, remove the tough outer leaves and trim the base. Neatly cut the tips off the remaining inner leaves.

Wash thoroughly in water and keep in a bowl of water with the lemon juice to prevent discoloring.

Bring a large pot of salted water to a boil and add the artichokes. Boil for 5 minutes.

Meanwhile, make the stuffing by mixing the mushrooms, diced bacon, and parsley in a bowl and seasoning with salt and pepper.

Drain the artichokes, then carefully lift off the cap of leaves and remove the hairy choke. Top the artichokes with the stuffing. Wrap each artichoke in 2 bacon slices (rashers), arranged in in criss-cross fashion, then tie with kitchen twine (string).

Heat a large skillet or frying pan over medium and add the butter and oil. Add the bacon-wrapped artichokes and fry them until golden, about 5 minutes.

Preheat the oven to 375°F/190°C/Gas Mark 5.

Put the carrots, onions, and bacon rinds in a heavy Dutch oven (casserole) and put the artichokes on top. Pour on the wine, then place on high heat and bring to a boil. Boil for 10 minutes until reduced.

Add the broth (stock), cover, and carefully place in the oven to cook for 30 minutes.

Remove the twine from the artichokes and place in a warmed serving dish. Strain the cooking juices over and serve.

SIDES AND VEGETABLES / ACCOMPAGNEMENTS ET LÉGUMES

TOMATOES STUFFED WITH RICE

TOMATES FARCIES AU RIZ

Preparation time: 45 minutes
Cooking time: 55 minutes
Serves 6

 v

scant 1 cup/6½ oz (180 g) long-grain rice
1 tablespoon/½ oz (15 g) butter
2 hard-boiled eggs
1 onion, chopped
2 tablespoons flat-leaf parsley, chopped
1 tablespoon chervil, chopped
6 large tomatoes
3 tablespoons dried breadcrumbs or
    1¼ cups/5½ oz (150 g) grated Gruyère cheese
salt and pepper

This type of recipe was originally created as a way to use up leftovers. It has become an everyday favorite, an economical and vegetarian dish to make in the summer, when tomatoes are in full season. The Mediterranean has a tradition of serving stuffed vegetables of all kinds, but *tomates farcies* have reached a nationally popular status. You can make a meat version by substituting the eggs for ground pork.

———————

Preheat the oven to 300°F/150°C/Gas Mark 2.

To prepare the rice, bring a large saucepan of salted water to the boil. Add the rice and boil for 10 minutes. Drain, then put the rice into a Dutch oven (casserole). Gently mix in the butter. Cover the dish tightly and cook in the oven for 20 minutes until the rice grains have become tender but remain whole.

Meanwhile, slice the top off each tomato to make a lid. Scoop out the seeds from the tomatoes with a small spoon, lightly salt the insides, and turn the tomatoes upside down for 30 minutes to release their liquid.

Increase the oven temperature to 375°F/190°C/Gas Mark 5. Chop the hard-boiled eggs and place in a bowl with the rice, onion, parsley, and chervil. Season with salt and pepper, then stuff each tomato with this rice mixture. Sprinkle with the breadcrumbs or cheese, top the tomatoes with their lids, and bake for 25 minutes until topping is golden and tomato lids are browned.

Remove from the oven and serve warm.

RATATOUILLE

RATATOUILLE PROVENÇALE

Preparation time: 25 minutes
Cooking time: 2 hours
Serves 6

Ratatouille is a summer vegetable stew cooked in Mediterranean olive oil. The recipe below is made the old-fashioned way with all the vegetables slowly simmered at the same time, as opposed to being cooked separately and then stewed together only briefly. It should be made only when the vegetables are in peak season. Leftover ratatouille is excellent, so it's always a good idea to make more for the next day. Serve with baked fish, roast and grilled meats, or an omelet.

---

1 lb 10 oz (750 g) eggplants (aubergines)
2¼ lb (1 kg) zucchini (courgettes)
4 oz (120 g) onions
1 lb 10 oz (750 g) bell peppers
1 lb 5 oz (600 g) tomatoes
1 clove garlic, sliced
5 tablespoons olive oil
salt and pepper

Cut all the vegetables into slices about ½ inch (1 cm) thick. Put them in a heavy Dutch oven (casserole) with the garlic, pour over the oil, season with salt and pepper. Cover and bring to a boil, then reduce the heat and simmer (covered) for 2 hours, adding a little water, as needed, if the vegetables start sticking to the pan. If desired, pound with a mortar and pestle to break up the vegetables slightly. Serve hot or cold.

PROVENÇALE SWISS CHARD

BETTES À LA PROVENÇALE

Preparation time: 10 minutes
Cooking time: 10 minutes
Serves 6

2¼ lb (1 kg) Swiss chard
3½ tablespoons/1¾ oz (50 g) butter
1 clove garlic, finely chopped
1 tablespoon flat-leaf parsley, chopped
salt

Swiss chard is a spring and summer vegetable, quick to prepare and a welcome green accompaniment to a meal. It's associated with the Mediterranean regions close to Italy, but is now grown more widely as it has adapted to a wide range of climates. The garlic in the recipe gives it a Provençale touch. Olive oil would probably be more authentic if it had to be really Provençale. Nevertheless, the creamy lactic touch of butter recommended here does suit the green leaves very well. This recipe omits the leaves, however they are delicious served as a side, blanched and pan fried, or folded into a quiche.

To prepare the chard stalks: Cut off the earthy ends, then strip the leaves from the stalks. Using a knife, remove the thin outer skin from the stalks. If the stalks are particularly tough, cut them into 1–1½-inch (2.5–4-cm) slices, then rinse and drain.

Bring a pot of lightly salted water to a boil. Boil the chard for 3–5 minutes, then thoroughly drain. Melt the butter in a large skillet or frying pan over high heat, add the pieces of chard and the garlic, and fry for 3–4 minutes. Sprinkle with the parsley and serve.

DESSERTS, PASTRIES, AND SWEETS

DESSERTS, PÂTISSERIES ET CONFISERIES

The French do like to end a meal on a sweet note. Dessert comes after cheese: At a dinner party, a full cheese platter will be offered to guests, while on an everyday basis it's not uncommon to take a bite of one or two cheeses between the main course and dessert. For the latter, this chapter offers many options: everyday dairy or fruit puddings, elegant-but-simple bistro-style desserts such as Light Chocolate Mousse (page 286) or Vanilla Crème Brûlée (page 280), ideas for *le goûter* —the afternoon snack—like Marbled Cake (page 314), Crêpes (page 294), or Madeleines (page 318), fancy pastries such as Paris-Brest (page 324); special occasion treats; and traditional sweet nibbles like Honey Nougat (page 346).

Milk, cream, butter, and eggs are common farmhouse ingredients almost everywhere in France, and form the base of a vast range of delicious desserts. Choose the best quality possible; their taste will shine through in the final dish, as flavorings such as vanilla are usually only subtly used. Buy free-range, organic eggs. For baking, whole (full-fat) milk is a good choice because it has a fuller taste and a richer texture: perfect, for example, in the cream of a Floating Island (page 284) or in crème brûlée. Bretons always bake with salted butter, which yields very tasty desserts without really giving a salty taste: it works well with Chocolate Cake (page 312), for example, and is worth the try. For whipping, choose 30–40 percent whipping cream. Otherwise, thick crème fraîche is a good alternative.

The French excel at preparing delicious and varied desserts from the simplest household ingredients. Many recipes here are very quick to make and can be improvised at the last minute, like French Toast (page 296) or crêpes. And even the easiest dish can be elevated to dinner-party dessert status, if accompanied by a scoop of ice cream, a little whipped cream, and some pan-fried apples or peaches, or perhaps with some homemade caramel (page 49) poured over.

French children—and some adults—always stop for an afternoon *quatre heures*. Baking a marbled cake, madeleines, or a simple chocolate cake (with or without children) on the weekend is a good idea to avoid buying commercially made versions at the grocery store. Also, even if French people often enjoy tartines of fresh bread spread with butter and jam with their coffee in the morning, many recipes in this chapter are suitable for breakfast, such as Far (page 268), Pain d'Épice (page 306), and Crêpes (page 294).

As for other dishes, there is an element of seasonality in desserts. Fruit tarts are very popular in France and are made all year round with fruit at its best: apples and pears in autumn, strawberries in spring, raspberries and peaches in summer, plums and figs at the end of the warm season, etc. Poached fruit, cooked in an aromatic liquid, such as pears and peaches (page 272), are a light and delicious option for dessert, on their own or enhanced by cream or ice cream and toppings. Chocolate desserts work all year too, but they tend to be associated with the winter and Easter.

Fancy pastries are usually bought at patisseries, so it's perfectly fine to bring a store-bought Saint-Honoré or a set of individual cakes to a dinner party. The recipes for this kind of dessert can be quite complex as they require you to master several different pastries and creams and assemble them together. But they are definitely not unfeasible, and this chapter also provides clear instructions if you wish to try your hand at them.

CLAFOUTIS

CLAFOUTIS

Preparation time: 30 minutes
Cooking time: 35 minutes
Serves 6

v

butter, for greasing
scant 1 cup/3½ oz (100 g) all-purpose
   (plain) flour
6 eggs
1 cup/8 fl oz (250 ml) milk
3 cups/1 lb 10 oz (750 g) black cherries,
   pitted (stoned)
1 tablespoon kirsch
3½ tablespoons/1½ oz (40 g) superfine
   (caster) sugar
salt

Clafoutis is a pudding from the region of Limousin, in south-central France, but variants exist in neighboring regions. There is a debate in France on whether to pit (stone) the fruit or not: some say it's best not to because the stones yield a lot of extra taste and the cherry juices won't be lost in the pudding; but it's easier to eat the dish without. Clafoutis batter is a little like a pancake batter, which is poured over fruit and then baked. Cherries are the most classic flavor, but other fruits work well too, such as mirabelle prunes, raspberries, or pan-fried slices of apples.

Preheat the oven to 400°F/200°C/Gas Mark 6 and butter an ovenproof dish.

Mix the flour with the eggs and a pinch of salt in a bowl. Add a little of the milk and beat into the batter until light and smooth. Add the remaining milk, a little at a time, beating between additions until the batter falls like a ribbon from the spoon, like crêpe batter.

Stir the cherries and kirsch into the batter. Pour into the prepared dish and bake for 35 minutes until set and top is golden brown.

Remove from the oven, then sprinkle with the sugar. Serve warm or cold.

Preparation time: 20 minutes,
   plus soaking time
Cooking time: 40 minutes
Serves 6

1 tablespoon/½ oz (15 g) butter
2¼ cups/9 oz (250 g) all-purpose (plain) flour
½ teaspoon salt
4 eggs
1¼ cups/9 oz (250 g) superfine (caster) sugar
4¼ cups/1¾ pints (1 liter) milk
1 tablespoon rum
generous 1 cup/9 oz (250 g) prunes, soaked
   in water for 24 hours

Far is a Breton specialty, usually available in boulangeries all around Brittany. The baking dish needs to be generously buttered: salted butter is preferred locally. *Far* means flour in Latin and evolved into *farz* in the Breton language. The word initially described a savory buckwheat porridge. The modern version appeared during the nineteenth century, when the dried fruit came from the southwest of France, brought back by Breton sailors who needed an unperishable source of vitamins on their ships. *Far* can be eaten for dessert after a light meal, and it's also perfect in the morning with coffee.

Preheat the oven to 425°F/220°C/Gas Mark 7 and grease an ovenproof dish with the butter.

Put the flour and salt into a bowl. Break in the eggs, one by one, mixing carefully between additions to remove lumps. Beat the batter to make it light. Whisk in the sugar, then the milk, then add the rum. Drain the prunes and add to the batter.

Pour the mixture into the prepared dish and bake in the oven for 20 minutes until the batter has set. Turn down the temperature to 350°F/180°C/Gas Mark 4 and bake for another 20 minutes until golden brown on top.

Remove from the oven and serve.

PEARS IN WINE

POIRES AU VIN

Preparation time: 15 minutes
Cooking time: 30 minutes
Serves 6

Pears cooked in red wine take on a lovely ruby color and delicious flavors from the sweet spices. You may have to adapt the cooking time to the fruit's firmness. Once pears ripen, they can turn bad very quickly, so this recipe is made with still-underripe pears to avoid this risk. It's also a good way to use up any leftover wine. A light dessert, *poires au vin* acts as a pleasant palate-cleanser, the perfect ending to a rich meal.

---

1 lb 2 oz (500 g) small, firm pears
⅓ cup/3½ fl oz (100 ml) red wine
1 cup/7 oz (200 g) superfine (caster) sugar
1 clove
pinch of ground cinnamon
small pinch of nutmeg

Peel the pears, leaving the stems (stalks) attached. Put them in a nonreactive pot with the wine, sugar, clove, cinnamon, and a scraping of nutmeg. Place over medium heat, bring to a simmer, and cook for 30 minutes, or until the pears are tender.

Arrange the pears in a dish with their stems upright and pour the cooking liquid over them.

PEACH MELBA

Preparation time: 30 minutes,
    plus chilling time
Cooking time: 25 minutes
Serves 6

 v

¾ cup/5½ oz (150 g) superfine (caster) sugar
2 cups plus 1 tablespoon/17 fl oz (500 ml) milk
5 egg yolks
1 vanilla bean, split lengthwise
6 peaches, peeled
red currant jelly, for coating
⅓ cup/1¾ oz (50 g) chopped toasted almonds

French cook Auguste Escoffier, chef at the London Savoy in the 1890s, was famously inspired to create the original version of this dessert upon hearing Australian soprano Nellie Melba perform in Wagner's *Lohengrin*. His recipe comprised a poached peach with vanilla ice cream doused in raspberry purée, all nestled in an ice-carved swan reminiscent of the opera. Perhaps less spectacular in presentation but equally seductive in taste, this take on the classic Melba involves cooled-down vanilla crème anglaise balanced out by the tartness of red currant jelly, with the mandatory peaches poached in syrup and a crunchy sprinkling of toasted almonds.

Begin preparing several hours in advance. Make a light syrup by dissolving ½ cup/3½ oz (100 g) of the sugar in 2 cups plus 1 tablespoon/17 fl oz (500 ml) water in a small pan. Bring to a boil and boil for 1 minute. Add the peaches and poach them for 5 minutes in the syrup.

Make a vanilla crème anglaise (see page 45) with the milk, egg yolks, vanilla bean, and remaining ¼ cup/1¾ oz (50 g) sugar.

Put the peaches in a bowl or a shallow plate, coat with the red currant jelly, and sprinkle with the almonds, then pour the crème anglaise around the peaches. Alternatively, layer the red currant jelly, peaches, and crème anglaise in individual dessert glasses. Chill in the refrigerator for a few hours before serving.

APPLE FRITTERS

Preparation time: 8 minutes
Cooking time: 15 minutes
Serves 6

Sweet fritters are popular all over France and come in many local varieties, such as the Lyonnaise *bugne*, the Languedocian *oreillette*, or the *chichi* from Marseille. They are often made in February or March for Mardi Gras, before Lent. But the fruit or flower varieties are made whenever they are in season: in the spring with acacia blossom and the autumn with apples. Keep the apples whole for this, coring them first without cutting them so you have horizontal slices with a hole in the middle.

For the batter
⅓ oz (10 g) fresh yeast
1 tablespoon warm water, plus more
    for mixing
2¼ cups/9 oz (250 g) all-purpose (plain) flour
1 tablespoon oil
1 egg white

For the fritters
vegetable oil, for deep-frying
3 dessert apples
granulated, superfine (caster) or
    confectioners' (icing) sugar, for sprinkling

Begin preparing the batter 2 hours in advance. In a small bowl, mix the yeast to a paste with the warm water. Put the flour in a large bowl and make a well in the center, then pour in the oil along with the yeast mixture into the well. Mix in warm water, a little at a time, until the batter falls like a ribbon from the whisk.

In another small bowl, beat the egg white for 1 minute with a fork. Stir this into the batter. Chill in the refrigerator for 2 hours.

Make the fritters: heat the oil in a deep-fryer to 350°F/180°C or until a cube of bread browns in 30 seconds.

Peel and core the apples and cut into even slices. Dip the apple slices, one by one, into the batter. Working in batches, carefully lower the apple slices into the hot oil and fry for a few minutes until golden and tender. Using a slotted spoon, carefully transfer onto some paper towels (kitchen paper) to drain. Sprinkle with sugar and serve immediately.

MONT BLANC

MONT-BLANC

Preparation time: 30 minutes,
  plus chilling time
Cooking time: 45 minutes
Serves 6

1 lb 2 oz (500 g) chestnuts
1⅔ cups/13 fl oz (375 ml) milk
scant 1 cup/6½ oz (180 g) vanilla sugar
½ teaspoon salt
3 tablespoons/1½ oz (40 g) butter
1 cup/8 fl oz (250 ml) heavy (double) cream
confectioners' (icing) sugar, for sprinkling
  (optional)

Taking on the appearance of a snow-capped mountain, this dessert is named after France's highest peak, Mont Blanc. The chestnut purée is often passed through a sieve to create a kind of vermicelli form, which gives it a lighter texture. Many variations of this winter dessert exist in pastry shops, sometimes with a meringue base. Its origins are not very clear: it may come from the Italian Piedmont, but also from Alsace, which has a very similar dish called *torche aux marrons*.

To prepare the chestnuts, carefully cut a cross in the rounded part of the shell of each one with a sharp knife. Bring a large pot of water to a boil and blanch the chestnuts in the water for 2 minutes. Drain, let cool slightly, and remove the shells. Cook the chestnuts for another 10 minutes in fresh boiling water.

Remove them from the water in batches and rub off the inner skins while they are still hot (the skin sticks to the nuts as they cool).

Place them in a saucepan with the milk, 1 teaspoon of the sugar, and the salt and bring to a boil. Reduce the heat and simmer for 30 minutes.

Remove the chestnuts and transfer to a food processor, then process to a purée. Moisten with a little of the cooking liquid, beat in the butter, then stir in the rest of the sugar. Chill in the refrigerator until completely cold—at least 1 hour.

Pile or pipe the chestnut purée into a pyramid shape on a serving dish. Whip the cream to stiff peaks and spread or pipe it onto the cold chestnut purée. Sprinkle with sugar, if desired, and serve immediately.

DESSERTS, PASTRIES, AND SWEETS / DESSERTS, PÂTISSERIES ET CONFISERIES   277

PARISIAN FLAN

FLAN À LA PARISIENNE

Preparation time: 10 minutes,
  plus chilling time
Cooking time: 45 minutes
Serves 6

v

2 tablespoons/1 oz (30 g) butter, melted,
  plus extra for greasing
1¾ cups/7 oz (200 g) all-purpose (plain) flour
½ cup/3½ oz (100 g) superfine (caster) sugar
4 eggs
vanilla sugar, to taste
4 cups/1¾ pints (1 liter) milk

Flan has been the name of any kind of baked custard that has existed in France for at least a thousand years, in many forms. Some versions involve cooking the mixture in a pie crust to make a kind of custard tart. Modern usage, no older than the late twentieth century, has matched this latter type of tart with the expression *flan à la Parisienne*, the dessert having become extremely popular in the capital's pastry shops as an easily transportable, inexpensive, and filling dessert after a quick lunch on the go. In Ginette Mathiot's time, though, flan à la Parisienne did not refer to the crust version, hence the discrepancy between the modern understanding of the name and her recipe, below, with no pastry; but it is still just as good and easier to bake.

Begin preparing the day before. Preheat the oven to 350°F/180°C/Gas Mark 4 and grease a round 9½-inch (24-cm) mold with butter.

Put the flour in a large bowl. Make a well in the center and put the superfine (caster) sugar, eggs, and melted butter into it, then beat to combine.

In a separate bowl, stir the vanilla sugar into the milk, then add to the flour and egg mixture. Beat the batter until completely smooth. Pour into the prepared mold, place in a roasting pan, and half-fill the pan with hot water. Bake in the oven for 45 minutes.

Turn out and let cool, then chill in the refrigerator overnight. Serve cold.

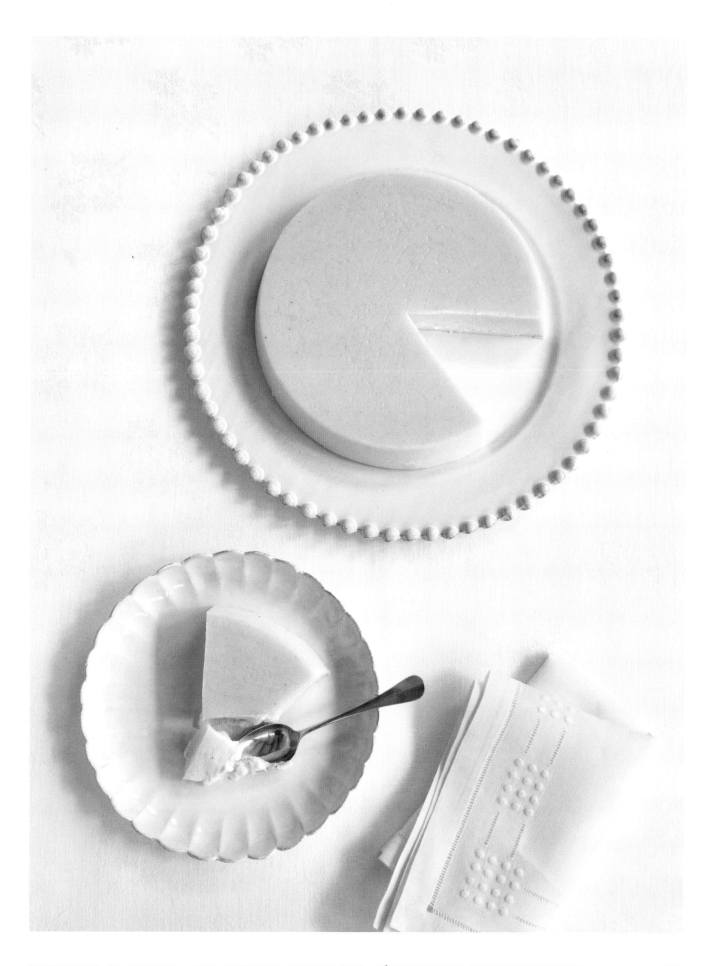

VANILLA CRÈME BRÛLÉE

CRÈME BRÛLÉE À LA VANILLE

Preparation time: 20 minutes,
   plus chilling time
Cooking time: 1 hour
Serves 6

2 cups plus 1 tablespoon/17 fl oz (500 ml) milk
2 cups plus 1 tablespoon/17 fl oz (500 ml)
   light (single) cream
4 vanilla beans, halved lengthwise
1 cup/7 oz (200 g) superfine (caster) sugar
10 egg yolks
scant ½ cup/3½ oz (100 g) brown sugar

A classic bistro dessert, crème brûlée is in fact surprisingly quick to put together, and is sure to please everyone at the table. Breaking through the caramel crust with a spoon to dive into the luscious cream is a wonderful experience. Crème brûlée has to be made in advance, which is quite handy when you have to plan a multiple-course dinner. The last step of "burning" the sugar is done immediately before serving. It's important to sprinkle the sugar as evenly as possible so it caramelizes well. Use a little sieve, if you have one. A kitchen blow torch works better than running the crème brûlée under the broiler (grill), but be really careful if using one.

Begin preparing at least 3 to 4 hours in advance. Preheat the oven to 300°F/150°C/Gas Mark 2.

Mix together the milk, cream, vanilla beans, and ½ cup/3½ oz (100 g) of the superfine (caster) sugar. Bring just to a boil over low heat, then remove from the heat and let cool.

Scrape the seeds out of the vanilla beans into the milk and save the empty beans for another use. Beat the egg yolks in a large bowl with the remaining superfine sugar until white and creamy. Pour the vanilla-flavored milk over the eggs and mix well. Pour into 6 individual ramekins or an ovenproof dish. Place the ramekins or dish in a roasting pan and half-fill the pan with hot water. Bake for 45–50 minutes, or until just set (the custard must not boil).

Let cool to room temperature, then refrigerate for 3–4 hours.

Shortly before serving, preheat the broiler (grill) to the highest setting. Sprinkle the custards with the brown sugar and put the dish under the very hot broiler, watching closely until just starting to caramelize: the sugar will form small balls on the surface. Alternatively, carefully wave a kitchen blow torch over the tops to caramelize the sugar.

Serve immediately.

CRÈME CARAMEL

CRÈME RENVERSÉE

Preparation time: 15 minutes,
  plus cooling time
Cooking time: 1 hour
Serves 6

1 cup/7 oz (200 g) superfine (caster) sugar
2 cups plus 1 tablespoon/17 fl oz (500 ml) milk
vanilla extract, coffee extract, liqueur,
  or other flavoring, to taste
6 eggs, lightly beaten

The essence of simplicity, this dessert never fails to please and always creates a moment of excited anticipation followed by admiring relief when the crème is turned out and the caramel flows down its sides. For many French adults, it's deliciously nostalgic. Orange blossom water or tangerine zest are lovely flavoring alternatives to the ones below. *Crème renversée* is versatile and suits informal meals just as well as dinner parties. Use individual molds for a fancier dinner party, and a rectangular cake pan or a fluted charlotte mold for a shareable version. Choose good-quality ingredients, and use whole (full-fat) milk, for a lovely creamy taste.

Begin preparing at least 2 hours in advance. Preheat the oven to 300°F/150°C/Gas Mark 2.

Make a dark caramel (see page 49) with ⅓ cup/2½ oz (70 g) of the sugar and 1 tablespoon water: Mix the sugar and water in a medium saucepan and place over low heat, stirring constantly, until the sugar dissolves. Increase the heat and bring to a boil without stirring; boil until the sugar is starting to caramelize, moving from light gold to deeper brown, and reaches 166–175°C (330–347°F) on a candy (sugar) thermometer.

Carefully remove the pan from the heat and stop the cooking by adding one or two drops of ice water to the pan. Pour the caramel into 6 individual molds or a large crème caramel mold to coat the insides and set aside.

In a large saucepan, bring the milk, the remaining sugar, and the chosen flavoring to a boil. Remove from the heat and, stirring constantly, add the eggs. Pour into the prepared mold(s) and place it in a large, deep roasting pan. Half-fill the pan with hot water, then bake in the oven for 45–50 minutes until set.

Remove from the oven and let cool. When ready to serve, dip the molds in hot water for 30 seconds and turn out onto individual plates or a serving dish.

DESSERTS, PASTRIES, AND SWEETS / DESSERTS, PÂTISSERIES ET CONFISERIES

FLOATING ISLAND

ÎLE FLOTTANTE

Preparation time: 20 minutes,
    plus cooling time
Cooking time: 1 hour
Serves 6

1 cup/7 oz (200 g) superfine (caster) sugar
6 eggs, separated
2 cups plus 1 tablespoon/17 fl oz (500 ml) milk

One of the sweet bistro classics, floating island is also a common household pudding and a children's favorite. A lightly sweetened meringue, light as air, swims in a pool of runny crème anglaise. The caramel on top gives a welcome crunch. You might also encounter *œufs à la neige*, a very similar dessert where the whipped egg whites are poached in individual portions rather than baked in a mold. It's worth buying good-quality, free-range eggs and fresh whole (full-fat) milk for this tasty dish.

Preheat the oven to 300°F/150°C/Gas Mark 2.

Using ¼ cup/2 oz (60 g) of the sugar, make a light caramel with 1 tablespoon water (see page 49). Pour into a large mold to coat the insides.

Whisk the egg whites to stiff peaks with a scant ½ cup/3 oz (80 g) of the sugar. Reserve the yolks for the crème anglaise.

Spoon the egg whites into the prepared mold, level the surface, and put the dish in a deep roasting pan. Half-fill the pan with hot water, then bake in the oven for 45 minutes.

Meanwhile, make the crème anglaise (see page 45) with the milk, remaining ¼ cup/2 oz (60 g) sugar, and reserved egg yolks.

Remove the meringue from the oven and let cool completely, then dip the mold in hot water for 30 seconds and turn out the meringue onto a serving dish. Surround with the crème anglaise and serve.

DESSERTS, PASTRIES, AND SWEETS / DESSERTS, PÂTISSERIES ET CONFISERIES 285

LIGHT CHOCOLATE MOUSSE

Preparation time: 20 minutes,
   plus chilling time
Serves 6

7 oz (200 g) semisweet (dark) chocolate
6 egg whites
2½ tablespoons/1 oz (30 g) superfine
   (caster) sugar

In this recipe, egg yolks are left out, which yields a very light mousse as the title suggests. Choose good-quality semisweet (dark) chocolate, preferably with at least 70 percent cocoa solids. Chocolate arrived in Europe in the first half of the seventeenth century, and Louis XIV and his wife Maria Theresa of Spain made a habit of drinking hot chocolate. The first mousse-like recipes were likely also created for him at that time. Chocolate mousse needs to spend a few hours in the refrigerator before being served from a large bowl or in individual portions, like they do in bistros.

Begin preparing 3 hours in advance. Place the chocolate with 2 tablespoons water in a heatproof bowl set over a pan of barely simmering water. Gently melt, stirring occasionally, to make a thick paste.

In a separate bowl, whisk the egg whites to soft peaks. Add the sugar and continue whisking until very stiff. Gently fold the hot chocolate into the egg whites. Pour into a serving bowl or individual dishes and refrigerate for up to 3 hours.

COFFEE CHARLOTTE

Preparation time: 10 minutes, plus infusing
   and chilling times
Cooking time: 20 minutes
Serves 6

¼ cup/1½ oz (40 g) ground coffee beans
1¼ cups/10 fl oz (300 ml) milk
4 egg yolks
1⅓ cups/5½ oz (150 g) confectioners'
   (icing) sugar
5 gelatin leaves or 2 tablespoons/⅔ oz (18 g)
   powdered gelatin
½ vanilla bean, split lengthwise
1⅔ cups/14 fl oz (400 ml) heavy (double) cream

CHARLOTTE AU CAFÉ

Charlotte is a very popular dessert, particularly for special occasions as it looks very pretty but is made quickly, and ideally the day before. The filling can be adjusted to your taste and the season. *Charlotte aux fraises*, with strawberries, is a favorite for spring birthday menus. A charlotte with poached pears and chocolate is also a well-loved classic. Flavored with chestnut purée and crushed *marrons glacés*, it could be shaped into a log for Christmas. The recipe below includes only a cream set in a small mold, but modern versions usually involve lining a larger mold with ladyfinger biscuits dipped in a flavored matching liquid—coffee, perhaps mixed with a little Cognac for a coffee charlotte, or berry syrup diluted in a little water or orange juice for a strawberry charlotte.

Begin preparing 3 days in advance: Mix the coffee and milk in a medium bowl, cover with plastic wrap (clingfilm), and place in the refrigerator to infuse for 2 days.

Put the egg yolks in a large bowl and mix with the sugar. Soak the gelatin leaves (if using) in a little cold water for 3 minutes.

Strain the coffee-infused milk into a pan, then add the vanilla bean. Bring to a boil. Mix into the egg yolk mixture, a little at a time, then return to the pan, and cook over very gentle heat, as for crème anglaise (see page 45).

Remove from the heat and remove the vanilla bean. Squeeze out any excess liquid from the gelatin leaves (if using) and add to the hot egg-yolk mixture (or add the powdered gelatin, if using). Stir until the gelatin dissolves, then let cool.

Meanwhile, whip the cream to soft peaks. Before the egg mixture starts to set, fold in the whipped cream. Divide among 6 individual molds and chill in the refrigerator for 12 hours, then dip the molds in hot water for 30 seconds and turn out onto a serving dish or individual plates. Serve immediately.

CHOCOLATE SOUFFLÉ

Preparation time: 10 minutes
Cooking time: 30 minutes
Serves 6

v

butter, for greasing
1⅔ cups/14 fl oz (400 ml) milk
¾ cup/5 oz (140 g) chopped semisweet
 (dark) chocolate
2 tablespoons/½ oz (15 g) all-purpose
 (plain) flour
2½ tablespoons/1 oz (30 g) superfine
 (caster) sugar
5 eggs, separated

Sweet soufflés are a magical dessert for a dinner party. They usually appear in posh restaurants, but are actually not complicated to replicate at home. Prepare the batter, pour into the prepared dish (or dishes if you wish to make individual portions), refrigerate, and bake just 30 minutes before you want to serve dessert. Other popular versions are flavored with lemon, orange, or Grand Marnier, a well-known bitter-orange flavored liqueur.

Preheat the oven to 325°F/160°C/Gas Mark 3 and grease a soufflé dish with butter.

Pour all but 2 tablespoons of the milk into a medium saucepan. Place over low heat and bring just to simmering point. Remove from the heat and stir in the chocolate until melted.

Pour the remaining milk along with the flour and sugar into a small bowl and mix to a smooth paste. Set aside.

Beat the egg yolks in a large bowl and pour in the chocolate milk, stirring. Stir in the flour and sugar paste.

In a clean mixing bowl, whisk the egg whites to stiff peaks and gently fold into the chocolate mixture. Pour into the prepared dish and gently level the surface. Place in the oven and bake for 10 minutes, then increase the temperature to 400°F/200°C/Gas Mark 6 and bake for another 20 minutes. Serve immediately.

Note
Avoid opening the oven door during baking to prevent the soufflé from collapsing.

RICE PUDDING

RIZ AU LAIT

Preparation time: 5 minutes
Cooking time: 25 minutes
Serves 6

4 cups/1¾ pints (1 liter) milk
½ vanilla bean, split lengthwise
1¼ cups/9 oz (250 g) short-grain (pudding) rice
½ cup/3½ oz (100 g) superfine (caster) sugar

A household, inexpensive warming pudding, the humble *riz au lait* was rehabilitated as a typical *"bistronomie"* dessert in the 2000s. The name was given by food critics to a style of restaurants where highly trained, high-end chefs decided to show off their talent in a relaxed and accessible bistro-style atmosphere, hence the contraction of the words *bistro* and *gastronomie*. *Riz au lait* is a good example of this. Stir the rice from time to time during cooking. With a little attention, it's a pudding really worth sitting down for. Children usually love it. It's also a perfect dessert to serve after a light meal, as it's naturally quite filling.

Pour the milk into a large saucepan with the vanilla bean and place over medium heat. Bring just to boiling point, then add the rice. Cover and gently simmer for 20 minutes, or until tender and most of the liquid is absorbed.

Remove from the heat, discard the vanilla bean, and gently mix in the sugar with a fork. Serve warm or cold.

CRÊPES

CRÊPES

Preparation time: 20 minutes,
    plus resting time
Cooking time: 3 minutes per crêpe
Serves 6

v

2¼ cups/9 oz (250 g) all-purpose (plain) flour
2 eggs
2 tablespoons vegetable oil
1 teaspoon salt
2 cups plus 1 tablespoon/17 fl oz (500 ml)
    milk, plus extra if needed
rum, kirsch, orange blossom water, or
    grated lemon zest, to taste
superfine (caster) sugar, for sprinkling

Each family has its recipe and rituals around crêpes. They are traditionally made for Candlemas, called in French *la Chandeleur*, on February second—but often really at any time of the year as a *goûter* (an afternoon snack) to make everyone happy. They are served with lemon juice and sugar, or a set of jams and chocolate spread. They can also be filled with sautéed apples and caramel for dessert, or sprinkled with sugar and orange zest and then flambéed with Grand-Marnier to make *crêpes Suzette*.

Begin preparing the batter about 2 hours in advance. Put the flour in a large bowl. Make a well in the center and break in the eggs. Add 1 tablespoon of the oil, the salt, and a little of the milk. Beat the batter with a whisk until light and smooth. Gradually add the remaining milk until the batter falls like a ribbon from the whisk.

Add the chosen flavoring. Rest the batter in the refrigerator for about 2 hours. It will thicken slightly.

When ready to cook the crêpes, stir the batter and thin with a little water or milk to return it to its original consistency.

Pour a very little of the remaining oil into a skillet or frying pan and place over high heat. Pour in a little of the batter, immediately tipping and turning the pan so that it spreads evenly. Cook until the crêpe is golden brown and can be lifted, then immediately turn over. Cook on the other side for 1 minute and sprinkle with sugar. Serve piping hot. Repeat with the remaining batter.

Note
The oil in the batter can be replaced by 2 tablespoons/1 oz (30 g) melted butter whisked into the batter just before making the crêpes.

FRENCH TOAST

PAIN PERDU

Preparation time: 10 minutes
Cooking time: 20 minutes
Serves 6

2 cups plus 1 tablespoon/17 fl oz (500 ml) milk
scant 1 cup/6 oz (175 g) superfine (caster) sugar
2 eggs
14 oz (400 g) day-old bread, cut into even,
   thin slices
9 tablespoons/4½ oz (125 g) butter
ground cinnamon or vanilla sugar, to taste

Pain perdu is France's answer to bread pudding, and a way to turn a few slices of almost-stale bread into a delicious snack. If you do not have bread, as Queen Marie-Antoinette famously said, then eat some brioche—and indeed, the same recipe is even better if made with day- (or two-day-) old brioche. In France, this is sometimes found as dessert in fashionable restaurants, dressed with fruit and a fancy sauce. At home, it is really nice as a quickly improvised breakfast.

Pour the milk into a shallow bowl with ¾ cup/5½ oz (150 g) of the superfine (caster) sugar and the eggs, then mix together. Dip the bread slices into the milk and egg mixture. The bread should not collapse, but merely be wet.

Melt a piece of the butter in a large skillet or frying pan over high heat. Working in batches, fry the bread slices for 1–2 minutes on each side until golden, adding more butter to the pan as necessary. Sprinkle with the remaining superfine sugar and some ground cinnamon or vanilla sugar. Repeat with the remaining bread. Serve hot.

VANILLA ICE CREAM GLACE À LA VANILLE

Preparation time: 10 minutes, plus cooling
and freezing times
Cooking time: 15 minutes
Serves 6

4 cups/1¾ pints (1 liter) milk
1 vanilla bean, split lengthwise
8 egg yolks
¾ cup/5½ oz (150 g) superfine (caster) sugar
2 cups plus 1 tablespoon/17 fl oz (500 ml)
    Sweetened Whipped Cream (page 44)
    (optional)

This vanilla ice cream is made from a crème anglaise base, which can be enriched with whipped cream. The vanilla gives it a wonderful aroma, but the same base can be used to make all kinds of different flavored ice creams, for example, by incorporating melted chocolate, instant coffee, pistachio paste, or fruit purées such as strawberry or raspberry. Serve as soon as it's ready, or, if you have stored it in the freezer, transfer to the refrigerator for 30 minutes to soften. Serve with poached fruit, a chocolate cake, or Apple Tart (page 338).

Place the milk and vanilla bean in a large saucepan. Bring just to the simmering point, then remove from the heat and set aside to infuse.

Whisk the egg yolks and sugar in a clean mixing bowl for at least 10 minutes, or until the mixture becomes white and foamy.

Remove the vanilla bean from the milk, then scrape out the seeds into the pan, saving the bean for another use.

Pour the vanilla milk onto the egg mixture, a little at a time, folding well between additions. Return to the pan and place over very low heat to gradually thicken, stirring all the time, until it coats the back of the spoon—about 10 minutes. Remove from the heat and continue whisking until creamy and smooth. Let cool completely.

Pour the custard into an ice-cream maker and freeze following the manufacturer's directions. For extra creaminess and volume, stir the whipped cream, if desired, into the ice cream just before it reaches the freezing point.

MERINGUES

MERINGUES

Preparation time: 30 minutes,
   plus drying time
Cooking time: 40 minutes
Serves 6

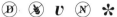

2 egg whites
⅔ cup/4½ oz (125 g) superfine (caster) sugar

There's something magical about meringues. It's all chemistry, though: The albumin in the whisked egg whites imprisons air bubbles, giving them a snow-like look, and the volume is further increased by cooking. The quantity of sugar may seem like a lot, but it's necessary for the right texture to be maintained. Dip meringues in melted chocolate and stick two together. Or cover with whipped cream and grate dark chocolate on top. The history of meringue and its different styles is complicated, but we do know that cook and author La Varenne had an early recipe in his 1651 *Le Cuisinier français.*

Preheat the oven to 200°F/100°C/Gas Mark ½ and line a baking sheet with wax (greaseproof) paper.

Put the eggs whites in a large bowl and whisk for 2 minutes, then add a quarter of the sugar. Continue whisking until the whites are very stiff, then delicately fold in the remaining sugar.

Place 6 small mounds of the meringue mixture on the prepared baking sheet, well-spaced apart. Bake for 35–40 minutes, without allowing to color. Turn off the oven and leave the meringues inside for 1 hour until completely dry, then serve.

Note
The quantities can be multiplied to suit your needs.

ALMOND MACAROONS

MACARONS AUX AMANDES

Preparation time: 25 minutes,
  plus cooling time
Cooking time: 25 minutes
Serves 6

butter, for greasing
2⅓ cups/9 oz (250 g) ground almonds
3 egg whites
1¼ cups/9 oz (250 g) superfine (caster) sugar
confectioners' (icing) sugar, for sprinkling

The recipe shared here is a traditional regional one, in the Nancy style, quite different from the colorful modern macarons known worldwide for their infinite range of flavors. It was written long before these became fashionable in high-end Parisian pâtisseries. Nowadays, the spelling "macaroon" typically refers to these cookie-like versions, which are made with either ground almonds or coconut. This recipe is easy to make and handy for using up leftover egg whites. The latter you can stock in the freezer (for instance when making Mayonnaise, page 35) and use up for meringues or macaroons when you have the desired quantity.

Preheat the oven to 300°F/150°C/Gas Mark 2 and line a baking sheet with buttered parchment (baking) paper.

Put the almonds in a large bowl and mix in the egg whites, a little at a time. Stir in the superfine (caster) sugar and mix well. Using your hands, form the dough into balls, then slightly flatten, and place on the prepared sheet. Bake for 20–25 minutes, or until lightly browned.

Let cool on a wire rack, sprinkle with confectioners' (icing) sugar, then serve.

POUND CAKE

QUATRE-QUARTS

Preparation time: 20 minutes,
  plus cooling time
Cooking time: 40 minutes
Serves 6

v

approx. ⅔ cup/5½ oz (150 g) butter, plus
  extra for greasing
3 eggs
approx. 1⅓ cups/5½ oz (150 g) all-purpose
  (plain) flour
approx. ¾ cup/5½ oz (150 g) superfine
  (caster) sugar
grated zest of 1 lemon

Quatre-quarts translates as "four quarters," because it is made of equal quarters (in weight) of each ingredient. Nothing beats a good *quatre-quarts* for le *quatre heures*, also known as *le goûter*, the afternoon snack for every child and child-at-heart. Serve on its own or with a bit of jam to spread on the slices. This simple cake is said to originate from Brittany, where it would have been made with salted butter, which is a good option as it nicely enhances the cake's flavor.

Preheat the oven to 325°F/160°C/Gas Mark 3 and line an 8½ × 4½-inch (21 × 11-cm) loaf pan with buttered parchment (baking) paper.

Weigh the whole eggs, in the shell, and measure out their weight in equal quantities of the flour, sugar, and butter. Melt the butter and let cool. Separate the eggs and place the yolks in a large bowl with the sugar. Beat until the mixture is pale and flows like a ribbon from the whisk.

Little by little, fold in the flour and butter in alternate spoonfuls. Add the lemon zest.

In a separate bowl, whisk the egg whites to stiff peaks, and then fold into the cake batter. Pour into the prepared cake pan, filling it by around two-thirds. Bake for 30–40 minutes, or until a cake tester inserted in middle into the center comes out clean. Remove from the oven and let cool slightly before turning out. Serve sliced.

PAIN D'ÉPICE

PAIN D'ÉPICE

Preparation time: 10 minutes,
   plus cooling time
Cooking time: 1½ hours
Serves 6

v

butter, for greasing
2 tablespoons superfine (caster) sugar
¾ cup/8¾ oz (250 g) dark honey
2 teaspoons baking soda (bicarbonate of soda)
2¼ cups/9 oz (250 g) all-purpose (plain) flour
grated zest of 1 orange
2 teaspoons pumpkin pie spice or mixed
   ground spices, such as anise seeds,
   cinnamon, cloves, cardamon, ginger,
   nutmeg, and pepper

Several places in France, such as Dijon, Reims, and the Lorraine region—mostly in the northeastern quarter of the country—have different types of gingerbread cake as one of their specialties. But pain d'épice has become quite popular everywhere in France, and artisanal versions can be found on almost every market, usually made with local honey. The "real" professional recipe requires an extremely long resting time for the dough, as long as six months in some versions! The straightforward, homemade method below yields a different type of texture, more cake-like than the bread-style ones, but it's just as flavorsome.

Preheat the oven to 300°F/150°C/Gas Mark 2 and grease an 8½ × 4½-inch (21 × 11-cm) loaf pan with butter.

Place the sugar, honey, and baking soda (bicarbonate of soda) in a large saucepan with ¾ cup/6 fl oz (180 ml) water. Place over low heat and cook, stirring until melted.

Remove from the heat and let cool a little before stirring in the flour, orange zest, and spices. Pour the batter into the prepared loaf pan, filling around halfway. Grease a piece of aluminum foil with butter, cover the loaf pan, and bake for 1½ hours, or until a cake tester inserted into the center of the loaf comes out clean.

Remove from the oven and let cool slightly before turning out. Serve sliced.

Note
For a moister gingerbread cake, after you have turned out the loaf from the oven, wrap it with plastic wrap (clingfilm) and let it stand for 24 hours before cutting it.

Preparation time: 40 minutes, plus resting,
  rising, and chilling time
Cooking time: 30 minutes
Serves 6

v

¼ oz (10 g) fresh yeast, or 2½ teaspoons
  (1 × 7-g packet) active dried yeast
4 tablespoons/2 fl oz (50 ml) milk, warmed
2½ cups/11 oz (300 g) all-purpose (plain)
  flour, plus extra for dusting
pinch of salt
scant ⅓ cup/2 oz (60 g) superfine (caster) sugar
3 eggs
9 tablespoons/4½ oz (125 g) butter, softened,
  plus extra for greasing
1 egg yolk

Making brioche at home is a process that stretches over a long period of time, but no step is complicated. It just needs a little effort to knead and some patience. The smell wafting out of the oven when it is baked— ideally in time for breakfast—is heavenly. Every region of France can boast one or several types of brioche, from the *pompe marseillaise* to the northern *cramique*, from the *pastis des Landes* near Bordeaux to the Alsatian Kugelhopf (page 310). The following version is the classic *brioche à tête* you will find at the bakery next to the croissants and pains au chocolat, with a plump base supporting a smaller round "head" of dough.

Begin preparing the day before. If using fresh yeast, mix it with the warm milk, stir to dissolve, and set aside for 10 minutes. Place the fresh yeast batter (or dried yeast, if using), flour, sugar, and salt—ensuring the salt does not directly touch the yeast before mixing—together in a large bowl or in the bowl of a stand mixer fitted with the dough-hook attachment and mix together. Mix in the warm milk (if not already added with the fresh yeast) and the eggs to make a very soft, sticky dough. Knead for 5 minutes with the dough hook, or by hand. Cover with buttered plastic wrap (clingfilm) and let rise in a warm place overnight, until doubled in size.

When risen, add the butter, a lump at a time, to the dough, either in the mixer or by hand. To add it by hand, put the dough onto a floured work counter, bury a lump of butter in it, then knead the butter in with an up-and-down motion until the dough is silky and smooth, with no visible butter. When all the butter is incorporated, cover again, and let rise in the refrigerator until doubled in size, 4–8 hours. Chill in the refrigerator overnight.

The next day, preheat the oven to 400°F/200°C/Gas Mark 6 and butter and flour a brioche mold or round cake pan.

Turn out the dough onto a floured work counter, shape two-thirds of it into a ball, and place in the prepared mold or pan to half-fill it. Shape the remaining dough into a small ball and place it on top. Dust the handle of a wooden spoon with flour and push it vertically through the top ball to join it to the bottom one. Let rise in a warm place for 1 hour or at room temperature for 1½–2 hours.

Beat the egg yolk in a small bowl. Brush the dough with the beaten egg yolk to glaze and then bake for 30 minutes, or until golden brown.

KUGELHOPF

KUGELHOPF

Preparation time: 30 minutes, plus soaking
  and rising times
Cooking time: 1 hour
Serves 6

v

1 cup/4½ oz (125 g) raisins
scant 1 cup/7 fl oz (200 ml) milk
1 oz (25 g) fresh yeast
scant ½ cup/3½ oz (100 g) butter, plus extra
  for greasing
4½ cups/1 lb 2 oz (500 g) all-purpose
  (plain) flour
2 eggs
12 almonds
confectioners' (icing) sugar, for sprinkling
salt

The Alsatians are very proud of their kugelhopf, a buttery brioche richly laden with raisins (sometimes soaked in rum) and topped with crunchy whole almonds. It's obviously a cousin to other Eastern European cakes from Germany or Austria. Kugelhopf should be baked in the traditional mold, which is made of terracotta and often painted with colorful, decorative patterns. It has a round, fluted shape with high sides and a hole in the middle, making the cake look a little like a hat, which is what the name relates to. Serve as a morning or afternoon treat with coffee or tea.

Begin preparing 6 hours in advance. Place the raisins in a small bowl, cover with water, and let soak for 15 minutes.

Meanwhile, place the milk in a large saucepan and heat until it is lukewarm. In a small bowl, mix 2 tablespoons of the warmed milk with the yeast. Place the butter in the pan to melt into the remaining warm milk.

Place the flour and eggs in a large bowl and mix in the warm milk and butter, yeast batter, and a pinch of salt until a dough forms. Knead the dough until combined and it starts to pull away from the bowl but is still sticky, and then knead in the drained raisins.

Grease a kugelhopf mold liberally with butter and place an almond at the bottom of each section of the mold. Half-fill the mold with the dough and set aside, covered, in a warm place to rise for 6 hours.

Preheat the oven to 325°F/160°C/Gas Mark 3. Place the kugelhopf in the oven and bake for 15 minutes, then raise the temperature to 350°F/180°C/Gas Mark 4 and bake for another 45 minutes, covering with aluminum foil if necessary to prevent it from browning too much. Sprinkle with confectioners' (icing) sugar before serving.

CHOCOLATE CAKE

GÂTEAU AU CHOCOLAT

Preparation time: 30 minutes,
    plus cooling time
Cooking time: 50 minutes
Serves 6

v

This is a classic, foolproof chocolate cake, where the eggs are separated and the whites beaten until firm, adding volume and lightness to the final texture. Take care not to break the beaten egg whites when folding into the chocolate mixture: Start by adding just a little and stir gently to loosen the batter. Then add the rest in two or three steps, cutting through the mixture and lifting it from the bottom with a spoon to cover the whites and eventually mix them in completely, with no traces left. Serve as an afternoon treat or for a birthday celebration.

For the cake
scant ½ cup/3½ oz (100 g) butter, plus extra
    for greasing
generous 1 cup/7½ oz (210 g) chopped
    semisweet (dark) chocolate
6 eggs, separated
scant 1 cup/4¾ oz (135 g) all-purpose
    (plain) flour
generous 1 cup/7½ oz (210 g) superfine
    (caster) sugar
1½ teaspoons flavoring, such as rum, kirsch,
    or orange blossom water
candied fruit, such as cherries, oranges,
    and angelica, to decorate

For the chocolate frosting (icing)
⅓ cup/2 oz (60 g) chopped semisweet
    (dark) chocolate
4 tablespoons/2 oz (60 g) butter
2 very fresh eggs, separated

Bake the cake: Preheat the oven to 300°F/150°C/Gas Mark 2 and grease a cake pan with butter.

Place the butter and chocolate in a large saucepan over very low heat, stirring until melted. Remove from the heat and stir in the egg yolks, one by one, followed by the flour and sugar.

In a separate bowl, whisk the egg whites and desired flavoring to stiff peaks. Fold into the chocolate batter, as described in the headnote. Pour into the prepared cake pan and bake for 50 minutes.

Meanwhile, make the chocolate frosting (icing): Place the chocolate and butter in a small saucepan over very low heat, stirring until melted. Remove from the heat and mix in the 2 egg yolks. Whisk the 2 egg whites to soft peaks and then fold these into the chocolate mixture. Set aside.

When the cake comes out of the oven, let cool, then cover with the chocolate frosting (icing) and decorate with candied fruit.

MARBLED CAKE

GÂTEAU MARBRÉ

Preparation time: 20 minutes,
  plus cooling time
Cooking time: 1 hour
Serves 6

10½ tablespoons/5½ oz (150 g) butter, plus
  extra for greasing
1½ cups/11 oz (300 g) superfine (caster) sugar
4 eggs, separated
⅔ cup/5 fl oz (150 ml) milk
2½ cups/11 oz (300 g) all-purpose (plain) flour
1½ teaspoons baking powder
⅓ cup/3 oz (90 g) grated semisweet
  (dark) chocolate
vanilla extract or grated lemon zest, to taste

A quintessential *goûter*, marbled cake became popular in the 1950s. Individually packed industrial versions have not managed to overshadow the homemade cake, which is also very satisfying to make. Many French children try their hand at baking for the first time with it. It's also very transportable, great to pack for an after-school snack, a picnic, or a sports competition.

Preheat the oven to 300°F/150°C/Gas Mark 2 and grease an 8½ × 4½-inch (21 × 11-cm) loaf pan with butter.

Beat the butter and sugar in a large bowl until pale and creamy, then add the egg yolks and milk.

In a separate bowl, combine the flour and baking powder. Mix this into the egg yolk and milk mixture.

In another bowl, whisk the egg whites until stiff, then fold into the cake batter, ensuring everything is evenly incorporated.

Evenly divide the batter into two bowls. Fold the chocolate into one bowl and the vanilla or lemon zest into the other. Put alternate spoonfuls of the white and chocolate batters into the prepared pan, filling it two-thirds full. Bake for 1 hour, or until a cake tester insterted into the center comes out clean.

Remove from the oven and let cool before turning out.

CHOCOLATE LOG

BÛCHE AU CHOCOLAT

Preparation time: 40 minutes,
   plus cooling time
Cooking time: 20 minutes
Serves 6

Bûche is a classic Christmas dessert in France and some other French-speaking countries. The tradition takes its roots in ancient pagan rituals. A big log (called a Yule log) would be burnt during the winter solstice as a token for the gods, to guarantee a successful harvest during the following year. The version imitating the piece of wood appeared in the nineteenth century. It's often a sponge cake layered with rich buttercream and decorated with tiny meringue mushrooms and little festive-themed figures. Individual logs appear in pastry shops in December, and a large one for the big day is usually specially ordered or made at home. Nowadays, many versions exist, including ice-cream-based ones. It can be a little too rich for after a big meal, so could also be made for an afternoon tea during the festive season.

---

butter, melted, for greasing
4 eggs
¾ cup/5½ oz (160 g) superfine (caster) sugar
1⅓ cups/5½ oz (160 g) all-purpose (plain) flour
2 teaspoons baking powder
1 teaspoon vanilla extract
1 quantity Buttercream (page 48)
1 tablespoon coffee extract or 3½ oz
  (100 g) melted and cooled semisweet
  (dark) chocolate
salt

Preheat the oven to 325°F/160°C/Gas Mark 3 and grease a jelly roll pan with butter. Line it with a sheet of wax (greaseproof) paper of the same size. Brush this paper with melted butter, too.

In a large bowl, whisk the eggs and sugar for 10 minutes until pale and tripled in volume. Fold in the flour, baking powder, a pinch of salt and vanilla. Pour the batter into the prepared pan and bake for 15–20 minutes until slightly springy to the touch but firm.

Turn out while still hot onto a clean dish towel and then use this to help you roll up the cake, starting with one long edge: the towel holds it securely and prevents any splits or cracks. Allow the cake to cool, still rolled up in the dish towel.

Ensure the buttercream is soft and at room temperature, then mix in the coffee extract or cooled chocolate.

Carefully unroll the cake and spread the inner surface with half of the buttercream. Roll up again and place on a serving plate. Spread or pipe the remaining buttercream onto the outside of the cake, covering all surfaces.

MADELEINES

Preparation time: 20 minutes, plus resting
and cooling times
Cooking time: 10 minutes
Makes 12 madeleines

9 tablespoons/4½ oz (125 g) butter, softened,
plus extra for greasing
2 extra-large (UK large) eggs
¾ cup/5½ oz (150 g) superfine (caster) sugar
1¼ cups/5½ oz (150 g) all-purpose (plain)
flour, sifted
1 teaspoon vanilla extract, or grated zest
of 1 lemon

This traditional little cake was originally baked in
a scallop shell, which later evolved into the modern
molds we know. It's not very clear which Madeleine
gave their name to it: a medieval one baking for pilgrims
leaving for Compostelle; a seventeenth-century cook
from Commercy in Lorraine; or, a century later, a servant
to Stanislas Leszczynski, duke of the same province,
who saved a dessert situation by baking her mother's
recipe. In any case, since Marcel Proust published his
1913 *À la recherche du temps perdu*, *"la petite madeleine"*
has also become a metaphor for anything that brings
back the nostalgic and sensory memory of past times
in someone's life, as it famously did for him when he
dipped the little cake in his tea.

Preheat the oven to 400°F/200°C/Gas Mark 6 and grease
12 madeleine pans with butter.

Place the eggs and sugar in a large bowl and whisk
with an electric whisk until the mixture turns white
and triples in volume.

Slowly fold in the flour and butter with a spoon, then
stir in the vanilla or lemon zest. Rest the batter in the
refrigerator for at least 2 hours (this will help the cakes
rise correctly in the oven).

Pour into the prepared pans and bake for 8–10 minutes
until well-risen and golden.

Remove from the oven and let cool before turning out.

FINANCIERS

FINANCIERS

Preparation time: 20 minutes, plus resting
    and cooling times
Cooking time: 20 minutes
Makes 12 financiers

½ cup/4¼ oz (120 g) butter, softened,
    plus extra for greasing
4 egg whites
⅔ cup/4½ oz (125 g) superfine (caster) sugar
scant 1 cup/3½ oz (100 g) all-purpose (plain)
    flour, sifted

Making financiers is a good way to use up leftover egg whites. In this recipe, you may substitute about one half of the flour for ground almonds. The ancestors of financiers were probably little cakes called *Visitandines*, made by nuns from the convent of the same name in Lorraine, a region near Alsace in eastern France. They were made popular in the nineteenth century when pastry chefs started selling them in shops in Nancy. They changed the shape from oval to rectangular, making the cakes reminiscent of little gold bars, and some of their clients would have been bankers and businessmen, hence the name.

Preheat the oven to 350°F/180°C/Gas Mark 4 and grease 12 small financier molds with butter.

Place the egg whites and sugar in a large bowl, then whisk with an electric whisk until stiff and glossy. Slowly fold in the flour and butter with a spoon. Half-fill each of the prepared molds with the batter and bake for 20 minutes.

Remove from the oven and let cool before turning out.

CHOCOLATE ÉCLAIRS

ÉCLAIRS AU CHOCOLAT

Preparation time: 45 minutes,
    plus cooling time
Cooking time: 20 minutes
Serves 6

v

Antonin Carême, chef and pastry chef at the turn of the nineteenth century, loved choux pastry. He modernized the recipe and inspired many creations based on it, including *duchesse*, an oblong cake that later evolved into éclairs. The name (meaning "lightning") was given because of the rapidity with which it can be engulfed: it's easy to hold in one hand and extremely delicious. Éclairs are a pastry store favorite, where they can be chocolate or coffee flavored. Making them at home requires a little practice. But even if they are not as neat as the ones on the pâtisserie counter, they will still be delicious.

For the éclairs
butter, for greasing
1 quantity Choux Pastry (page 42)

For the crème pâtissière
½ vanilla bean, split lengthwise
2 cups plus 1 tablespoon/17 fl oz (500 ml) milk
heaped ¼ cup/1¾ oz (50 g) all-purpose
    (plain) flour
⅓ cup/2½ oz (75 g) superfine (caster) sugar
1 whole egg
3 egg yolks
scant ½ cup/3½ oz (100 g) grated semisweet
    (dark) chocolate

For chocolate frosting (icing)
⅓ cup/2 oz (60 g) chopped semisweet
    (dark) chocolate
4 tablespoons/2 oz (60 g) butter
2 very fresh eggs, separated

Bake the éclairs: Preheat the oven to 200°C/400°F/Gas Mark 6 and grease a baking sheet with butter.

Pipe or spoon the choux pastry into fingers on the prepared sheet. Bake for 20 minutes and let cool.

Next, make the crème pâtissière (see page 46), adding the grated chocolate immediately after you remove the pan from the heat (after the mixture comes to a boil), mixing thoroughly until melted and fully incorporated.

Make the chocolate frosting (icing): Place the chopped chocolate and butter in a small saucepan, then place over low heat to gently melt. Remove from the heat and mix in the 2 egg yolks. Whisk the egg whites to soft peaks in a separate bowl and then fold these into the chocolate mixture.

When cooled, slit the éclairs along the side, fill with the chocolate crème pâtissière, and top with the chocolate frosting. The frosting will set as it cools.

PARIS-BREST

PARIS-BREST

Preparation time: 45 minutes, plus chilling
   and cooling times
Cooking time: 45 minutes
Serves 6

v

For the choux pastry
3 tablespoons/1½ oz (40 g) semi-salted butter
½ cup/2½ oz (65 g) all-purpose (plain) flour
2 whole eggs

For the crème pâtissière
3 cups (750 ml) whole (full-fat) milk, hot
scant 1 cup/3½ oz (100 g) all-purpose
   (plain) flour
¾ cup/5½ oz (150 g) superfine (caster) sugar
5 egg yolks

For the praline filling
scant 1 cup/7 oz (200 g) butter, softened
6¾ oz (200 g) almond and hazelnut chocolate
   spread (see Notes)

To finish
butter, for greasing
1¾ cups/7 oz (200 g) slivered (or flaked)
   almonds, toasted
confectioners' (icing) sugar, for sprinkling

The name refers to a cycling race running from Paris to Brest, the westernmost town in France, in Brittany. The bike-wheel-shaped pastry was created sometime at the turn of the twentieth century. Several pastry chefs, working in shops along the route, claim its invention. In any case, this ring of choux pastry filled with a praline cream quickly became a huge success. It's still a pastry store classic and has been endlessly reinvented. The classic version is still a winner, though; it takes a long time to make at home but is worth the effort.

The day before, make the choux pastry dough (see page 42) with ½ cup/4½ fl oz (125 ml) water, the butter, flour, and whole eggs (omit the sugar). Let cool, then chill in the refrigerator overnight.

Next, make the crème pâtissière (see page 46), with the milk, flour, superfine (caster) sugar, and egg yolks. Transfer to a clean bowl, cool, cover with plastic wrap (clingfilm) directly touching the surface of the cream, and chill in the refrigerator.

Next, make the praline filling: Beat the butter and almond and hazelnut chocolate spread together in a bowl. Mix in the well-chilled crème pâtissière and beat together. Store the praline filling in the refrigerator for 12 hours.

On the day: Preheat the oven to 500°F/250°C/Gas Mark 9 and grease a baking sheet with butter.

Pipe the choux pastry dough onto the sheet in a ring, 10 inches (25 cm) in diameter, like a bicycle wheel. Bake for 10–12 minutes, or until the pastry is well-risen and golden brown. Turn the oven off and leave the pastry to dry for 3–4 minutes with the oven door open. Remove from the oven and let cool to room temperature.

Put the chilled praline filling in a pastry (piping) bag with a fluted tip (nozzle). Once the pastry is completely cold, carefully split it in half with a sharp knife and cover the bottom with praline filling, using the pastry bag to make swirls. Sprinkle the praline filling with all but a few almonds. Cover with the choux pastry lid and sprinkle the Paris-Brest with the remaining almonds and confectioners' (icing) sugar.

Notes
To make 6 individual portions, pipe the choux pastry into 6 rings, 8 cm (3¼ inches) in diameter, and then bake as instructed.

Almond and hazelnut chocolate spreads are available at specialty stores.

SAINT-HONORÉ

SAINT-HONORÉ

Preparation time: 1¾ hours, plus resting
 and cooling times
Cooking time: 45 minutes
Serves 6

Saint-Honoré is the patron saint of pastry chefs. His name was given to this pastry in 1846 by its creator, a *pâtissier* named Chiboust whose store was on the rue du Faubourg-Saint-Honoré, in the center of Paris. Making it is a bit of a pastry masterclass, since it's an architectural dish involving five essential elements of French pastry: choux pastry; pie dough (shortcrust pastry)—or sometimes puff; pastry cream; Saint-Honoré cream; and caramel. If you master Saint-Honoré you can probably make almost any other French pastry. It has also recently enjoyed renewed popularity in France.

For the base
butter, for greasing
1 quantity Choux Pastry (page 42)
all-purpose (plain) flour, for dusting
1 quantity Basic Pie Dough (page 41), chilled
1 egg, beaten
½ quantity Crème Pâtissière (page 46)
1 cup/7 oz (200 g) superfine (caster) sugar

For the Saint-Honoré Cream
2 gelatin leaves or 1 teaspoon/¼ oz (6 g)
 powdered gelatin
2 egg yolks
¼ cup/1¾ oz (50 g) superfine (caster) sugar
1 tablespoon/¼ oz (10 g) all-purpose
 (plain) flour
½ cup/4 fl oz (125 ml) milk, warmed
1 teaspoon vanilla extract
2 egg whites

Make the base: Preheat the oven to 400°F/200°C/Gas Mark 6 and grease 2 baking sheets with butter.

Place the choux pastry into a pastry (piping) bag fitted with a large plain tip (nozzle).

Dust a work counter with flour and roll the pie dough (shortcrust pastry) out to a thickness of ¼ inch (5 mm). Cut into a 9-inch (23-cm) round and place on one baking sheet. Prick all over with a fork and brush with the egg.

Starting 1 inch (2.5 cm) inside the edge of the round and using half of the choux pastry, pipe it in a spiral onto the pie dough, finishing in the center, leaving space between the lines to allow it to puff up in the oven. Use the remaining choux pastry to make small choux buns, piping them onto the other baking sheet. Place both in the oven and bake for 15 minutes, then remove the choux buns and continue cooking the dough round for another 5–10 minutes until golden and cooked through. Once cooled, fill the small choux buns with the crème pâtissière.

With 1 cup/7 oz (200 g) superfine (caster) sugar, make a light caramel (see page 49). Carefully dip the buns in the caramel, then immediately stick them around the outer edge of the dough round.

Make the Saint-Honoré cream: Soak the gelatin leaves in a cold water for 5 minutes, or if using powdered gelatin, sprinkle it into ¼ cup/2 fl oz (60ml) cold water, and leave to bloom for 5 minutes. Place the egg yolks and sugar in a heatproof bowl set over a pan of barely simmering water. Whisk for 2–3 minutes until pale and thick, then add the flour, milk, vanilla, and the well-drained gelatin leaves or the softened powdered gelatin. Cook the custard until it has thickened, without allowing it to boil. Remove from the heat and let cool. Whisk the egg whites until they form stiff peaks and fold them gently but thoroughly into the lukewarm custard.

Fill the center of the cake with the Saint-Honoré cream. Serve immediately.

MILLE-FEUILLES

MILLE-FEUILLES

Preparation time: 2½ hours, plus resting and
  cooling times
Cooking time: 20 minutes
Makes 6

𝑣

1 quantity Puff Pastry (page 40)
1 egg, beaten
1 quantity Crème Pâtissière (page 46)
confectioners' (icing) sugar or superfine
  (caster) sugar, for dredging

For a weekend lunch or a special occasion—or to make
any occasion special—the French like to visit pâtisseries
and pick out a variety of pastries for their guests, and
mille-feuilles often make the cut. The combination of flaky
puff and smooth pastry cream is irresistible. The name
refers to the multiple layers, both in the puff pastry itself
and in the finished dessert. Mille-feuilles can be served
with tea or as a plated dessert, made at the last minute.

Preheat the oven to 350°F/180°C/Gas Mark 4.
  Make the puff pastry. Roll the dough out into a 14 ×
14-inch (36 × 36-cm) square. Prick all over with a fork
and place on a slightly damp but ungreased baking
sheet. Bake the pastry for 15–20 minutes until it is dry
and crisp.
  Using a serrated knife, cut the square into 3 equal
4½ × 14-inch (12 × 36-cm) rectangles, and each of these
rectangles into 6 small 4½ × 2½-inch (12 × 6-cm) rectangles.
  Once cooled, spread some crème pâtissière over one
of these and cover with a second pastry strip. Spread this
layer with more crème pâtissière and finish by placing
the third pastry strip on top. Dredge very generously with
sugar. The sugar can be branded in a diamond pattern
with a red-hot skewer if desired.

QUICK RUM BABA

BABA AU RHUM RAPIDE

Preparation time: 15 minutes,
 plus cooling time
Cooking time: 20 minutes
Serves 6

Rum is very often present in French desserts. Most house-holds have a bottle just for flavoring cakes, pastries, and pancakes. It's produced in the French Caribbean islands, Martinique and Guadeloupe, and in Réunion Island in the Indian Ocean. Baba au rhum probably came into existence on a whim from Stanislas Leszczynski, the Polish stepfather to Louis XV and duke of Lorraine. He deman-ded a moist version of a babka-style Eastern European leavened cake, which was therefore drizzled with Tokay wine. The resulting pastry was later reinterpreted by Parisian pastry chef Nicolas Stohrer, inventor of the modern baba, around 1735. The version below is an unleavened shortcut—quite easy and delicious.

For the baba
butter, for greasing
3 eggs, separated
½ cup/3½ oz (100 g) superfine (caster) sugar
scant 1 cup/3½ oz (100 g) all-purpose
 (plain) flour
½ teaspoon baking powder
3½ tablespoons/1¾ oz (50g) currants (optional)
Crème Pâtissière (page 46), for decorating
 (optional)

For the syrup
⅔ cup/4½ oz (125 g) superfine (caster) sugar
scant 1 cup/7 fl oz (200 ml) rum

Make the baba: Preheat the oven to 400°F/200°C/Gas Mark 6 and generously grease an 8-inch (20-cm) savarin mold or ring mold with butter.

In a large bowl, mix the egg yolks, sugar, flour, baking powder, and currants, if using. In a separate bowl, whisk the egg whites until stiff, then mix half of them into the egg yolk mixture to make a stiff batter. Carefully fold in the remaining whites. Pour the batter into the prepared mold. Bake for 20 minutes until golden.

Make the syrup: Place 3½ tablespoons/1¾ fl oz (50 ml) water with the sugar and rum in a medium saucepan and bring to a boil over low heat. Immediately remove from the heat and pour the rum sauce over the savarin. Let soak and cool before turning out. The center of the cooled baba may be filled with crème pâtissière just before serving.

APPLE TURNOVERS

CHAUSSONS AUX POMMES

Preparation time: 2½ hours,
    plus resting time
Cooking time: 30 minutes
Serves 6

v

Turnovers of all types, savory or sweet, seem to appear in almost every cuisine of the world. The characteristic French turnover is sweet *chaussons aux pommes*, one of the classic *viennoiseries* on offer in French boulangeries, along with croissants, pains au chocolat, and pains aux raisins. Children are often given some money to grab them on their way back from school. Turnovers may be filled with apple purée or half a baked apple. A lemon-filled turnover is called a *bichon*.

For the apple purée
2¼ lb (1 kg) cooking apples, quartered and
    stems (stalks) removed (do not peel or core)
pinch of grated lemon zest
superfine (caster) sugar, to taste (optional)

For the turnovers
butter, for greasing
9 oz (250 g) Puff Pastry (page 40)
all-purpose (plain) flour, for dusting
1 egg yolk, lightly beaten
scant ⅓ cup/2 oz (60 g) superfine (caster) sugar

Make the apple purée: Put the apples in a nonreactive pot with ½ cup/4 fl oz (120 ml) water. Cover and cook over a low heat for 15–20 minutes. Drain and then place the cooked apples into a blender. Process until smooth, then pass through a sieve to remove any seeds (pips). Stir in the lemon zest and a little sugar, if needed. Let cool and then measure out 6 oz (175 g). Store the leftover purée in the refrigerator for another use.

Make the turnovers: Preheat the oven to 425°F/220°C/Gas Mark 7 and grease a baking sheet with butter.

Roll the puff pastry out very thinly on a floured work counter. Cut out even rounds 5 inches (12 cm) in diameter using a bowl or cookie cutter. Place a good tablespoon of apple purée on each one. Fold in half, moisten the edges with a little water, and press down to seal, forming a crescent shape. Place on the prepared sheet. Brush with the egg yolk to glaze and sprinkle with the sugar. Bake for 30 minutes until puffed and golden brown.

Remove from the oven and let cool a little before serving.

Note
Jam turnovers can be made by replacing the apple purée with a jam of your choice

PALMIERS

PALMIERS

Preparation time: 2½ hours,
    plus resting time
Cooking time: 20 minutes
Serves 6

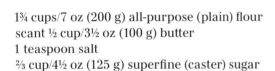

1¾ cups/7 oz (200 g) all-purpose (plain) flour
scant ½ cup/3½ oz (100 g) butter
1 teaspoon salt
⅔ cup/4½ oz (125 g) superfine (caster) sugar

These pastries get their name because they are shaped like the palms of a palm-tree—or, if you prefer, like an elongated heart. Larger versions of the crunchy and flaky biscuits can be found in boulangeries, but the more industrial versions, sold as little hearts in a box, are also popular. They are perfect to use up scraps of leftover puff pastry, very pretty, and easy to make. When handling scraps of puff, do not knead or overwork them, just lay them together in a single layer on a lightly floured counter and press them out with a rolling pin to make them stick together. Then roll out the pastry as usual and proceed with the recipe.

Make puff pastry with the flour, butter, salt, and 2 tablespoons water (see page 40).

Preheat the oven to 425°F/220°C/Gas Mark 7.

Sprinkle a work counter with some of the sugar and roll out the pastry to about ¼ inch (5 mm) thick, in a strip about 4–8 inches (10–20 cm) wide. Fold the short ends of the pastry in so that the 2 edges meet in the middle, then fold again in the same way.

Cut the pastry crosswise into slices ½ inch (1 cm) thick. Open the slices out slightly to form heart shapes. Sprinkle the baking sheet with sugar and put the heart shapes flat on the sheet. Bake the palmiers for 15–20 minutes, turning them over once during cooking.

Remove from the oven and let cool before serving.

TARTE TATIN

TARTE TATIN

Preparation time: 35 minutes
Cooking time: 30 minutes
Serves 6

Caroline and Stéphanie Tatin ran a hotel in Sologne, a beautiful hunting area south of Paris. The sisters are often considered to be the inventors of this famous tart. The story goes that in 1899 one of them, in a hurry while preparing a meal for hunters, shoved apples in the oven, forgetting to include the usual pastry underneath, which she added on top later, thus creating a delicious tart in which the apples caramelize under the lid of the pastry. This type of upside-down tart may have existed before that, but tarte tatin wouldn't have become such a French classic without the culinary mishap story and pretty name.

For the pie dough (shortcrust pastry)
1 quantity Basic Pie Dough (page 41)
all-purpose (plain) flour, for rolling

For the caramel
½ cup/3½ oz (100 g) superfine (caster) sugar

For the filling
1 lb 2 oz (500 g) apples, peeled, cored, and thinly sliced (about 5 cups sliced)
2 tablespoons/1 oz (25 g) superfine (caster) sugar
3 tablespoons/1½ oz (40 g) butter

heavy (double) cream, to serve (optional)

Make the tart shell: Preheat the oven to 400°F/200°C/Gas Mark 6.

Make the pie dough (shortcrust pastry) and allow it to rest.

Make the caramel: Put the superfine (caster) sugar and 1–2 tablespoons of water in a flameproof tart pan with a solid bottom, preferably made of solid metal, or an ovenproof skillet. Place the pan over medium heat and make a fairly dark caramel (see page 49). Ensure the bottom of the dish is coated in caramel and let cool.

Make the filling: Arrange the apple slices close together in a ring over the caramel and sprinkle with the sugar. Dot with the butter.

On a lightly floured work counter, roll out the pastry to a thickness of ¼ inch (5 mm) and place over the apples, tucking the pastry into the pan all around so the fruit is completely covered. Bake for 30 minutes.

Remove from the oven and immediately turn out onto a serving dish with the caramelized apples on top, then serve, with fresh cream if desired.

APPLE TART

TARTE AUX POMMES

Preparation time: 2½ hours,
  plus resting time
Cooking time: 40 minutes
Serves 4

butter, for greasing
all-purpose (plain) flour, for dusting
1 quantity Puff Pastry (page 40)
1 egg, lightly beaten
1 quantity apple purée (see page 332)
4–5 apples, peeled, cored, and thinly sliced
white (granulated) sugar, to taste

This is the French brasserie classic apple tart, with apple purée under the apples, and the thin slices perfectly arranged in overlapping rows on top. When baking with apples, try to choose the variety based on how you will use it: for the topping, you need a baking apple that holds its shape during cooking, such as Golden Delicious or Granny Smith; while the purée requires the more fluffy flesh of a dessert apple, such as a Gala or Red Delicious. Or look for heirloom varieties locally with different taste profiles and textures.

Preheat the oven to 350°F/180°C/Gas Mark 4 and grease a baking sheet with butter.

Make the puff pastry. Dust the work counter with flour and roll out the puff pastry to a thickness of 1/8 inch (3 mm). Cut the sheet into a square, reserving four strips of pastry to form a border all around the square. Dampen the surface around the edges of the square and stick the strips in place. Transfer to the prepared baking sheet and flute the edges with a pastry crimper or back of a knife. Brush the border strips with the lightly beaten egg to glaze. Prick the dough all over with a fork to prevent the center of the tart from rising too much.

Spread the apple purée to cover the pastry square, excluding the borders. Arrange the apple slices in an overlapping fashion so they completely cover the purée. Sprinkle the apple slices liberally with sugar.

Bake for 30–40 minutes until the tart is cooked through and the sugar forms a very shiny glaze.

RASPBERRY TARTLETS

TARTELETTES AUX FRAMBOISES

Preparation time: 35 minutes, plus resting
and cooling times
Cooking time: 15 minutes
Makes 12

v Ⓝ

butter, for greasing
1 quantity Basic Pie Dough (page 41)
1 quantity Sweetened Whipped Cream
(page 44) or Crème Pâtissière (page 46)
(optional)
3 cups/1 lb 2 oz (500 g) raspberries or other
soft fruit
⅓ cup/3½ oz (100 g) red currant jelly

These pretty, glazed raspberry tartlets are a lovely way to showcase fresh and delicate seasonal fruit, by making something elegant without spoiling the taste. The first raspberries in France are more of an end-of-summer fruit. They are always best bought from local harvests and grown *de pleine terre*, meaning they are actually planted in the soil, which makes for a far better taste.

Make the pie dough and allow it to rest.

Preheat the oven to 325°F/160°C/Gas Mark 3 and grease twelve 2½-inch (6-cm) tartlet pans with butter.

Roll out the dough to a thickness of about 1/8 inch (3 mm) and cut into twelve rounds a little larger than each pan (use the pans as a guide). Line the molds with the pastry. Place wax (greaseproof) paper and pie weights (baking beans) in each tartlet and blind-bake for 10–15 minutes. Remove the paper and pie weights and allow the tartlets to cool.

Shortly before serving, if desired, spread with whipped cream or crème pâtissière before arranging the raspberries inside the tartlet cases.

Make a red currant syrup by placing the jelly in a small saucepan with 3 tablespoons of water. Heat gently over low heat for a few minutes until the mixture becomes syrupy and liquid. Dip a pastry brush into this syrup and glaze the fruits with it, and serve.

STRAWBERRY TARTLETS / TARTELETTES AUX FRAISES

For strawberry tartlets, use the same quantity of strawberries and hull them before placing in the tartlets. For currant tartlets, replace the fruit with 6 cups/1 lb 8 oz (700 g) of red currants. Remove the currants from their stems (stalks) before placing in the tarts. You can also make larger tarts with this recipe; just divide the dough and raspberries between six 4-inch (10-cm) tart pans.

CHOCOLATE TRUFFLES

Preparation time: 25 minutes,
  plus cooling time
Cooking time: 5–10 minutes
Makes 40 truffles

Chocolate truffles are not complicated to prepare. In France, they are usually made around Christmas time. They make for a nice seasonal treat to be enjoyed at the end of a meal, with coffee. They can also be brought to a dinner party as a thoughtful homemade gift to the host. It's important to choose good-quality chocolate as its taste will come through strongly. You may flavor your truffles with a tablespoon of Cognac or Armagnac for an adult version.

1½ cups/9 oz (250 g) chopped good-quality
  semisweet (dark) chocolate
2 tablespoons milk
2 egg yolks
5 tablespoons/2½ oz (75 g) butter, diced
½ cup/2 oz (60 g) unsweetened cocoa powder

Begin preparing 4 to 5 hours in advance. Place the chocolate and milk in a medium saucepan over very low heat and stir until melted.

Remove from the heat when it has formed a very smooth paste. Stir in the egg yolks, then the butter. Beat the mixture for 2–3 minutes, then let cool for 4–5 hours.

Roll small balls the size of a walnut and then roll in cocoa powder. Put in white paper cases and place in a box. Store in the refrigerator and eat within 48 hours.

342

CRYSTALLIZED CHESTNUTS

MARRONS GLACÉS

Preparation time: 3½ hours, plus soaking time
Makes 2¼ lb (1 kg)

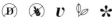

2¼ lb (1 kg) large chestnuts
5 cups/2¼ lb (1 kg) sugar

Marrons glacés is a seasonal treat often bought in boxes from pastry shops or *confiseries*—specialty candy (sweet) stores. Chestnuts are historically an important food in regions where it's difficult to grow crops, like Ardèche or the Cévennes, and these crystallized versions are a festive celebration of a precious fruit. It is best to avoid industrial-made ones, which are overly sweet. The solution is to make them at home, which is quite a lengthy process though not very difficult. The finished chestnuts can be eaten as is or used in pastry, for example crushed to make a filling for a Chocolate Log (page 316) or as a topping for Mont Blanc (page 276).

Begin preparing at least 3 days in advance. Peel the outer skin from the chestnuts without breaking them. Place in a large saucepan and cover with cold water. Bring to a simmer and cook over low heat at just below the boiling point for 3 hours.

Discard the water and, very carefully, immediately peel off the inner skins from the chestnuts, being careful not to break the chestnuts. Make a light syrup with the sugar and 1⅓ gallon/10 pints (5 liters) of water. Let cool to 68°F/20°C on a candy (sugar) thermometer. Put the chestnuts into the syrup then let soak for 12 hours.

Set a wire rack over a baking pan and set aside. Place the chestnuts in a heatproof bowl (reserving the syrup) and set over a pan of simmering water. Gently reheat the chestnuts, then remove with a slotted spoon and drain on the wire rack, allowing them to drip into the pan underneath.

Place the syrup in a large sauce pan over very low heat until it reached 77°F/25°C. Remove from the heat, then lower the chestnuts into the syrup and leave for another 12 hours.

Remove and drain as before, then heat the syrup to 91°F/33°C. Leave the chestnuts in the syrup for a final 12 hours.

Preheat the oven to its lowest setting. Remove the chestnuts and place into a heatproof metal sieve. Heat the syrup to 293–302°F (145–150°C)—the hard-crack stage. To check the consistency without a thermometer, remove a small quantity of syrup with a teaspoon, dip your fingers in cold water and immediately into the syrup on the spoon: a ball should form that is able to be cracked between your fingers or teeth.

Carefully lower the chestnuts into the syrup and then remove after 1 minute. Transfer to a baking sheet, then place in the oven for several hours until dry.

HONEY NOUGAT

NOUGAT AU MIEL

Preparation time: 10 minutes,
   plus cooling time
Cooking time: 20 minutes
Makes 1 lb 2 oz (500 g)

Nougat is a confection principally associated with Montelimar, a town in Provence. It's a traditional candy (sweet) originally made with the local harvest of almonds and inspired by East-Asian recipes, which arrived via Spain and Italy. Use good-quality honey as its taste will come through in the nougat: something with a nicely aromatic taste like orange blossom, heather, or acacia. Avoid strong forest honeys for this. Nowadays nougat is usually store-bought but it used to be easily made at home, as in the following recipe.

flavorless oil, for greasing (optional)
all-purpose (plain) flour, for dusting (optional)
3½ cups/14 oz (400 g) mixed almonds,
   hazelnuts, and pistachios
⅔ cup/5½ oz (150 g) honey
lemon, for rubbing

Preheat the oven 350°F/180°C/Gas Mark 4 and lightly grease a marble slab or baking sheet with oil, or dust it with flour and cover with a sheet of rice paper.

Place the nuts on an ungreased baking sheet and cook in the oven for 5 minutes to lightly toast. Let cool and then roughly chop them.

Put the honey in a large saucepan over medium heat, bring to a boil, and cook for 10 minutes. Add the nuts and return to a boil. Stirring constantly, boil until the syrup reaches 248°F (120°C) on a candy (sugar) thermometer—the firm-ball stage. To check the consistency without a thermometer, remove a small quantity of syrup with a teaspoon, dip your fingers in cold water and immediately into the syrup on the spoon: when rolled between your fingers, the syrup should form a small, soft ball, the size of a pea.

Remove from the heat, then pour onto the prepared slab or baking sheet. Rub the lemon over a rubber spatula, then use to level the surface. Cover with another leaf of rice paper. Cover with a cutting (chopping) board and place a weight on top. Let cool.

Once cool, cut into squares to serve.

QUINCE JELLIES

PÂTE DE COING

Preparation time: 5 minutes, plus drying time
Cooking time: 30 minutes
Makes 1 lb 5 oz (600 g)

9 oz (250 g) quinces
flavorless oil, for greasing
1¾ cups/12 oz (350 g) superfine (caster) sugar,
   plus extra for sprinkling

Quinces, which appear in the autumn, tend to be neglected, as they are hard work to peel and core, and impossible to eat raw. But their wonderfully aromatic taste is fully worth the effort. *Pâtes de fruits* are a slightly old-fashioned but still popular—and very charming—candy (sweet). When carefully prepared with fresh ripe fruit—such as apples, apricots, and plums—they are delicious, and a lovely way to preserve seasonal flavors. They make a very elegant gift, too.

Begin preparing 5 days in advance. Peel and cut the quinces into quarters, remove the cores, and place in a large saucepan. Put the peel, cores, and seeds in a cheesecloth (muslin) bag and add them to the pan along with enough cold water to cover the fruit. Bring to a simmer and cook over medium heat until tender—about 45 minutes.

Lightly grease a marble slab with oil and sprinkle with some sugar. When the quinces are tender, drain them. Transfer to a blender, then add 1¼ cups/9 oz (250 g) of the sugar, and process until smooth. Return to the clean pan and cook over very low heat, stirring constantly, until the paste comes away from the sides of the pan.

Pour the paste onto the prepared slab. Sprinkle with the remaining sugar. Place in the refrigerator and set aside to dry for 4 days.

Once dried, cut into small squares. Stored in an airtight container lined with wax (greaseproof) paper, the jellies will keep for months.

INDEX

Page numbers in *italic* refer to the illustrations

RECIPE NOTES

Butter is always unsalted, unless specified otherwise.

All pepper is freshly ground black pepper, unless otherwise specified.

If unavailable, superfine (caster) sugar can be substituted in the US with granulated sugar by weight.

Vegetables and fruits are assumed to be medium size, unless specified otherwise. When using the zest of citrus fruit, buy unwaxed or organic.

Eggs are US size large (UK size medium), unless otherwise specified, and preferably organic and free-range.

All crème fraîche is full-fat (30–40-per cent fat); if you cook with half-fat crème fraîche it may split. Heavy cream (or UK whipping cream) can always be substituted for crème fraîche. UK double cream can also be substituted but the result may be richer, as it typically has a higher fat content (48 per cent).

Unless otherwise specified, use a light olive oil, or a flavorless oil such as sunflower or peanut (groundnut).

Unless otherwise specified, fish are assumed cleaned, scaled, and gutted.

While most broths (stocks) are gluten-free, some store-bought broths and bouillon cubes may contain gluten, so if you are following a gluten-free diet or cooking for those who do, please check the packaging before purchasing and preparing store-bought broths.

Cooking times and temperatures are for guidance only, as individual ovens vary. If using a fan oven, follow the manufacturer's instructions to adjust the oven temperatures as necessary.

To test whether your deep-frying oil is hot enough, add a cube of stale bread. If it browns in 30 seconds, the temperature is 350–375°F/180–190°C, which is about right for most frying. Exercise a high level of caution when following a recipe involving any potentially hazardous activity including use of open flames, melted sugar and deep-frying. In particular, when deep-frying, add the food carefully to avoid splashing, wear long sleeves, and never leave the pan unattended.

Some recipes involve mixing or blending very hot liquids—work in batches, and fill no more than half a blender to avoid burns.

When sterilizing jars for preserves, wash the jars in clean, hot water and rinse thoroughly. Heat the oven to 275°F/140°C/Gas Mark 1. Place the jars on a baking sheet and place in the oven to dry. Remove from the oven and fill while the jar is still hot. Do not fill hot jars with cold food, as this may cause them to shatter.

Some recipes include raw or very lightly cooked eggs, fish, shellfish, or meat. These should be avoided by the elderly, infants, pregnant women, convalescents, and anyone with an impaired immune system.

All herbs are fresh, unless otherwise specified. All herbs, shoots, flowers, and leaves should be picked fresh from a clean source. Do exercise caution when foraging for ingredients, which should only be eaten if an expert has deemed them safe to eat. In particular, do not gather wild mushrooms yourself before seeking the advice of an expert who has confirmed their suitability for human consumption.

As some species of mushrooms have been known to cause allergic reaction and illness, do take extra care when cooking and eating mushrooms and do seek immediate medical help if you experience a reaction after preparing or eating them.

Both imperial and metric measures are used in this book. Follow one set of measurements throughout, not a mixture, as they are not interchangeable. All spoon measurements are level, unless specified otherwise.
1 teaspoon = 5 ml
1 tablespoon = 15 ml
Australian standard tablespoons are 20 ml, so Australian readers are advised to use 3 teaspoons in place of 1 tablespoon when measuring small quantities.

When no quantity is specified, for example of oils, salts, and herbs used for finishing dishes, quantities are discretionary and flexible.

GINETTE MATHIOT (1907–1998), legendary French food writer and the foremost authority on home cooking in France, taught three generations of French families how to cook. Author of more than 30 best-selling cookbooks covering every aspect of French cuisine, she brought together recipes for classic French dishes in her definitive works, including *I Know How to Cook* and *The Art of French Baking*.

KEDA BLACK is a prolific French-Scottish food writer and critic, and an expert on French home cooking. She is the author of more than 20 cookbooks and collaborates with chefs.

DAVID LEBOVITZ is a cook and pastry chef living in Paris. He is the author of 9 cookbooks, including *My Paris Kitchen* and *L'appart*, and has been featured in *Bon Appétit*, *The New York Times*, and *USA Today*.

Phaidon Press Limited
2 Cooperage Yard
London E15 2QR

Phaidon Press Inc.
111 Broadway
New York, NY 10006

phaidon.com

First published 2024
© 2024 Phaidon Press Limited

Classic French Recipes originates from *Je sais cuisiner*, by Ginette Mathiot © Éditions Albin Michel S.A., 1932, 1959, 1965, 1984, 1990, 2002, 2019 first published in English by Phaidon Press Limited in 2009; and *Je sais faire la pâtisserie*, by Ginette Mathiot © Éditions Albin Michel S.A., 1938, 1966, 1991, 2003 first published in English by Phaidon Press Limited in 2011.

ISBN 978 1 83866 679 8

A CIP catalogue record for this book is available from the British Library and the Library of Congress.

Commissioning Editor: Hélène Gallois Montbrun
Project Editor: Baptiste Roque-Genest
Production Controller: Adela Cory
Design: Hans Stofregen
Layout: Cantina

Introduction, chapter openers and recipe headers: Keda Black

Photography: Marie-Pierre Morel

Printed in China

The Publisher would like to thank Deb Aaronson, Natacha Arnoult, Evelyn Battaglia, Hilary Bird, James Brown, Julia Hasting, David Lebovitz, João Mota, Marie-Pierre Morel, Claire Rogers, Ellie Smith, Tracey Smith, Clara Soupart, Caroline Stearns, Phoebe Stephenson, Ana Rita Teodoro, Emilia Terragni, and Vaisselle Vintage for their contributions to the book, as well as Astier de Villatte for the tableware featured on pages 79, 81, 89, 95, 135, 151, 163, 167, 177, 191, 207, 209, 219, 223, 235, 239, 245, 271–5, 279, 283–9, 293, 303–17, 321–35, 339, 341, and 345.